KT-403-266

Books should be returned on or before the
last date stamped below

31 JUL 2004    12 OCT 2007

22    2003    30 SEP 2004    -8 MAR 2008
14 N
JUN 2005

16 JUN 2003    7 MAY 2008

-8 OCT 2003

22 MAR 2004    -8 APR 2006    19 MAY 2008

-7 JUN 2007    16 MAR 20

14 SEP 2009

12 OCT 2007    21 APR 2011

17 AUG 2012

-3 MAY 2012

-4 JAN 2013

ABERDEENSHIRE LIBRARY
AND INFORMATION SERVICE
MELDR    Lewis, William J.
Under the red duster : the Merchant

184 p. : ill. ; 25 cm.

940.545

1471662

A L I S
1471662

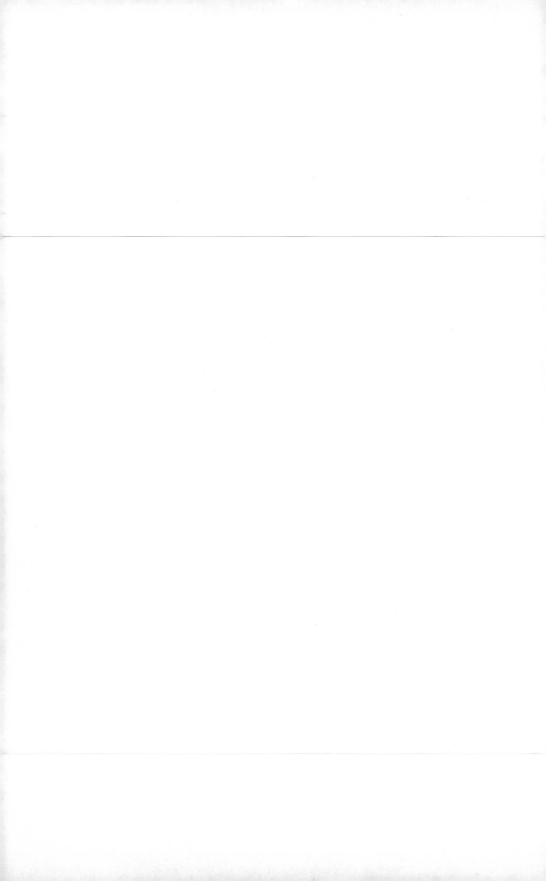

# Under the Red Duster

# Under the Red Duster

## The Merchant Navy in World War II

### William J. Lewis

**Airlife**

940.545

Copyright © 2003 William J. Lewis

All illustrations created by David C. Bell

First published in the UK in 2003
by Airlife Publishing Ltd

**British Cataloguing-in-Publication Data**
A catalogue record for this book
is available from the British Library

ISBN 1 84037 383 0

All rights reserved. No part of this book may be reproduced or transmitted in any form or by any means, electronic or mechanical including photocopying, recording or by any information storage and retrieval system, without permission from the Publisher in writing.

Typeset by Phoenix Typesetting, Burley-in-Wharfedale, West Yorkshire
Printed in England by Biddles Ltd., Guildford and King's Lynn

*Contact us for a free catalogue that describes the complete range of Airlife books.*

**Airlife Publishing Ltd**
101 Longden Road, Shrewsbury, SY3 9EB, England
E-mail: sales@airlifebooks.com
Website: www.airlifebooks.com

This book is dedicated to merchant seamen who served during World War II and to my wife Patricia, without whose attention the book might have been written in half the time.

# Contents

# Introduction

The seeds for this book were planted sixty years ago when, as a child of just four years, I first began to take notice of the horrors which were taking place all around me in war-torn Swansea when the eerie, orange glow of incendiary and high explosive (HE) bombs lit up the night skies and blood-red flames leaped high into the air over the docks and town. Despite my tender age, the awful memories of those days come flooding back from time to time to haunt me: memories of the communal Anderson shelter which was blown out of the earth and sent flying through the air to become embedded in the roof of my mother's house in the Townhill district of the town; memories of the torn-up corpses which littered our bedrooms. The twisted, burned-out buildings, the water trucks, the fires, the fire-hoses which twisted and turned like massive sinuous snakes through the wrecked streets and piles of rubbish which were once houses and shops, reduced to skeletal steel remains. The wrecked ships which had been drawn up along Swansea's beach after hitting mines in the Bristol Channel. The snaking lines of bewildered, homeless people wandering dazedly through the bomb-shattered streets. The solitary workman who had been blown through the passage of my mother's home by an HE bomb whilst seeking shelter there from yet another air raid. It was a truly horrendous time for children in those days. There was no room for illusions, no time for childish play, time only for survival as the bombs rained death from the darkened skies.

Despite the terror from the skies and beneath the sea, however, it was perhaps the stringent rationing which depressed a war-weary people most as bacon and ham were reduced to just 4 ounces (113 g) per week, butter to 2 ounces (57 g), margarine to 4 ounces, cheese to 2 ounces, cooking fat to 4 ounces, sometimes dropping to 2 ounces, 8 ounces of sugar, 2 ounces of tea, one egg (when available) and two or three pints (1.1–1.7 l) of milk per week depending on availability. One packet of dried skimmed milk was available every four weeks, 1 pound (454 g) of preserves every two months, one packet of dried eggs every four weeks, and 12 ounces (340 g) of sweets every four weeks. Survival in such a situation became an art. I recall that whenever I asked mother for anything which she did not have and could not afford, or which was simply not available, her standard reply was, 'No, you can't. There's a war on.' They were not 'good old days'; they were hideous days.

It was not for another sixteen years, however, that I realised that both world wars were in danger of becoming forgotten by younger generations in the mists of time, and it occurred to me that they were really much more than just another piece of history – they had changed the whole world. They had changed people's lives and attitudes, and the shape of our towns, cities and countryside, and I vowed that one day, when the hurly-burly of everyday life had moderated and slowed to a more leisurely pace, I would document all that I had learned and experienced and been told so that the younger men and women of succeeding generations might understand just what sacrifices were made by their forebears.

Following in my family tradition, I had become a merchant seaman in 1954, and after meeting and sailing with men who had served in that service throughout both world wars, some of them in their seventies by then, and listening to the tales they told of the war years, I began to realise that the memories of those participants should be recorded, conserved and cross-referenced. Over the succeeding years, I came to hear of many acts of extreme courage under fire from the merchant seamen, and slowly but surely I came to realise that without those men, Britain would surely have collapsed under the Nazi jackboot. I also came to realise that, apart from the families concerned, very few people knew of the courage displayed by that unarmed essential service, and it is this which has prompted me to record here a few of the stories I was told so many years ago by family members and by the men with whom I sailed. That was also the time when I first began to make a private study of maritime history in general, and merchant navy history in particular. What I found, in addition to the courage and fortitude displayed by those men, was something truly appalling.

Having been born and raised within the seafaring fraternity of Swansea, I learned at a very early age of the desperation of the depression years of the 1920s and 1930s. The massive unemployment, the hunger, the back-street, rat-infested hovels in which people were forced to live, the disease, the heartbreak, the hopelessness, the workhouses. The scale of poverty in those days was truly formidable. Unemployment and deprivation were soulless terms for a soulless existence. Poverty destroys one's appetite for education. It smothers opportunity and kills off life's chances. Education was reserved for the wealthy simply because the poor wretches who kept them living in the lap of luxury could ill afford the time for education. It was a time when every honest heart cried out in moral outrage at the subterranean, sunless labyrinthine world of the poor where life became a waking nightmare of poverty, degradation and squalor. All these things I knew from people who had first-hand experience of it all. Then war came, and a people lost in poverty and squalor suddenly found new hope and a unity of purpose when the whole country was mobilised and employment became readily available to all. For the merchant seamen however, life at sea was very grim. Each and every one of them took their ships and 'rust-buckets' to sea with few illusions, in the sombre knowledge that many of them would never return.

On 3 September 1939, when Britain declared war on Nazi Germany, quite a large proportion of the British merchant fleet was in a most appalling condition, most of it having been put into mothballs during the depression. Although it was the largest merchant fleet in the world with approximately 30 million tons, dwarfing even that of the United States, most of the ships were so old and decrepit that they should have gone to the breaker's yard years before. Many of them were unseaworthy, being no more than rotting rust-buckets subject to constant breakdowns of one kind or another, and always at severe risk of foundering at sea in severe weather conditions. Many ships simply disappeared without trace in the deep oceans without even having enough time to send out the international distress signal when foundering in storms after breaking up through years of neglect, their steel plates so thin from the ravages of rust that they would not have stood the strain of a weld, let alone the pounding of wind and sea. And the conditions suffered by the seamen who had themisfortune to sail aboard such vessels were harrowing.

That savage neglect of both ships and men can be laid squarely at the feet of the owners of the vessels, many of whom were no more than greedy, grasping peddlers of death, looking for profits at any cost, and eagerly supported by equally avaricious shareholders and successive governments, even at the cost of the lives of the men who served them. Cocooned in their protected and privileged world, the ship owners prospered as their crews died. Whilst the wages of the crews, barely above subsistence level at best, were cut to starvation level during the 1930s the owners, together with some unscrupulous directors and favoured shareholders, lived their lives of luxury ashore and in safety, jealously defending their own interests and lifestyles.

Merchant seamen unfortunate enough not to be employed by one of the reputable companies of the British merchant fleet were forced to wait for a ship to be loaded, and then take their chances along with the many others for the few berths available. It was a similar situation to the dock workers and miners who were forced to stand at closed gates in all kinds of weather, waiting pathetically to be chosen for a day's work. Even then, it was not uncommon for a sailor to have to tuck £5 into his discharge book before showing it to any skipper aboard whose ship he wished to embark. If he was lucky (or perhaps unlucky) enough to be signed on, he was then provided with a straw mattress – a 'donkey's breakfast', but was obliged to provide the rest of his bedding and cutlery out of his own pocket.

Living and working conditions aboard such ships might have come straight from a Dickens novel, as might the dictatorial powers of the owners. Like the feudal barons of ancient days, their fleets were their serfdoms and the crews who manned them, their serfs. For any serf to have the audacity to revolt against that established order was virtually unheard of. Those with the temerity to do so were very swiftly consigned to virtual oblivion. Unemployment was very high in the merchant navy in the 1920s and 1930s, as indeed it was in most other walks of life throughout the length and breadth of Britain, and ship owners who ever had cause, whether just or unjust, saw to it that such men were automatically 'blackballed' and never boarded another ship again. Berths were for willing, subservient serfs, serfs who 'knew their place' and kept to it.

Morale was all but non-existent aboard those ships. In the stygian blackness of the holds, lazarettes, forepeaks, engine rooms, steering flats and forecastle heads, where the deck crews' and black gang's (stokers') accommodation was to be found, the rats ran freely, feeding upon whatever scraps of food they could find or, if foodstuffs were being carried, upon the cargo itself. In galleys, cabins, mess rooms, pantries etc., where the condensation ran in rivulets down bulkheads and over steel decks, soaking clothes, mattresses, blankets etc., cockroaches ruled, wandering at will over tables, work surfaces, food and bunks. In food storage lazarettes, weevils grew fat as they feasted on the crews' meagre rations.

Accommodation for the crews was all communal, usually in the most austere conditions under the forecastle head or aft, on or under the poop deck. It stunk of mildew, rat droppings and cockroaches, whilst hygiene and toilet facilities, where they existed at all, ranged from the primitive to the horrendous. Such food as was made available aboard some of the worst ships was usually half rotten, badly cooked and liberally seasoned with the same verminous filth as that in which the men lived and worked, which would not have been tolerated in even the foulest and most spartan of workhouses. Maggot-ridden meat, which butchers ashore usually paid other people to get rid of, was a comparative luxury in comparison with the weevil-infested stocks of flour, and bread they were forced to eat because there was nothing better. The margarine which was used to go on such offerings was usually rancid, and it was always a good idea to boil their suspect water supplies before consumption. Such companies as these came to be referred to amongst seamen as 'starvation lines'. (Ships' officers used separate food stocks and water reserves.)

The skippers and mates of such vessels ruled with an iron hand, showing no mercy or compassion whatsoever to the men under their command, and casting the stigma of mutiny on anyone who dared to complain. Such officers as those backed the companies for whom they worked to the hilt in return for the few crumbs of comfort which directors saw fit to throw their way, and most were guilty of lining their own pockets from company funds which were made available for ships' stores and equipment. Their power was absolute, and nothing short of slave labour and absolute obedience was ever tolerated.

As was the case with their Royal Naval counterparts, such had been the lot of merchant seamen for hundreds of years. Hangings, floggings, keel-haulings, beatings and brutality of every description were normal, everyday events until well into the nineteenth century. Their spirits broken by severe frugality and cruelty, continuous punishments and severe repression, such treatment was looked upon as 'nothing more than such verminous scum deserved'. The skipper of a clipper ship in the mid 1850s even developed the habit of shooting any member of his crew who did not move quickly enough when an order was given. He was later tried and hanged for murder.

Over the centuries, those savage conditions continued unabated beyond all measure of human decency, and as though shipboard life was not bad enough, the ship owners' greed for profits at any cost knew no bounds. Ships foundered at sea through years of neglect; overloading was a normal practice, and if ships sank, so what? There was more money to be made from a shipwreck than from cargo safely delivered.

In my early youth, even before I started my own seagoing career, I knew several 'Cape Horners' (one of whom was my own grandfather), who had served their time in sail, and who told horrendous tales of the savagery of incredibly cruel skippers and mates; of trying to round Cape Horn in the depths of the southern winter against the prevailing westerlies, and having to 'run down the eastern', having failed to make any way through the Drake Passage which separates the Atlantic from the Pacific. Even to this day, there are the remains of several of those ancient sailing ships drawn up on the shore at Port Stanley having been irreparably damaged by the severe storms which ravage that area and written off by insurance companies. In fact, I have, in the distant past, been aboard two of them, and marvelled at how ordinary mortals suffered as they did in the furtherance of their employers' greed.

The first champion of the merchant seamen was a man by the name of Samuel Plimsoll. Born in Bristol in 1824, he later became a successful businessman, dealing mostly in coal. Once Plimsoll went on board the ship which was to transport his coal, and was appalled at the shocking conditions under which merchant seamen were forced to live and work. Very soon after that experience, it became his goal in life to try and improve the lot of those men, upon whom Britain depended so heavily and whom she treated so unjustly.

He soon came to realise that the only way he could achieve his aims was through Parliament. After contesting the Derby seat at a by-election in 1861 and failing, he was finally elected as Liberal MP for Derby in 1868, serving until 1880. He began gathering evidence of the 'floating coffins' which were being used by some of the unscrupulous ship owners, and the way in which they were using those ships to claim exorbitant insurance settlements when they foundered, as they so often did.

In 1876, eight years after his election, he finally succeeded in getting Disraeli's Conservative government to pass the Merchant Shipping Act, which introduced marks on ships' sides to stop them being overloaded. That mark became known throughout the world as the Plimsoll line. He later became known as the 'Sailors' Friend', and was the first man ever to have taken any interest in the welfare and well-being of merchant seamen.

Over the years, legislation was enacted which did improve the sailors' lot. It was not very much, but a few small steps in the right direction. Between the two world wars, all the men of power throughout the closed shop of the British establishment, at every level from senior government ministers to shipping and Civil Service clerks, were only too well aware of the atrocious conditions which existed in the merchant navy. No one in a position of power, however, was prepared to do very much about the situation. The shipping magnates were far too powerful and wealthy for mere governments to risk incurring their wrath.

They did, however, come to a sort of compromise. In a rather farcical series of exercises designed mainly to avoid embarrassment, the Government and the ship owners introduced certain recommendations, laying down minimum standards in regard to crew accommodation, food, hygiene and safety at sea. These became known amongst lower-deck ratings as 'the Board of Trade Whack', and were referred to as such until well into the 1950s. However, governments, owners and the captains who served them at sea were well aware that recommendations are not laws, and therefore, not legally enforceable. The recommendations were, for the most part, totally ignored. Many decent skippers who, doing their utmost to enforce them in an effort to improve conditions aboard their commands and offer some crumbs of compassion to their crews, very quickly found themselves without a command. This tended to act as a very efficient deterrent to merchant captains who, after having seen or heard about those fellow officers who had ended up 'on the beach' having dared to try and improve the lot of their crews, simply toed the company line in order to keep their jobs. It was a form of despotism, a despotism which cast a long, dark shadow over fleet owners and successive governments alike. Compassion is a frail thing.

On nearly all the small, dirty, smelly, festering coastal steamers which were in and out of port every few days, crews were obliged to provide their own food, eating and drinking utensils and blankets, grateful even for a berth aboard those rusting, stinking hulks. In the Britain of the 1920s and 1930s, 'a land fit for heroes' as it was declared after the First World War, poverty, unemployment, serfdom and servility were a way of life for the vast majority of the population of Britain, and they were castigated and reviled with a contempt born of the arrogant superiority of the wealthy minority, figures of fun for the morally bankrupt and socially inept society which ruled over them.

Such horrifying conditions had become an accepted way of life simply because people at the lower end of the social scale were – and remained until very recently – uneducated, with few rights, leaving them living in squalor in disease-ridden back-street hovels with open sewers where vermin roamed free, where toilets were communal and running water from an outside tap was a comparative luxury. The merchant seamen were in even worse straits. Similar horrifying conditions existed aboard the many tramp steamers which plied the lucrative coastal and Far Eastern trade routes, with the difference that they were remote from the outside world and separated for many months from friends and family.

There were, of course, many exceptions in the shipping industry – family shipping businesses, small companies and the very large companies that operated either passenger or passenger/cargo combinations – and although they, like the more ruthless owners demanded their 'pound of flesh' at all times, they did feel a certain amount of responsibility towards their ships and the men who sailed in them. Such ship owners took a genuine interest in their vessels, visiting them from time to time and listening to complaints and suggestions from their crews. The small companies owned mainly tramp steamers built on the north-east coast of Britain, home of some of the finest shipbuilding expertise in the world. Cheap to build and economical to run, they were very basic but eminently seaworthy vessels which served their owners well for many years, many of them for far more years than they were originally designed for. Although these owners provided no better wages for their crews than the others, they did at least operate clean, safe ships which afforded better living and working conditions, even though the food provided was at all times meagre.

There were also the 'in-between' ships, which were neither floating hellholes nor luxury cruise liners. As long as they turned over a good profit for their owners and shareholders without too much cost, the directors did not care how their ships were run. If these vessels were commanded by a bad skipper, their crews became prey to their greed simply because it became easy for them to pocket the cash the company made available for food, cleaning materials, small comforts such as blankets, decent mattresses etc., or even failing to replace faulty navigational equipment and even lifeboats. A good skipper aboard such a ship ensured that his crew received whatever became available which, even at best, however, was never enough. The Merchant Shipping Act, for example, laid down a minimum scale of fresh food, but also allowed for shipping companies to use a substitute ration of salted or canned meat, on the labels of which were printed, 'Not to be used without reasonable cause.' Most pre-war sailors, however, became well acquainted with salt beef or pork, as it was used by the more ruthless companies.

The very large companies such as the Cunard/White Star Line (those two companies merged in 1935), the Blue Star Line, the Blue Funnel Line, the White Funnel Line, Elders and Fyffes, the P&O Line and the Clan Line, being passenger or passenger/cargo combination vessels, ran very efficient ships to a very high standard of safety and hygiene. But although food standards and crew accommodation and conditions aboard such vessels was very much better than in tramp steamers, tankers and general cargo freighters, the rates of pay were exactly the same. However, crews did stand a much better chance of survival aboard such ships.

In a report issued by the London School of Hygiene and Tropical Medicine in 1938, it was stated that the mortality rate for men below the age of fifty-five was twice as high for merchant seamen as it was for the rest of the male population. Statistics issued later by the Registrar General showed that the death rate for merchant seamen was 47 per cent in excess of the national average. The main killer was tuberculosis, brought about by the damp, unhygienic and generally appalling conditions under which those men were forced to live and work.

Although it is true to say that the merchant navy of those days employed some very rough diamonds, hard cases, vagabonds and thoroughly disreputable characters, many of whom had 'shipped out' one step ahead of the law, no one can ever deny the massive contribution which was made by those men throughout the First and Second World Wars, and no matter what their social or intellectual status, nothing could excuse the atrocious and humiliating way in which they were treated.

Neither must it ever be forgotten that there was a large contingent of foreign seamen such as Malays, Chinese, Arabs, Somalis, East and West Indians and many others who had travelled to Britain to put their lives on the line in aid of the British war effort. They were all lumped together into the same melting pot of festering ships and the most appalling living and working conditions of any group of British workers throughout history. In conditions of unrelieved horror, they lived and worked in virtual isolation from the outside world, which was the nature of their work, condemned to a life of poverty, squalor and sudden, violent death. In spite of that, they played out what surely was one of the most important roles in the Allied victory, and were contemptuously tossed aside for their efforts.

Before the war, those foreign seamen, called 'Lascars', always served aboard ships which sailed to the warmer climes. When war began, however, and ships were likely to be sent to any destination by government order, the Lascars very often found themselves in cold, stormy seas. They suffered very badly from the change and did not like those new conditions but, as the official history of the merchant navy cold-bloodedly put it, 'They were always plentiful, almost invariably docile and gave no trouble.' When the ex-Italian passenger/cargo combination *Calabria* was transporting Lascar seamen to Britain, she was torpedoed and sunk by *Korvettenkapitän* Victor Schutze in U-103, 350 miles (650 km) west of Ireland. (Throughout this book distances are expressed in miles. The reader should assume statute miles for land and nautical miles for sea distances.) Four hundred and fifty Indian and twenty-two British seamen lost their lives in that incident and yet that tragedy does not even get a mention in either the Royal or merchant navy histories. Were they really that unimportant to government leaders and naval commanders?

Being civilians, merchant seamen had the right to 'pay off' the ship in which they sailed just as soon as it returned to any UK port, and although such a practice was quite common, not one of them ever left the service. After March 1941, for example, the Government assumed the power to prevent men from leaving the service and to direct former merchant seamen back to it under threat of imprisonment. The continuous flow of volunteers was such, however, that, even though the merchant service lost many thousands of men throughout the almost six years of war, the manning of merchant ships was never compromised. It was a situation where the unexplained met the unfathomable because, even though those men were well aware of just what they were letting themselves in for, the flow of volunteers continued unabated all through the war years.

It was upon those starving, ill-housed, underpaid and tuberculosis-ridden seamen then that Britain, and later Russia, depended between 1939 and 1945, to bring in the food, oil, arms, ammunition, weapons and raw materials which were so badly needed in the fight against Nazi tyranny. It was the lifeline upon which Britain was absolutely dependent. Without the rust-buckets, and the massive efforts of the pathetic crews who manned them, the RAF would not have been able to fight the Battle of Britain, simply because they would not have had any aeroplanes to fly, let alone fuel to fly them. When Operation Sea Lion was imminent, it is true that it was the RAF and the Royal Navy that stood between freedom and the Nazi jackboot, but only because the men of the merchant navy kept them supplied at enormous cost in men and ships. Without that civilian service, the Royal Navy could not have put to sea, the Army would have been immobile and impotent, and the population of Britain would have been starved into submission within six months of the opening of hostilities. In the euphoria of victory, the part played by the merchant navy has been almost totally ignored and, for the most part, forgotten. (In very recent times, and fifty-six years after the defeat of Nazi Germany, the merchant navy has, at long last, been recognised for the service it gave, with its own Merchant Navy Day, the first of which was held in September 2002.) Not for them, however, compensation for injuries and severe traumas suffered as a result of enemy action at sea. Not for them the recognition that other essential civilian workers received – just oblivion and a quiet ride to the nearest graveyard at the end of it all.

However, war or no war, the owners still worshipped the god of profits, and protected them to the bitter end. When ships were sunk, whether by accident or by enemy action, their owners shed no tears of sorrow for either the ships or their crews. Having come under the authority of the Ministry of Shipping, or Ministry of War Transport, as it later came to be known, merchant ships were insured to the hilt, many of them grossly over-insured, having been covered by guarantees of reimbursement under the Government's insurance scheme, and their crews, or what was left of them, simply fired.

Anything that could float and carry cargo was welcomed by the Government, and ships which had been mothballed throughout the depression, most of them stinking, rotting hulks by then, were pressed into service. The result of that sudden build-up of shipping meant that there was at last, full employment for the merchant seamen, but with very little in the way of remuneration. It also meant a massive influx of profits for the ship owners.

One would imagine that the Government, the Admiralty and the owners would have been deeply ashamed of their conduct towards that lifeline upon which Britain depended so heavily, but as in times past, if any of them were, it was never manifest. In comparison with prestige, glory and profits, life aboard merchant ships and the horrors of sudden or lingering death or mutilation at sea were as nothing. Disgraceful and scandalous as the situation for merchant seamen was, everyone turned a blind eye to their plight, without regard to their conditions. The merchant seamen, with bodies gnarled by age and illness, and characters shaped by wind and sea, or with fresh, expectant young faces looking eagerly for adventure, were plunged into the front line of the war at sea, with the mystic chords of memory stretching from one battle to another.

Before the war started, Karl Doenitz declared that Britain had broken the London Submarine Agreement of 1936 by arming merchant ships, thereby converting them to warships. That was his way of declaring 'open season' on the British merchant fleet whilst perpetuating the myth of his own honour. In his memoirs, he made no mention of the fact that German 'armed raiders' in the form of converted merchant ships or heavy and light cruisers were already on station at sea waiting to annihilate British merchant ships whenever and wherever they found them. The truth was of course that the guns with which most merchant ships were equipped were so antiquated that they posed more danger to the crews who operated them than they ever did to enemy targets at which they were aimed. Even so, it is also true that a submarine on the surface was always at a very great disadvantage in an artillery duel with merchant ships, owing to the vulnerability of the pressure-hull. So, even with such antiquated weapons, merchant ships were potentially lethal to the U-boats.

Whilst the smaller ships of the British merchant fleet were forced to make do with pathetically feeble old weapons, ranging from the humble .303 Bren guns to the 12-pounders and 3.7-inch naval guns of First World War vintage, the larger, faster and far more important ships carried the kind of armament which would make any destroyer captain green with envy (as in Operation Pedestal in August 1942). But even that kind of sophisticated armament was quite useless against a submerged submarine. It was designed mainly for air defence, but these ships did, on occasion, become involved in artillery duels with U-boats, and usually won.

It was in these circumstances then that the British merchant fleet came under the authority of the Ministry of Shipping in 1939 and, through the auspices of the Naval High Command, came to be official known as the British Mercantile Marine and was plunged into the front line of the war at sea. Many of the seamen had already tasted the vile fruits of total war at sea in the First World War, and it was the stark realisation of their darkest nightmares in which a whole generation of young men forfeited their youth. Shaped in the bitter crucible of war, they are now old men, yesterday's men, forgotten men.

At eleven o'clock on the morning of 3 September 1939, a sombre-voiced Prime Minister Neville Chamberlain informed the British population that they were once again at war with Germany. From that moment, and right up until March 1940, the newspapers and radio termed that short period the 'phoney war', as little or no action was undertaken – mainly because Britain had virtually nothing with which to wage war on land or in the air. There was no 'phoney war' at sea, however. War for the merchant seamen, and for their Royal Navy counterparts, began just twelve hours from the British declaration of war. At sea, the war raged with such fury that it presaged a long, bitter and blood-drenched conflict, which was to last beyond the German surrender in May, 1945.

At 23.00 hours on the evening that war was declared, the German U-boat U-30, commanded by *Kapitän-Leutnant* Fritz Julius Lemp, torpedoed and sank the 13,500-ton Donaldson liner *Athenia* 250 miles (460 km) to the north-west of Ireland, with the loss of 110 passengers and eighteen crew. The *Athenia* presented no more threat to Nazi Germany than the women and children she carried as evacuees to the United States. Lemp claimed to have mistaken her for an armed merchant cruiser, and upon his return to Germany, he was given secret orders to alter his ship's log accordingly. To add insult to injury, the German government immediately issued a statement that Winston Churchill had personally ordered that a bomb should placed aboard the *Athenia* in order that its resultant destruction would prejudice German–American relations. That rather silly statement received more than a little credence in some unfriendly quarters, notably amongst the American isolationists, many of whom were Communists.

That barbarous act then set the pattern for a long and dirty war against British merchant shipping, with ships being indiscriminately sunk without regard to their status. By the third week of November 1939, the U-boats had sunk sixty-six British ships. (Fritz Julius Lemp died at sea the following year when his boat was forced to the surface by the British destroyers *Bulldog* and *Broadway* and the corvette *Aubretia*. Lemp's was the U-boat from which the crew of *Aubretia* captured the German Enigma machine and its attendant cypher and code books.)

In the weeks that followed the sinking of the *Athenia*, Doenitz's sea-wolves struck time and time again at the merchant shipping that was so vital to Britain's, and ultimately Europe's survival. Even the mightiest of Britain's warships fell prey to the German U-boats, the first large casualty being the aircraft carrier, HMS *Courageous* which was torpedoed and sunk in the Western Approaches with the loss of 518 men. That was followed a month later by the sinking of the mighty battleship, HMS *Royal Oak* whilst swinging at anchor in Scapa Flow. Eight hundred and thirty-three men went down with her.

The losses in ships and cargoes alone was staggering, but what was happening to crews and passengers was truly appalling, and stunned all who heard of it into shocked immobility. In the terrifying minutes between a torpedo's steel-shattering explosion and the victim's final death plunge beneath the sea, those unfortunates who were not killed outright by the tremendous force of the initial explosion were all too often crushed by collapsing steel bulkheads, scalded to death by high-pressure superheated steam from ruptured pipes and exploding boilers, or drowned by the thousands of tons of freezing sea-water.

Fire at sea is probably the seaman's worst nightmare. When a tanker or any other vessel carrying fuel oil, ammunition or otherwise volatile cargo was hit, the resulting conflagration spread very rapidly, cascading from ruptured hulls into the surrounding sea. Scenes of men burning and struggling frantically in an ocean of blazing oil have been graphically described to me on many occasions, and I never cease to wonder how it was that these intrepid men kept on going back to sea after surviving such hideous terror.

By December 1939, the number of sinkings by the torpedoes, mines, bombs and shells of surface raiders had soared to terrifying proportions, so that within the short space of just four months, more than 220 merchant ships, representing a staggering

750,000 tons, along with more than 1,500 men, women and children, had gone to the bottom of the sea.

Nearly six years later, on 7 May 1945, three days after the German surrender in the west, the Canadian freighter *Avondale Park* was torpedoed and sunk by *Kapitän-Leutnant*, Emil Klusmeier in U-2336 in the Firth of Forth with great loss of life. The Nazi commander claimed not to have received any orders concerning the cessation of hostilities. Those two events, the sinking of the *Athenia* and the *Avondale Park*, marked the beginning and the end of the Battle of the Atlantic, the most prolonged and bloodiest campaign of the Second World War. It was a battle which Britain had to win at any cost because upon its outcome depended the outcome of the entire war worldwide. The merchant navy also had its fair share of heroes, with over 6,000 meritorious awards for gallantry being made.

Such pitiless action by German U-boat crews against virtually unarmed merchant ships followed strictly the letter of Doenitz's commands. However, although there are many oral accounts of submarine crews machine-gunning survivors in the water or in lifeboats, only one U-boat captain, Eck of U-852 and his officers, was eventually convicted by an Allied court of deliberately killing survivors in the water when he torpedoed and sank the Greek ship, *Peleus*. After the war, they were all tried, convicted and executed for acts of extreme barbarism. Indeed, even though many atrocities were carried out at sea, there were very few U-boat commanders who became involved in acts of barbarism.

In looking at tonnage losses, it becomes very easy to overlook the human tragedy involved in the war at sea. It is a tragedy in itself that the cost in human life has always been ignored. In fact, the seamen were told quite categorically that their ships and cargoes were of far more importance than they were. It was indelicate and cruel perhaps, but in the overall scheme of things, and in the face of the Nazi terror which was then sweeping relentlessly over the whole of Europe and the Middle East, it was true to a large extent. It is also true, however, that the merchant seamen have never, even to this day, received the accolades which have been heaped upon our armed services, services which, ironically, could not have functioned without the merchant fleet. Karl Doenitz's U-boat war was merciless and unremitting, and under his direction, U-boat commanders showed little or no mercy towards largely ineffectively armed merchantmen, and even less for the innocent passengers they sometimes carried.

In September 1939, the merchant navy employed some 120,000 officers and ratings. By May 1945, upwards of 35,000 of those men had perished with their ships and cargoes. (Casualty figures for merchant seamen vary considerably, ranging from 35,000 to 50,000.) Many thousands more were disabled in both body and mind after some of the most horrendous experiences at sea, my own father, brother and other family members amongst them. It was a far higher percentage of losses than any of our armed services.

Whilst many merchant navy officers who held commissions in the Royal Naval Reserve went off to man the corvettes and smaller vessels of the Royal Navy, the bridges, engine-rooms, decks, galleys, radio shacks and saloons were filled with men whose age in any other profession would have debarred them from military service. At one end of the scale there were 14- and 15-year-old deck and galley boys, and 16-year old bridge apprentices and radio operators, none of whom had ever really learned how to live, but who very quickly learned how to die. At the other end of the scale could be found uprooted pensioners in their seventies who had done it all before and knew what was to come. Wartime propaganda made much of the willingness of young men barely out of school, and even more of the older men who had come out of their well-earned retirement to serve once more under the 'Red Duster'. And it was with the sustained endurance of those merchant seamen, no matter what their age, that Britain's hope of victory against Nazi oppression lay. The merchant navy always got through, but they got through at a terrible price in loss of life, limb and ships. (Theoretically, the minimum age for young men wishing to become merchant seamen was sixteen in 1939/40. It was no strange sight, however, to see youngsters of fourteen and fifteen manning merchant ships, my own brother being one of them. My father became a merchant seaman at the age of fourteen in 1922, my grandfather and great-grandfather at thirteen and twelve respectively.)

Lacking the long traditions and cohesive *esprit de corps* which supported the men of the Royal Navy, the merchant seamen were victims of chaotic economic conditions, their employment was erratic and their futures uncertain. They were always very much aware of the poor and unjust treatment they received from the Government, employers and the Admiralty and a great many of its high-ranking officers, and of being grossly undervalued, even by the general population. Such perceptions were given greater force by the general unwillingness of the Royal Navy to give them adequate protection, and by the fact that a merchant seaman's pay stopped at the moment he abandoned his sinking ship. Unlike the men of the Royal Navy, the merchant seamen did not get survivor's leave whenever their ships were shot away from under them. All they were entitled to was their annual holidays and time off in lieu of Sundays spent at sea (actually at sea, not in port). Time spent fighting for their lives in open lifeboats or on flimsy rafts in the deep oceans, often with horrific injuries or with lungs full of oil and sea-water and very little, if anything, in the way of emergency supplies, was treated as an unpaid excursion. Merchant seamen died in the knowledge that they were dying unemployed, and the fact that such an awful situation had been allowed to develop by people who should have known better left an indelible mark in the minds of merchant seamen everywhere.

There existed between the merchant crews and the crews of the small escort vessels such as the destroyers and corvettes – especially the corvettes whose crews had been drawn mainly from the merchant navy – a mutual admiration which formed a bond of sorts between the two services, and neither would have changed places with the other. With its self-confessed air of superiority, the Royal Navy for the most part tended to look down on its entrepreneurial counterpart, whose losses were very often trivialised simply because merchant ships carried much smaller crews than naval vessels. No one ever seemed to stop to consider that merchant ships were being lost at such a tremendous rate that fatalities were mounting accordingly, so that by the war's end, the merchant navy had lost a far higher percentage of men than any of our armed services.

A very wide gulf separated the men of the two services and the Arctic convoys, especially the farce of PQ 17, provided the catalyst which brought about the widening of that gulf, which affected the men of the merchant navy for a very long time afterwards. In truth however, the services were so inextricably linked that they were totally dependent upon each other for their very existence. Without the merchant fleet, the Royal Navy could not have functioned. Without the Royal Navy, the merchant fleet would have been totally annihilated.

Whilst other civilian workers in reserved occupations such as the miners, dock workers, factory workers, policemen, aircraft and shipyard workers and others took home fat pay-packets through essential overtime working – and the miners and some dock workers even struck for more at various times even though it was illegal to stage strikes in times of national emergencies – and lived in their own homes and could buy goods on the black market, the merchant seamen and their families lived and died penniless and hungry. (I was a first-hand witness to that situation as a youngster throughout the war.) The people who held the country to ransom with their strikes and grievances knew full well that the government would be forced to give way to their demands simply because a whole industry could not be jailed and the commodity which they produced was vital to the British war effort. Never, however, through all the long, bitter years of savagery at sea, did the merchant seamen ever suggest strike action, and never was there any form of mutiny. The bitterness which their situation generated, however, fuelled a growing discontent within the merchant service which lasted for many years after the war had ended.

America's entry into the war in December 1941 only served to heighten their awareness of the shameful way in which they were treated compared with their American colleagues. American seamen were well fed, well treated and well paid. When the Arctic convoys began after Hitler's Operation Barbarossa, all American seamen employed on the Arctic route to northern Russia received 'danger money' at the rate of £16 per month over and above their already generous rates of pay. British seamen received just £2. 10s a month war bonus, nothing more – not even simple human justice or compassion.

During the early years of the war, merchant ships were being lost at such a tremendous rate that Britain had neither the resources nor the manpower to replace them, and in that respect, Karl Doenitz's assertion that his U-boat service alone could starve Britain into submission was no idle boast. In fact, his categorical promise to Hitler on that subject was actually achievable by mid-1941. However, Britain's merchant fleet was to receive a much-needed boost in that year from unexpected sources. When the German *blitzkrieg* of 1940/41 had conquered over half of Europe, quite a large proportion of the merchant ships of the conquered nations which were at sea at the time escaped capture. Their captains faced a most appalling dilemma, because the families whom they had left behind had come under German control. It was the Danes and Norwegians who were the first to suffer, in April, 1940. The BBC immediately put out broadcasts to those ships at sea offering them protection and payment for their services. The Germans were saying exactly the same things at the same time, urging the captains of those ships to return to their home ports. The exact same thing happened when The Netherlands and Belgium were occupied the following month, but not one of the ships of those conquered nations ended up in German hands. In 1941 yet another large tonnage of shipping was successfully diverted to Britain when Greece and Yugoslavia were invaded, the larger Greek fleet making a particularly important contribution. Britain received a further 480,000 tons of shipping when neutral Sweden offered 60 per cent of its merchant fleet on charter to Britain. The result of that astute action meant that the British merchant fleet had been expanded by more than 700 ships, representing a total of some 3 million tons of priceless shipping capacity.

Of the 30 million tons of British merchant shipping available in 1939, 4 million tons was requisitioned by the navy as armed merchant cruisers, Royal Fleet Auxiliaries or troopships. This left some 26 million tons for trade. British merchant ship losses for the year 1941 alone amounted to 4,300,000 gross tons, representing 1,300 vessels. Such massive losses were not replaceable at that stage of the war; but in 1942, merchant ship losses soared to an unprecedented 7,800,000 tons – 1,665 ships. The German U-boat force at the beginning of 1941 consisted of ninety-one boats. By the end of that year, and despite the loss of eighty-seven boats throughout that year, it had grown to 212. Britain did not have the manpower, financial resources or raw materials to be able to sustain such losses, but more help was at hand.

In 1941 the era of the American liberty ships began, and with them and such new vessels as Britain was able to build came a gradual improvement in shipboard life and conditions for the merchant seamen. Moreover, along with these very gradual changes came a limited increase in pay.

Liberty ships were mass-produced, prefabricated merchant ships with all-welded hulls, which were produced in the USA between 1941 and 1945 to replace the vast amount of tonnage lost to the Axis forces. They were the product of quite a large number of shipyards throughout the USA, and they formed the emergency part of a shipbuilding programme which had been started by the US Government some years earlier. That programme was for standard-design merchant vessels, of which 4,900 were built including 2,700 liberty ships. The total dead-weight was in excess of 40 million tons, 29,292,000 tons of which was accounted for by the liberty ships. Twenty-four of those were equipped as colliers, eight as tank carriers, thirty-six as aircraft transports and sixty-two as tankers (T2s).

The original design for those vessels had been produced by the Sunderland Company, on the Tyne, as long ago as 1879, and it was adopted by the US Government because it combined simplicity of design and operation, rapidity of construction, large cargo-carrying capacity and the remarkable ability to be able to withstand anything that the natural elements could throw at them. However, it has since been discovered that in very cold conditions the steel that was used to build those ships tended to crack quite easily, especially where there were welded joints. It must of course be borne in mind that the standard of steel technology in the 1940s was nowhere near as high as it is today, and consequently, some of those ships foundered a sea in what were then mysterious circumstances. Since the discovery of the RMS *Titanic* by Dr Bob Ballard in 1985, a close inspection of that vessel's hull has revealed the selfsame faults in the steel that was used to build her as was used in those liberty ships. Even so, they made a very significant and valuable contribution to the Allied war effort.

Because the entire American capacity for turbine engines was geared up for naval fighting ships, the liberty ships were fitted out with triple-expansion steam engines and steam-driven auxiliary machinery. With a dead-weight tonnage of 10,500, their overall speed was something in the order of 10 or 11 knots (18.5–20.3 kph).

Under a lend-lease agreement between Britain and the USA, 200 of those vessels were built for the British Mercantile Marine by the New England Shipbuilding Corporation in Portland, Maine, all of which were prefixed with the abbreviation SAM (Superstructure aft of midships, the forward part of the bridge being almost on the centre line). Each of those SAMs were 421 feet (128.3 m) in length, 57 feet (17.4 m) in the beam, with a draught of 27 feet 8 inches (8.4 m) when loaded to their marks. One 2,500-horsepower, triple-expansion steam-drive engine gave them an economical speed of between 10 and 11 knots. They were to serve Britain well for quite a number of years after the war had ended. In fact, I actually sailed on two of them myself during the 1950s.

The last of the liberty ships is the SS *Jeremiah O'Brien*, which is now in the National Defense Reserve Fleet at Suisun Bay on the San Francisco waterfront, commemorating the largest merchant shipbuilding venture in maritime history.

This book briefly tells the stories of some of Britain's merchant navy ships and the men who so loyally served in them. And it is to those men that this book is dedicated.

# 1   Convoy SC 7

This is the story of the first successful massed U-boat battle of the Second World War, and it has been told to me on many occasions over the years by men who sailed in it in the various ships which were involved. My father was one of those men and, if my memory serves me correctly, he sailed aboard a Welsh tramp steamer called the *Botusk*, which was owned by the Reardon Smith Company of Cardiff. A second mate I once sailed with in the 1950s was also on that convoy, serving aboard another Welsh tramp steamer called the *Beatus* which, along with her sister ship, the *Fiscus* – both owned by the Cardiff shipping company of Sir William Seager, perhaps better known as Tempus Shipping – was torpedoed and sunk almost within hailing distance of Northern Ireland and safety.

Although the Battle of the Atlantic had been going on since the very first day of the war with the sinking of the Donaldson liner, *Athenia*, the destruction of SC 7 was the first of the massed, big-action U-boat battles. It was a battle that should have served as a timely and valuable warning to the British government and the Admiralty of what could be expected from Karl Doenitz's U-boat fleet in the months and years ahead. In fact, those warnings had been very much in evidence from the very first day of the war but, as with so many other warnings that had been in evidence from as early as 1933, it went unheeded.

All the lessons that had been learned by the Royal Navy about convoy work during the First World War had all been meticulously documented and filed away in the Admiralty archives, and were readily available to anyone in the Naval High Command who desired to read them. Nobody did, preferring instead to prevaricate and bicker between themselves, the Chiefs of Staff of the Royal Air Force and government ministers as to the best way to fight the war at sea, each with their own pet ideas and very few with any real idea at all. It was a case of 'all of one accord, but very far from a meeting of minds'.

A prime example of this attitude is displayed in a written opinion of Winston Churchill's in 1940, and recorded in Volume 2 of his war memoirs, *Churchill, the Second World War*: 'The submarine should be quite controllable in the outer seas, and certainly in the Mediterranean. There will be losses, but nothing to affect the scale of events.' He went on to say, 'That opinion was not incorrect. Nothing of major importance occurred in the first year of the U-boat warfare. The Battle of the Atlantic was reserved for 1941 and 1942.' He failed to mention the 4,800,000 tons of British merchant shipping which had been lost to the U-boats between September 1939 and December 1940, nor did he mention the subject of this particular story, convoy SC 7, or the following one, HX 79. Moreover, this opinion contradicted the statement he made about his first request to the Director of Naval Intelligence in 1939 for information about the U-boat position in the Atlantic: 'I was at once informed that the enemy had sixty U-boats and that a hundred would be ready early in 1940. The number of long-range endurance vessels were formidable, and revealed the intention of the enemy to work far out in the oceans as soon as possible.' In fact, the number of long-range U-boats in the service of the German *U-bootwaffe* in 1939 was just twenty-six boats, not sixty, with another thirty small coastal vessels operating around the British coasts.

This story also shows the Royal Navy's inability to protect convoys, simply because they had neither the suitable escort vessels nor enough fully trained men available when war broke out. Whilst air force Chiefs of Staff and high-ranking naval flag officers at Whitehall argued and bickered between themselves, it was left to the men at grassroots level to do the very best they could with the woefully in-adequate tools at their disposal.

Whilst Coastal Command was clamouring for Lancaster bombers to protect Britain's vital merchant ships, Bomber Command would not release any because they were intent only on bombing German cities. Whatever that strategy may have achieved is open to question, except of course for the odd occasions when vital strategic targets were hit. Having said that, however, it is also true that, just as the Navy was desperately short of escort ships, Bomber Command was desperately short of long-range bombers at that time. Bearing in mind the circumstances under which the Royal Navy was forced to fight a vicious and highly dangerous enemy in possession of a small fleet of brand new U-boats and surface vessels, the only wonder is that they managed to do that job at all.

Anyone with any knowledge at all of naval warfare in the Western Ocean would surely have known that, to send convoys of slow, rapidly ageing tramp steamers with too few and totally inadequate escorts across an Atlantic Ocean completely dominated by German U-boats and, at the time, German heavy surface ships, was idiocy enough even in summer; in winter it was little short of murder. Like sacrificial lambs to the slaughter, the merchant seamen involved were nothing more than cannon-fodder for the Naval High Command and good practice shoots for Doenitz's U-boat fleet, and even though the Government, Bomber Command and high-ranking staff officers at Whitehall were aware of the situation, they willingly went along with it. It was a betrayal, a disgrace and a tragedy that so many brave men and fine ships of both Britain's maritime services were needlessly lost because of silly quarrels and prevarication by people with a wealth of education but not very much in the way of intelligent thought between them. This may seem a rather unkind statement, but the Lords of the Admiralty had seen it all before during the First World War. They knew full well the serious blunders and disasters which had been caused by their own senior officers between 1914 and 1918, just as the Chamberlain government of 1939 knew of the chaos, confusion and mayhem that Churchill had caused when he was First Lord of the Admiralty in that war, yet still he was once again made First Lord in 1939.

It is just as well that Hitler had been premature in involving Germany in a war with Britain, when the *Kriegsmarine* was woefully below strength in both ships and men and Karl Doenitz, who had requested 300 U-boats as being the absolute minimum needed to starve Britain into submission, had received just twenty-six ocean-going boats and thirty small coastal vessels by September 1939. Even with such a small number, however, the German submarine commanders were well enough able to find all the targets they could possibly want in the crowded sea lanes of the Western Ocean without too much danger to themselves. They roamed the Atlantic at will, sinking British merchant ships with complete impunity because the Royal Navy had no defence against them.

Opposed by a very few sloops, merchant cruisers and slow, lightly armed corvettes – which was the sum total of what the Navy could provide during the first eighteen months of the war, convoys held no terrors for the U-boat crews. The slow, all-too-few, antiquated escorts were vastly overextended and overwhelmed by the intensity of the pack attacks, so that they were very soon reduced to the level of rescue ships whilst all around them, erupting merchant ships were being torpedoed at will and their crew being killed and mutilated without mercy.

Such was the situation in the Western Ocean on 4 October 1940 when convoy SC 7 gathered in the sheltered waters of Sydney, Cape Breton, at the entrance to the Gulf of the St Lawrence River. They were destined to lose twenty-one ships in just two horrendous nights of mass, unrestricted slaughter. The following convoy, HX 79 was to lose fourteen ships in just one night of complete chaos. The total cost in tonnage lost to the British Mercantile Marine in SC 7 alone was 152,000 tons whilst the U-boats escaped unscathed.

The eastern Canadian port of Three Rivers is situated at the confluence of the St Maurice and St Lawrence rivers, very near to the St Lawrence estuary. It lies approximately 100 miles (160 km) east of Montreal and 80 miles (128 km) west of Quebec, about 800 miles (1,280 km) from the open sea. Throughout the war, Three Rivers ceased to be just a quiet backwater harbour sandwiched between the mighty

St Lawrence River and the vast Canadian pine forests, becoming instead one of the most important ports for the loading of the vast quantities of steel, aircraft, armaments and timber being shipped from Canada to Britain across the 3,000 miles (5,500 km) of treacherous and uncompromising Western Ocean. (The USA was still neutral at that time but, being sympathetic to the British cause, many thousands of tons of arms, ammunition and raw materials were being dispatched through Canada under the lend-lease agreement.)

It was at Three Rivers, in September 1940, that two rapidly ageing Welsh tramp steamers, the 4,885-ton *Fiscus* and *Beatus*, sister ships belonging to the Tempus line's fleet of just four vessels, were loading steel and timber. My father's ship, the *Botusk*, owned and operated by the Reardon Smith Company was, I believe, loading grain at Montreal.

The *Beatus*'s cargo was made up of heavy steel ingots which had been stowed in her lower holds, whilst her remaining cargo space in the tween decks had been used up with baulks of Canadian timber. She also carried a deck cargo of planks to a height of some 12 feet (3.6 m). Such a state of loading, being full cubic and dead-weight capacity was a sailor's dream, and highly satisfying to her skipper, Captain Brett. It was a cargo which could very well make the difference between life and death to her crew, with or without the attentions of Doenitz's U-boats. The even vertical distribution of weight would make her stable in high seas, and the timber would keep her afloat longer in the event of a torpedo strike. The cargo which had been loaded into the *Fiscus*, however, was a seaman's nightmare. Whichever clerk of Bumbledom had planned the loading of that ship had very firmly seen to it that she would roll onto her beam ends every inch of her voyage back to the UK. Even worse, however, was the fact that, being loaded only to her marks with a full dead-weight cargo of steel ingots topped off with a few crated fighters, she would go to the bottom like a stone should a torpedo strike. With too much weight too low down in her holds her skipper, Captain Ebenezer Williams, a dour and, by nature, confirmed pessimistic North Walian, was not a happy man.

Like the *Beatus* and the *Fiscus*, the *Botusk* was just an ageing, overworked Welsh tramp steamer, well past her 'sell-by' date, and all three ships carried crews drawn mainly from the South Wales ports. Amongst those crews were many young boys of between fourteen and seventeen years of age – children by today's standards. In the dark and dangerous days of the 1940s however, they were forced to grow up very fast indeed.

All three ships duly sailed from their ports of loading on or about 1 October, and all three joined convoy SC 7 on the 4th. My father's ship, the *Botusk*, was about four hours astern of the *Beatus* and the *Fiscus*, and dropped her hook into the frigid waters off Cape Breton Island in the late afternoon of the 4th.

My father told me that the crew of the *Botusk* lost all hope of getting through the U-boat packs when they saw the thirty-two ageing rust-buckets assembled on the leaden-grey waters of Sydney harbour, and their hearts dropped when it became apparent that the convoy commodore vessel was the 26-year-old 3,000-ton *Assyrian*, another ancient rust-bucket which would have been far more suited to the subtropical coastal trade rather than the North Atlantic at the start of the winter storms.

Also included amongst those antiquated relics of another age were the three Great

Lakes steamers, the *Trevisa*, the *Eaglescliffe Hall* and the *Winona*, each of them weighing in at just 1,800 tons and all even older than the *Assyrian* and those other elderly veterans which had been especially built to withstand the mighty seas of the North Atlantic. The *Botusk* herself was a 21-year-old, 3,000-ton tramp, and along with the *Beatus* and the *Fiscus*, the pride of the whole sorry collection. Of the others, my father could only describe them as 'a sad armada of geriatric piles of scrap', all about to challenge the mighty Western Ocean, which was then totally dominated by hostile U-boats.

Proudly led by the diminutive *Assyrian*, a three-island steamer more suited to some maritime museum or breaker's yard than the North Atlantic, convoy SC 7 finally left Sydney on 5 October, and as though the sight of such a curious collection of junk was not enough to prompt U-boat skippers to rub their hands with delight, the ships designated to escort and protect them, the Canadian armed yacht, HMCS *Elk* and the 1,000-ton sloop, HMS *Scarborough*, were not exactly designed to strike terror into the hearts of the enemy. In fact, they would have been more likely to roar with laughter. They certainly failed to inspire confidence in any of the merchantmen. My father described them as 'having about the same effect as a dose of senna-pods'.

Wrapped up in a gloomy basket of cynicism then, with melancholy weighing heavily on their shoulders, the seamen hove the hooks up from the sea bed and they began to get under way. That October day was one of the very rare occasions when the Western Ocean wore its more serene face. The weather was fine and clear, with little more than a fresh breeze blowing out from the north-north-west, but bringing with it the stupefying cold of a fast-approaching Canadian winter, the awful dead smell of the Arctic tundra, and a warning that the Western Ocean would not remain benign for very long, and was about to bare its considerable fangs.

Throughout the following two days, the wind speed steadily increased and the leaden grey seas rose ominously until, by the 7th, it was up to severe gale force 9 to storm force 10. It was also on the 7th that the tiny HMCS *Elk*, running short of fuel and unable to withstand the mountainous seas then slamming into her frail hull with the force of large steam-hammers, turned back, leaving HMS *Scarborough* as the one remaining escort vessel. Four other ships, including the pitiful 1,800-ton *Trevisa*, also broke ranks and were left to straggle along far astern as best they could.

As the storm increased in intensity and the fast-running seas rose to un-precedented heights, the remainder of the convoy fought desperately to hold ranks as they rolled and pitched slowly eastwards, uncomfortable but unmolested. Carrying a full dead-weight of steel in her lower holds, the *Fiscus*, as her deadly cargo silently promised, was rolling her scuppers under as she took the green over her blunt bows, her red-leaded foredeck constantly awash with boiling white foam. As with all the other ships in the convoy, the crew of the *Botusk* fought a hard battle just to stay on station, but from her wheelhouse, my father was hard put to be able to see the *Fiscus* at all through the murk and wind-driven rain and spray. She appeared to be spending more time under the sea than on the surface, and I shudder to think how her crew must have suffered just to be able to stay upright on such a crazily rolling deck.

Still unmolested on the 16th, when they had reached the northernmost point of their route in co-ordinates, 60 degrees north by 15 degrees 30 minutes west, their hopes were high as they began steering a more southerly course of 135 degrees. As they came within four days' steaming time from the North-western Approaches, the hard-pressed HMS *Scarborough* was joined by the sloop HMS *Fowey* and the flower class corvette, HMS *Bluebell*. It was at that point that they heard the piteous pleas for help from the tiny *Trevisa*, one of the three Great Lakes steamers which had been so thoughtlessly included by some bureaucrat who had probably never even seen the sea. *Trevisa* was by then straggling far astern. The U-boats had found their first victim. There were no survivors. As though conspiring together with the German forces, the wind and sea ceased their violent raging, and the merchant crews waited, tense and nervous, for the approaching onslaught.

They did not have long to wait. Just before midnight on the 16th, *Kapitän-Leutnant* Bleichrodt in U-48 was scanning the darkness of an apparently empty North Atlantic when he suddenly sighted the ponderous mass of rolling and pitching steamers heading straight towards his boat, approximately 180 miles (288 km) north-west of Rockall, that lonely, forlorn and windswept outcropping of rock on the Western Ocean shipping lanes. Immediately, he sent out a wireless message to the BdU (the U-boat headquarters at Lorient, on the west coast of France) for assistance, then began stalking his helpless prey.

Immediately Bleichrodt's message was received, Doenitz ordered his North Atlantic force into action. In the general area at the time were Otto Kretschmer in U-99, Engelbert Endrass in U-46, Fritz Frauenheim in U-101, Joachim Schepke in U-100 and Karl-Heinz Moehle in U-123. Just thirteen months into the war, those five ace U-boat commanders had already accounted for seventy-eight merchant ships between them. They stationed their vessels in a north-west/south-east line ahead of the projected convoy track, and there waited to spring a lethal trap.

Slowly and with infinite patience in the darkness, Bleichrodt coaxed the surfaced U-48 into position about a mile off the port flank of the convoy, and there remained, silently watching the ghostly silhouettes slide past across the moonpath.

At approximately 05.00 hours on the 17th, when the three escorts were farthest away from him, Heinrich Bleichrodt began a lone attack with a fan of four torpedoes which sank three conveniently overlapping ships within minutes of each other. The first to go was the 3,840-ton *Scoresby*. Hit on her starboard side by just one torpedo, she took on an immediate list and sank within ten minutes, taking all of her engine-room crew down with her. Moments after the *Scoresby* was hit, the French tanker *Languedoc* was hit by two torpedoes which literally ripped her apart when her cargo of fuel oil ignited with a tremendous roar that reverberated over the ocean like the crack of doom. A massive fireball immediately engulfed the vessel from stem to stern, and all that could be seen of the furiously burning wreck from the bridge of the *Botusk* was a black pall of rolling oily smoke relieved only by a vast sheet of blood-red flame as the tanker disintegrated. Mere moments later, she was gone; there were no survivors. The third ship to be hit by that same salvo was the 4,670-ton *Haspenden*. She too went down within minutes of being hit, and also took most of her crew down with her.

Contrary to instructions contained in the German BdU's handbook for submarine commanders, Bleichrodt made the almost fatal mistake of attacking on the surface just as a grey dawn was beginning to creep over the south-eastern horizon, leaving himself wide open to air attack from bases in Northern Ireland. A Sunderland flying-boat of Coastal Command, the first air cover to find the convoy, spotted U-48 on the surface and immediately dived to the attack. Although the Sunderland's bombs did no damage to the U-boat, Bleichrodt was force down. The escorting sloop, HMS *Scarborough* then gave chase, wasting most of that day hunting it. By the time she had broken off the engagement empty-handed, she was so far astern of the convoy that she was never able to catch up, leaving just one sloop and one smaller corvette as sole escorts for a thirty-ship convoy in an ocean teeming with enemy U-boats.

As the Asdic pings bounced off U-48's hull, Bleichrodt took his boat down to 600 feet (183 m) and there prepared to wait out *Scarborough*'s attack. For the following eight hours, the deadly thuds of exploding depth-charges kept the U-boat's crew's nerves jangling. Fortunately for them, however, the charges had been set for a depth of 400 feet (122 m), and Bleichrodt's only thought throughout that long and terrifying ordeal was that the convoy was escaping his attentions.

During the early hours of 18 October, U-38, commanded by Heinrich Liebe, came upon the convoy quite by chance, and immediately began shadowing. Reporting its position to Doenitz, an updated message was sent out to his waiting wolf-pack, and the scene was set for the first mass slaughter in the Battle of the Atlantic.

Liebe, meanwhile, had made a rather unenthusiastic attack, damaging just one ship, the freighter *Carsbreck*, whose cargo of timber kept her afloat until she reached safety, before breaking off the engagement. Soon after Liebe's withdrawal on the morning of the 18th, the escort was reinforced by the arrival of the sloop *Heartease*, bringing the total escort strength up to two sloops and one corvette, none of which had received any training in working with each other, thereby making the whole a very fragmented group whose members were, in effect, at odds with each other. At that point, however, the convoy was just 150 miles (275 km) away from the west coast of Ireland, and well within range of air cover.

Optimism reigned amongst the merchant crews, and even Captain Ebenezer Williams felt his pessimism lift just a little with the knowledge that within the following twenty-four hours they would be safe. At 19.00 hours on the evening of the 18th, however, on a fine, clear night, convoy SC 7 sailed into the cross-hairs of the U-boat trap awaiting it.

Karl-Heinz Moehle, commanding U-123, and the least experienced of Doenitz's aces, almost bungled the whole operation as he opened the attack by failing to sink the 5,458-ton *Shekatika* which, at that point, was quite a long distance ahead of the main body of the convoy. Before the escorts were able to co-ordinate their defence, however, the more experienced Engelbert Endrass in U-46 reacted very quickly, and at 20.15 hours fired off his first salvo. Within the space of ten minutes, the Swedish freighter, *Convallaria* had capsized. Her cargo of pulpwood kept her over-turned hull afloat for a further fifteen minutes before she finally sank. A little while later, one of the lookouts aboard the *Beatus* spotted the low profile of a submarine as it was silhouetted against the moonglow then reflecting off the black water, off her port bow. Captain Brett, alerted by the lookout's warning, had barely enough time to transmit an urgent warning of an imminent U-boat attack (SSS) before the port side of his ship was ripped out by the force of the exploding torpedo, creating a 40-foot (12 m) gash in her Number 2 hold. The resulting inward pressure of water coupled with the blast of the torpedo caused the bulkheads separating the Number 2 hold from the engineroom and Number 1 hold to collapse, causing rapid flooding throughout three-quarters of her length. A quick inspection of the carnage wrought by that one torpedo was enough to reveal that, despite her cargo of timber, the *Beatus* was doomed. Accordingly, Captain Brett issued orders to abandon ship. No lives were lost.

No sooner had the *Beatus* been torn apart than the commodore aboard the *Assyrian* issued orders for the convoy to scatter. Whether or not that was an ill-advised order is not for me to say, but as the ships pulled out of line to go their separate ways, the slaughter began with enthusiastic fervour by the U-boats.

The next ship to go was the British steamer *Creekirk*, taking her crew and cargo of iron ore to the bottom in seconds. Minutes later, another British steamer, the *Empire Miniver* suddenly lurched out of line with steam and black, oily smoke gushing from her funnel and ruptured hull as her crew fought to lower the boats.

At that time, the sloop *Heartease* had left the convoy to stand by the steamer *Carsbreck*, which had been severely damaged following an earlier attack by U-38, and with the *Scarborough* still many miles astern, the two remaining escorts could do little more than chase around in ever-decreasing circles while, manoeuvring on the surface with complete impunity, the U-boat skippers gleefully moved in for the *coup de grâce*. In the following three hours, another five ships were sunk and the *Shekatika* again damaged. How that ship ever made port safely is a mystery, but somehow she did, which is a tribute to the seamanship skills and devotion to duty of her skipper and crew.

The 2,118-ton Dutch vessel *Boekolo*, commanded by Captain J. de Groot, had managed to get clear away from the furious assault. However, being a master mariner with many years' experience, and irretrievably imbued with the lore and sacred code of seafarers, and being aware that astern of him fellow mariners were struggling and dying in the cold, oil-coated waters of the North Atlantic, his conscience dictated that he return to help in the rescue of men in the water.

The *Beatus*, meanwhile, thanks to her carefully considered cargo, had taken forty minutes to sink, allowing all of her crew to get safely away in the boats. Together with his twenty-seven man crew in two lifeboats, Captain Brett spotted the *Boekolo* racing towards them at her best speed. They were soon spotted from the bridge and, very courageously if very foolishly, and also contrary to strict orders not to stop their vessels under any circumstances, Captain de Groot paid the ultimate price of stopping his ship to pick them up. The first of the two boats was already alongside when Joachim Schepke in U-100 surfaced just 500 yards (450 m) from the scene of de Groot's mission of mercy and, without hesitation or consideration for the safety of the men alongside, put one torpedo into the *Boekolo*'s Number 4 hold. She immediately developed a heavy port list and began to settle rapidly at the stern, sinking some eight minutes later. There were no casualties.

Not all the ships of SC 7 had scattered independently. In fact, most of them were still on station when Otto Kretschmer in U-99 began to move in for his twenty-fifth kill of the war. He had found himself right in the middle of the convoy, coolly picking off his targets at will, as though on a training exercise. Missing one ship on the convoy's flank, his torpedo hit another vessel, which was carrying a full cargo of ammunition. In the time it took for the flash of the exploding torpedo to expire, she had been blown to smithereens, leaving virtually nothing but a massive black cloud of billowing smoke above a maelstrom of confused water and debris to mark her passing.

Almost at once Kretschmer found a gap in the line of ships and, with almost contemptuous ease, wheeled through it, only to find the ancient and slow-moving veteran, *Assyrian*, bearing down on him, desperately trying to nail him with her archaic 12-pounder whilst firing a succession of star shells over the U-boat. For forty minutes, he twisted and turned to avoid the angle of the pursuing freighter and the small but deadly gun. On his final turn, he managed to fire off one torpedo, missing the *Assyrian* by a few feet, but destroying another ship, the *Empire Brigade*, which was just astern of the *Assyrian*.

Captain Ebenezer Williams was not alone in his horror and bewilderment at the sinkings going on all around him, however. My father and the crew of the *Botusk*, then just ahead of the *Fiscus*, stood on deck watching as the night of chaos and confusion continued unabated. All around, ships were burning, blowing up, sinking, some settling slowly and tiredly while others simply broke in half, with one section sticking ludicrously out of the sea until the imprisoned air trapped inside finally leaked out. The British steamer *Sedgepool*, with her bows blown off, knifed down into the sea with her screw still turning at full revolutions, hastening her and her crew into the final oblivion of the cold, Stygian depths.

The night sky was alive from the flickering light of burning and exploding ships. Burning timber and oil added to the chaos of the debris-littered sea. Canadian timber that had been scheduled for use as pit props, and floating spars trailing deadly, razor-sharp steel wire lashings and rope were tearing the bare flesh of men in the water to ribbons as they strove to climb onto anything which was floating. Many of those men were crushed to death as succeeding explosions churned the oil-soaked debris into maelstroms of floating death, producing lurid images of carnage.

Fearing for the safety of his ship and crew, Captain Williams rang down for full revolutions and ordered the helmsman to pull the heavily laden vessel off station as the ship began to steam ahead of the column in a pathetic attempt to escape the carnage of the U-boats. The pitifully slow and all-too-few escorts had been completely overwhelmed by the furious, uncompromising attack and, with little or no chance of engaging any of the U-boats, were then reduced to the level of rescue ships. Captain Williams knew this and decided to take his chances alone. The wily old fox Otto Kretschmer was there, however, ready and waiting for just such an opportunity, like an old and starving wolf waiting in ambush for an injured prey.

With just one well-aimed torpedo, the ancient hull plates of the *Fiscus* were ripped open as though they were made of cardboard and, with all her reserve buoyancy cancelled out by the dead weight of steel in her lower holds, she went to the bottom within seconds of being hit, taking Captain Williams and his entire crew down with her. Two of those crew members were 14- and 15-year-old galley boys.

The massacre of SC 7 could not, by any stretch of the imagination be called a battle. It was no more than a mass slaughter of men and ships with His Majesty's Navy completely impotent in the face of the overwhelming odds. The awful slaughter continued all through the night of 18 October and well into the early hours of the 19th. It was only when most of the U-boats had expended all their torpedoes by 04.00 hours on the morning of the 19th that they faded away into the approaching dawn. By that time, SC 7 had lost twenty-one ships out of a total of thirty-three which had sailed from Cape Breton two weeks earlier. Two others had been severely damaged, and two stragglers had been picked off.

It had taken just seven U-boats to effect the destruction of SC 7, and not one of them had even been damaged, let alone lost. Kretschmer, Moehle and Frauenheim had used up all of their torpedoes and, since it was torpedoes that determined the length of time that a U-boat could stay at sea, they were forced to return to their base. Kretschmer, it turned out, had sunk six ships and Moehle four, nearly a half of the convoy's total losses between two skippers.

As Kretschmer, Moehle and Frauenheim were leaving the scene, word came through from Lorient of a fast convoy of forty-eight ships, quite a large proportion of which were tankers, which was fast approaching their position on almost the same course as SC 7. Those U-boats that still had torpedoes were then joined by Liebe in U-38 and Gunther Prien in U-47, he who had torpedoed and sunk the British battleship *Royal Oak* inside the anchorage of Scapa Flow. The extreme violence of the previous night was about to be repeated some 200 miles (320 km) further west. On that occasion, however, the heat and fury was to be far more intense and the cost in human lives far greater. Oil burns far more fiercely than wood, and before the next dawn had crept over the wintry horizon, twelve ships of convoy HX 79 had gone to the bottom in a conflagration so great that it could be seen for many miles over the horizon.

The winter of 1940/41 was one of the worst in living memory in the Western Ocean. U-boat operations were severely curtailed and Allied losses dropped accordingly. While the British were being kept busy attempting to improve the Navy's defence against the U-boats, Doenitz and his commanders were gearing themselves up for a renewal of their wolf-pack attacks. As the weather eased in the spring of 1941, Allied losses began mounting once more as the U-boats again stalked the shipping lanes. Another year would pass before Doenitz had the U-boat numbers he had been pleading for; but the strategy for waging the most devastating kind of submarine warfare had already been found.

Captain Brett and his crew from the *Beatus* were all safely picked up by the corvette *Bluebell*, whilst the survivors of the Dutch vessel *Boekolo* were rescued by the sloop *Fowey*. All were landed safely at Gourock on 20 October. My father's ship, the *Botusk*, survived the U-boat attacks unscathed, only to be caught up in another, equally frightening experience while approaching the Scottish coast in fog.

All was eerily quiet in the wheelhouse as the fog came down, settling over the ocean like a grey, damp shroud in which the surviving ships became enveloped. As they proceeded cautiously at slow speed, the eerie silence in the midst of that all-embracing miasma was suddenly broken by the urgent shout of a lookout right up in the bows; there was a mine off her port bow. The *Botusk* had inadvertently overrun a British minefield while approaching the coast. Her luck held, however, and she came through unscathed again.

After that unnerving episode, my father joined the Elders and Fyffes Line, which operated fast, modern passenger/cargo combinations between Barry docks and the Caribbean. He stayed with Elders and Fyffes until February 1942 when he felt the need for a change of venue. At that time, the U-boat war in the Caribbean was at its height and no effort was being made by the US Navy to organise a convoy system. As a result, all ships, sailing independently, no matter how fast they were, became easy prey for the U-boat crews. By May of that year, however, he found himself in an entirely different – and colder – sea war. Little did he realise when he left the Elders and Fyffes Line what horrors awaited him on the Arctic convoys.

My father once said to me that he was no hero, and if one thinks of heroes as dashing, nerveless macho men running dementedly about waving guns, then he certainly was not. He hated violence of any kind. It is significant, however, that, in common with many thousands of other 'non-heroes' of the merchant fleet, he spent the entire Second World War as a deep-sea sailor, and if that is not heroic, then I cannot imagine what is.

# 2  A Tale of Two Ships

This is the story of two rapidly ageing tramp steamers, both of which were owned and operated by Welsh shipping companies and sailed mainly out of ports along the South Wales coast. It was related to me many years ago when, as a youth of sixteen, I was serving aboard another Welsh tramp steamer, the *Fairwood Oak*, which was exactly 50 per cent of the total fleet owned by a Swansea family who lived in Upper Killay very near to the Fairwood Common. Hence the names of their ships, *Fairwood Oak* and *Fairwood Elm*.

An able seaman aboard that ship was an ancient mariner whose only known name was 'Scouse', and who had made his home in Swansea – home being the place he would stay between ships, which would either be the local seaman's mission or the bar of some docklands pub. Scouse had served in the merchant navy from the age of fourteen, a career which began in 1892 with a voyage aboard a Swansea square-rigger around the dreaded Cape Horn to Lima, employed in the copper trade.

Having served his time in sail before going into steam, he had served through both world wars as an able seaman. He had also, over the years, become a past master at spinning yarns, and whether in the seaman's mess or sitting on one of the hatches in flying-fish weather, he would regale anyone who had a mind to listen with tales of ships and the sea. Scouse was also well versed in sea lore and super-stition and his tales were consequently enjoyable, outrageous, plausible, sad, funny, ridiculous, ludicrous, creepy and self-indulgent, and might well have contained truth, half-truth and outright lies all at the same time.

One balmy evening whilst on course for Freetown, Sierra Leone, the watch below were gathered on the Number 1 hatch, drinking tea, coffee or cocoa and smoking an endless supply of cigarettes. Scouse began relating the story of a tramp steamer aboard which he had served during the early days of the Second World War, the *Newton Pine*. Being a 16-year-old 'man of the world' I listened with a certain amount of amusement and scepticism to what I considered to be the fanciful ravings of an old relic of the sea. However, as the years, ships and voyages passed, my adolescent mind matured and I became more familiar with sea lore and stories of the merchant navy at war from other ageing old shellbacks, and I quickly learned never to doubt their tales. From them I learned that Scouse was a well-known character amongst the seafaring fraternity of Swansea and other ports around the country and indeed, the world, and that most of the tales he told were perfectly true.

There is nothing very glamorous or romantic about the tramp steamers of old. Squat, box-like vessels with straight, blunt bows and counter sterns, they sported one single funnel amidships, usually belching out billows of black, oily smoke which could be seen for many miles over the horizon. They were usually what is called 'three-island steamers', sporting fore and aft well-decks between a high fore-castle head, beneath which could usually be found the deck crew's and black gang's accommodation on the older ships such as the *Fairwood Oak*, and a high midships section which housed the bridge officers' and engineers' cabins, pantry and saloon. On the larger, more modern tramps, the catering staff's accommodation would also be found amidships. Above that was the boat deck, which usually sported four open lifeboats that in most cases had not been in the water from the day they were first fitted into the davits and two companion ladders, one on either side leading up to open bridge-wings encompassing a tiny wheelhouse in the centre, and a monkey island atop that. Just beneath the bridge would be found the captain's and mates' cabins. The galley would, in most cases, be situated just aft of the midships super-structure, either forward or aft of the bunker hold, depending on whether the ship was a coal or oil burner and whether her engineroom was aft or midships. There was a high poop deck aft, with perhaps a small boat deck above the aft accommo-dation, depending on the ship's size and the number of crew she carried. Tramp steamers were built more for efficiency rather than for speed and comfort. Relatively cheap to build and run, they served their owners well for many years – most of them for many more years than they had originally been designed for.

These vessels, when owned by avaricious companies of dubious integrity, were usually beaten-up 'rust-buckets' plying the lucrative Far East or European coastal trade routes and using cheap labour – usually Somali, Chinese, Middle Eastern or West Indian seamen. Many of them sailed under flags of convenience which meant that rules of safety at sea, conditions of employment, food and lower deck pay could usually be ignored. The 'Board of Trade Whack' definitely did not apply on vessels such as those. Poorly maintained and provisioned, these ships were owned by people who cared more for profits than for their ships and the men who sailed in them.

Unloved and unlovely, when viewed from outboard these ships were as ugly as sin. When viewed from inboard, however, they were positively grotesque. It is nevertheless a fact that any seaman aboard any ship, no matter how old or ugly she may be, becomes deeply attached to the vessel. Just before their ship enters port merchant seamen can hardly wait to get ashore. Best gear will be laid out neatly, shoes will be highly polished, haircuts given, and a general air of euphoria prevails. After a few days ashore, however, when they have had their fill of ale and women, they will become agitated and restless, eager to get back on board and into jeans, sea-jersey, woollen hat, sea-boots and knee-length woollen stockings. Their ship is their livelihood, their centre of recreation and their home.

The war at sea was a long, bloody affair, with no quarter asked or given, and although the larger, more important ships were quite adequately armed against air attack, the smaller, older ships, especially the tramp steamers, were not. In most instances, all they had in the way of defence were antiquated weapons of First World War vintage which would have been far more at home in a museum than on the deck of a ship at war. In any case, it was not very often that merchant ships were in a position to make use of their pathetically limited armaments. When attacks against merchant ships did occur, they usually took place at night from an unseen enemy, and the exploding torpedo ripping their ship apart was the first and only indication of danger that merchant seamen had. By the time that danger had registered in minds befuddled with sleep, it was too late for anything other than a mad scramble for the boats and rafts. Therefore, whenever an opportunity arose to put their relics of another age to good use, the merchant seamen, with a verve born out of frustration, desperation and extreme anger at what they saw as cowardly attacks, did so with an efficiency which at least equalled that of their Royal Navy counterparts.

Whilst many of the larger ships used Defensively Equipped Merchant Ships' (DEMS) crews or naval gunners, the smaller, less important tramps were obliged to use their own crew members. And if you do not believe that merchant crews could handle their weapons efficiently, then read the stories of the *Newton Pine* and the *Sarastone*.

Buenos Aires, the capital of Argentina, is situated on the southern shore of the Rio de la Plata, 150 statute miles (240 km) from the open Atlantic Ocean. Its summer climate is warm, sunny and pleasant. A sprawling and cosmopolitan megalopolis, it is one of the world's major ports as well as the national centre of commerce, industry, politics and culture. It has always been a firm favourite of seamen everywhere. The city itself has a charm which is all its own with plenty of interesting places to visit, from centres of culture and learning or lowlife drinking dens. The population can be charming, the women obliging and the ale plentiful. For the more discerning minds, Buenos Aires can also be a Mecca of cultural and intellectual interest.

Berthed snugly inside the large basin just opposite the Plaza Roma, the SS *Newton Pine*, loaded to her marks with Argentinian wheat and barley, was a typical, nondescript tramp steamer of 4,412 tons. Built in 1925 for the Graig Shipping Company of Cardiff and registered in that city, she left Buenos Aires on 27 November 1940 bound for Freetown, Sierra Leone, with her 1,134-ton cargo. She carried a crew of thirty-seven men, and was armed with a 12-pounder gun forward and a 4-inch low-angle (LA) naval weapon aft, both of them sorry, outdated reminders of a war fought two generations earlier. In command of the vessel was Captain C.N. Woolner, a master mariner with many years' experience and a stern but fair and loyal disciplinarian. An imposing figure in any company, he was never a man to suffer fools gladly, and was as sturdy and reliable as the ship he commanded.

With squat, beetle-like tugs fore and aft, the *Newton Pine* left the sanctuary of her berth on a fine, sunny morning to brave once again the unpredictable Atlantic Ocean, then teeming with enemy U-boats. Approximately twenty-four hours after passing through the Darsena Norte and nosing her blunt bows slowly into the great river, she passed by the wreck of the German pocket battleship *Graf Spee* just to the south and east of Montevideo, and entered the Atlantic Ocean.

Closely following the recommended Admiralty route given to him by the British Consul in Buenos Aires, courtesy of the captured Enigma decoding machine, Captain Woolner took his ship to sea unescorted and, upon clearing the estuary of the Rio de la Plata, set a course of 090 degrees, due east on a compass heading, as far as 20°W longitude. From there, his course would change to 005 degrees, east by north a half north, which would take the vessel direct to Freetown. That course would take the *Newton Pine* 2,000 miles (3,700 km) out into the vast Atlantic wastes before changing course again, and would involve a total voyage of some 5,000 nautical miles (9,300 km) instead of the 4,000-mile (7,400 km) it would normally have taken to reach Freetown at her best speed of 9 knots (16.7 kph). Although it was a far costlier route, it was infinitely preferable to the bottom of the South Atlantic.

Sailing first eastwards and then on a more northerly heading across that vast and fickle ocean must have seemed like a receding nightmare to Captain Woolner and his crew as they cruised through sun-drenched days and balmy, star-studded tropical nights of unsullied loveliness. Yet, 6,000 miles (11,100 km) away from his position on latitude 24°53'S, in the wild northern reaches of that great ocean, convoy HX 90 was pounding through high winds and heavy seas into the cross-hairs of the wolf-pack which was to virtually destroy it.

Also unknown to Captain Woolner at the time was the fact that, the German battle-cruiser *Admiral Scheer* has prudently moved southwards to the waters off Bermuda, where it sank the SS *Port Hobart* on the 24th. This followed the *Scheer*'s attack on HX 84, in which it sank five ships of the convoy. This number would have been greater but for the courage of Captain Fegan and his crew, of the British armed cruiser *Jervis Bay* – the only vessel available to protect the convoy – who attacked the *Admiral Scheer* and sacrificed themselves while giving the convoy time to scatter, avoiding further losses. Also loose somewhere in the Atlantic at that time were no less than seven German armed raiders, the *Atlantis*, the *Orion*, the *Widder*, the *Thor*, the *Pinguin*, the *Komet* and the *Kormoran*. All were replenishing from various supply ships in pre-designated parts of the Atlantic, and all were carefully disguised as innocent merchant ships of neutral nations, using many different flags to disguise themselves.

The *Newton Pine*, however, was but a tiny speck in that vast expanse of ocean, and it is doubtful if a man of Captain Woolner's character would have been seriously disturbed by the news, even had he known. Being a very sophisticated man in the ways of ships and the sea in general and war at sea in particular, he had developed a stoic calm and patience, and never worried himself unduly about things which *might* happen. He never allowed his guard to drop, however, and kept his guns' crews sharp and efficient, with frequent practice shoots. As a result, the *Newton Pine* carried a very efficient gun crew.

After a peaceful and uneventful voyage, the *Newton Pine* crossed the Equator on the morning of 13 December, and by that afternoon was just seventy-two hours' steaming time west of Freetown. In the area of the doldrum calms, the crew experienced idyllic weather conditions with a light easterly breeze – very unusual for that area – which, although not even strong enough to cause a ripple on the glassy-calm surface of the sea, brought some welcome relief from the blazing sun as the ship zigzagged her weary way north by east. Under powder-blue skies by day and star-studded black velvet by night, it was 'flying fish' weather all the way.

Ten minutes before the end of the first watch at 15.50 hours on that day the Second Mate, who was due to go off watch at 16.00 hours, was alarmed to see a torpedo break the surface about 1,500 yards (about 1.4 km) off the starboard quarter. With the instincts of the career seaman, he ordered hard-a-port in order to steer the ship away from the torpedo track. As he ran back to the starboard bridge wing, he threw the switch which operated the alarm bells before reaching the extremity of the bridge just in time to see the torpedo for the second time, clearly visible in the limpid blue water, pass along the ship's side about 20 feet (6 m) away.

My old shipmate Scouse was in the wheelhouse at the time, and was therefore in a position to give us all a first-hand account of the proceedings. The Second Mate alerted the Captain, who arrived on the bridge at the double less than a minute later and, according to Scouse, actually saw the torpedo for himself breaking the surface across the bows some way ahead of the ship. Without pausing he issued orders to the helmsman for a course change to 315 degrees, north-west on a compass heading, a course which was designed to put the ship stern-on to the direction from which the torpedo had appeared to come. At that point, there was no sign of the attacking submarine.

Thirty minutes later, when the skipper and his First Mate were in the chartroom composing a wireless report to warn all ships in the area of the presence of an unidentified enemy submarine, all hell seemed to break loose as the sound of gunfire suddenly shattered the still silence of that tropical day. Both men charged out onto the bridge wing to see shells bursting in the sea astern of them. On the surface, about 4 miles (7.5 km) off her port quarter, they saw for the first time the long, sinister outline of a submarine, her fore gun spitting fire as her shells sought out the unarmoured plates of the *Newton Pine*.

Captain Woolner immediately issued instructions for a course change designed to place the submarine directly astern and in line with the ship's 4-inch gun before giving the order to return fire. The scene had dramatically changed from one of peaceful tranquillity under a powder-blue tropical sky, to a desperate battle for survival against a superior enemy hell-bent on their destruction.

As the submarine constantly changed course in order to position itself for the best possible firing angle, so Captain Woolner changed course accordingly to keep it directly in line with his 4-inch on the stern, so presenting the smallest possible target whilst at the same time directing his own fire from the bridge. The ageing vessel shook from stem to stern as, with a tremendous roar followed by a tongue of fire, the *Newton Pine*'s first shell arched across the few miles of ocean separating the two antagonists, leaving the groaning plates of the vessel shuddering under the force of the gun's recoil, the sound reverberating through her ancient hull like some monstrous musical concerto.

That first shell fell short and slightly to port of its target, sending up a geyser of white water into the still air. Another tremendous burst sent her second shell screaming across the decreasing space between the vessels; it was in line with the submarine, but still short. Increasing the range and deflection of the 4-inch, the third shell burst very close to its target, no doubt sending shivers of alarm through the men in the conning tower, and a salutary warning to its skipper of what could be in store for him and his crew – a warning which, through arrogance or sheer stupidity, went unheeded.

Steaming at her best speed of 9 knots (16.7 kph), it was obvious that the *Newton Pine* was rapidly being overhauled, as the distance shortened, so the submarine's shells crept ominously closer. Soon, they were bursting just 50 yards off the stern of Woolner's ship, and as the submarine came ever closer, the *Newton Pine* began to be straddled by shells, which were then being fired from two guns simultaneously.

By that time, the submarine had crept close enough for Captain Woolner to have a good look at her and to be able to identify her as an Italian vessel, although there was no sign of any markings. She had an exceptionally long conning tower, square at its fore end, with two big guns mounted just forward of it.

Working frantically behind their unprotected 4-inch, the *Newton Pine*'s gunners were well into their rhythm and using to good effect the lessons they had learned in their regular firing drills. Their shells were falling very close to and directly ahead of the submarine, showering her foredeck with cataracts of white spray. Still the warning went unheeded.

Captain Woolner knew that it was only a matter of time before his ship was overwhelmed and torn to shreds by the far superior firepower of that submarine, and it showed in his grim face as he gripped the after bridge rail, his tense body rigid, silently willing his own pathetic shells to score a hit.

A shell from the enemy vessel suddenly burst just a few feet off the ship's port side, just aft of her midships superstructure, and he decided that the time had come for drastic evasive action. Ordering the 4-inch to cease firing, he ordered the helm hard-a-starboard, swinging the ship through a 60 degree arc. In so doing, he put the submarine on his starboard quarter, a move which was designed to spoil the enemy's aim whilst giving his own gunners a better view of their target.

The tactic worked well, and the submarine's shells began to overshoot the steamer, bursting in the water about 100 yards off her port bow. Captain Woolner then ordered the 4-inch to recommence firing and, to a hearty cheer from the watching crew, that very first shell scored a direct hit on the submarine's vulnerable pressure-hull, right on the waterline. She almost disappeared under a massive cloud of smoke and spray, and even before it had properly cleared, a second shell exploded immediately ahead of her conning tower, mangling her forward guns and killing several of her crew, who could be seen from the decks and bridge of the *Newton Pine* being hurled unceremoniously into the sea as the submarine rolled almost onto her beam ends. She was then seen to straighten herself up briefly with just the top half of the conning tower visible above the sea. A few seconds later, she sank beneath the waves. The masthead lookout aboard the *Newton Pine* reported seeing her half surface on two occasions before she finally disappeared altogether, and Scouse himself, who had earlier been relieved of his watch, said that he actually saw the submarine go down bows first. (Whether or not this was actually the case I am not in a position to know because there is no official record of it; but Scouse's word is good enough for me.)

The attacking vessel turned out to be the Italian submarine *Foca*, which was reported to have been sunk in the Mediterranean some time in December 1940. However, it appears that the skipper, perhaps not finding the Mediterranean to his liking, had ventured out into the South Atlantic in search of easier, less well-protected prey in safer waters, finally meeting his end at the hands of the *Newton Pine*'s gunners.

At that stage, Captain Woolner was not quite certain whether the submarine had actually been sunk or had merely submerged to make a torpedo attack. With two shell holes in her pressure-hull, however, it is highly unlikely that she would have been able to make a successful dive, and perhaps even less likely that she would have been able to launch a torpedo attack with her insides mangled and quite a lot of her crew possibly dead. Not wanting to take any unnecessary risks, however, Woolner ordered a smoke-float dropped astern, and when the black, oily smoke had formed a thick screen between himself and the submarine's last known position, he steamed off to the north-east at top speed. A constant lookout was kept for the remainder of that day for the possible reappearance of the submarine, but it was not seen to surface again.

From start to finish, the entire action had lasted no more than thirty minutes. In the space of that half-hour, the *Newton Pine* had fired off just twenty-two rounds of 4-inch ammunition, whilst it was estimated by Captain Woolner that the submarine had fired between fifty and sixty rounds. The merchant ship suffered no casualties or damage in the exchange.

In the German BdU's handbook for U-boat commanders, it clearly states that 'the U-boat is not constructed for gunnery action because of its limited stability and its low, unsteady gun and observation platform, which are directly exposed to the sea's action. Strictly speaking, the U-boat is inferior to every other surface warship in an artillery battle. The U-boat, as opposed to its surface opponent, is rendered completely vulnerable in every artillery battle since just one hole in its pressure-hull can prevent a boat diving and thus easily leads to the loss of the boat.' Perhaps Italian submarine skippers were not conversant with that handbook.

The plucky *Newton Pine* was to survive for just another fourteen months of the war, until 15 February 1942. Then, whilst in an outward-bound convoy bound for Halifax, Nova Scotia, she fell astern of the convoy in heavy weather and was never heard from again. At first, it was assumed that she had simply foundered in the storm force winds and finally succumbed to the raging seas. However, it was later claimed that she was torpedoed and sunk by U-704.

Was it merely the fickle fortunes of war which granted victory to *Newton Pine* against far superior odds? Or was it the determination of a well-drilled crew about to have their ship shot away from under them? Perhaps it was a mixture of both explanations. It is a fact, however, that the *Newton Pine* was not unique. Whilst she was engaged in her deadly duel, the 2,473-ton SS *Sarastone* was held in the grip of a force 9 gale in the Bay of Biscay whilst trying desperately to hold station in convoy OG 47 out of the west Wales deepwater port of Milford Haven and bound for Gibraltar.

The *Sarastone* was a typical three-island collier of her time and, like the *Newton Pine*, was a small, sturdy, if ageing and overworked, tramp steamer. Built in 1929 for the Stone and Rolfe Shipping Company, which operated from the small Welsh market town of Llanelli, she, like most of the old tramp steamers, was plagued with recurring engine problems. To Captain John Herbert and his crew, however, the *Sarastone* was home, and its recalcitrant machinery an accepted fact of their lives. They had far worse problems in 1940.

Leaving Barry docks on 7 December 1940 loaded to her marks with 4,080 tons of Welsh coal for Gibraltar, in more peaceful times she would have steered a course of 255 degrees from Barry to Ilfracombe before changing course again to 225 degrees to head to the south-west of the Bishop's Rock Light on the Long Ships chain off Land's End before crossing the busy sea lanes of the English Channel. From there, she would have lumbered her slow, plodding way south, hugging doggedly to the coast for most of her wearisome 1,100 mile (2,000 km) voyage to Gibraltar, apart from the exposed crossing of the Bay of Biscay.

Unfortunately, however, like all other merchant vessels outward bound from anywhere along the western seaboard of the UK, she was under the direct orders of their lordships at the Admiralty, and the Captain had been instructed to entrust the safety of ship and crew to the doubtful protection of the Royal Navy at Milford Haven. No criticism of the men of the Royal Navy is intended; they did the very best they could with the woefully inadequate tools at their disposal. Thanks to the inadequacies of successive governments and the senior flag officers of the Naval High Command of the 1920s and 1930s, who had signed away most of Britain's naval strength, and contrary to popular belief, the Royal Navy in the early 1940s did not 'rule the waves'.

Nevertheless, it was some little comfort to Captain Herbert and his crew to have the protection of the convoy around him, as there was some kind of safety in numbers. The U-boat war in the Atlantic was becoming more and more dangerous, but the powers that there were at the time saw fit to arm the *Sarastone* with just one 12-pounder peashooter and two light machine-guns. However, it was not the pathetic defensive armament they possessed which troubled Captain Herbert so much as the course they were to steer.

The South-western Approaches to the Bristol Channel ports had effectively been blocked by British minefields very early on in the war, so in common with all other convoys of the time, OG 47 had been directed north about Ireland. From there they were to steam west for 200 miles (370 km) out into the Atlantic before changing course to the south until they reached a point just to the east of the Azores. They would then change course again to the east towards the Straits of Gibraltar. It was there, they all knew, that the U-boats would be waiting for them. The distant waters of the Atlantic were deep and unfamiliar to the lumbering *Sarastone*, and if she should suffer another of her many breakdowns, she would be a long way from repair facilities and therefore in great danger, not only from her German enemies, but also from the seaman's ancient enemy, the sea itself.

Nine hundred miles (1,700 km) later at 43°10'N, 13°20'W the convoy was approximately 250 miles (460 km) west of Cape Finisterre on a southerly heading at a mean speed of just 7 knots (13 kph). The *Sarastone*, like all the other ships, was being battered by a force 9 gale and seas of over 50 feet (15 m) in height which were rolling in from the north-west with incredible velocity. Rolling her scuppers under most of the time and pitching to frightening angles as she breasted the enormous seas, she was 'taking the green' in vast cataracts over her forecastle head with every pitch and yaw and, rolling almost onto her beam ends, the tremendous seas boiled over her low well decks in a frenzy of seething white water that smashed against her superstructure like battering rams before pouring out from her scuppers in Niagaras of foaming white.

Whilst she was labouring in the fearsome grip of that gale, *Sarastone*'s chief engineer reported to Captain Herbert a serious defect in the port boiler. The skipper became understandably worried when the chief went on to say that the boiler would have to be shut down, leaving the vessel with only half power, which in turn meant a top speed of just 4 knots (7.5 kph) in good weather. In the heavy seas and high winds which they were then experiencing, they could count themselves fortunate if they made 2 knots – not a happy prospect for a slow, ageing tramp steamer battling a severe gale in the deep oceans.

Captain Herbert immediately informed the Commodore of his plight and was ordered to proceed independently for the time being, and to rendezvous with the convoy by 12.00 hours on 22 December. Five hours later the *Sarastone* was lost to sight of the other ships and completely alone in a sea teeming with underwater enemies. Making just about 2 knots (3.7 kph) in the heaving ocean, she barely made steerage way as the wind and sea raged around her. This situation concerned Captain Herbert even more than Doenitz's U-boats.

The engineers made frantic efforts to repair the faulty boiler, but without the proper equipment they could do nothing. Fortunately, the weather began to moderate the following day, but by that time the starboard boiler was beginning to feel the strain and was also starting to give trouble. Captain Herbert decided that his best course of action was to steer for Lisbon whilst he still had steerage way. He consequently ignored the proposed rendezvous with the convoy and hauled his ship around to the east in a determined effort to close the Portuguese coast with all possible haste.

The tramp steamers were bitches of the first order, and with just two knots steerage way, the *Sarastone*'s bitchiness knew no bounds. Rolling, pitching and corkscrewing to impossible angles, she flung herself all over the ocean as her helmsman, with a touch equalling that of a worldly-wise lover towards a sheltered virgin, eventually brought her round to a course of 123 degrees true, south-east by east on a compass heading.

Just one hour after her course change, the Radio Operator intercepted a wireless message from the Admiralty reporting enemy submarines operating to the south of her position, and quite near to her point of rendezvous with the convoy. The Italian submarine *Moncenigo* was shadowing convoy OG 47 and attacked it later that day.

As the day and night passed, so the weather began moderating, and by the morning of the 22nd, the *Sarastone* found herself in relatively calm seas with a light north-westerly breeze rippling the surface and the long Atlantic swells almost directly astern. With the horizon-line in sharp and clear focus and a crimson sun in the ascendancy in the south-east, the Chief Engineer nursed his one remaining boiler until she was averaging about 5 knots (9 kph) in a calm sea and her skipper and mates were confident that they would make landfall at Lisbon on the evening of the 24th. Christmas in neutral Portugal was something that none of her crew had anticipated, and they contemplated their good fortune with relish.

The first sign of unwanted company came towards the end of the afternoon watch at approximately 15.50 hours when the Second Mate sighted what he had at first thought to be a fishing boat about 4 miles (7.5 km) off the starboard beam. He immediately summoned Captain Herbert to the bridge. The unknown vessel was obscured by a westering sun which by that time was quite low down on the horizon in the south-west. Although Captain Herbert could make virtually nothing of the strange vessel, he became suspicious. The *Sarastone* was at that time about 300 miles (550 km) from the nearest land, with some 600 fathoms (1,100 m) of water beneath her keel, and Herbert quite rightly reasoned that such a place was a most unlikely spot to meet a small fishing boat.

A highly cautious man where unidentified vessels were concerned, the skipper gave orders for all hands on deck, then went back to studying the low-profile vessel. Some minutes later, the dark object moved out of the line of the sun, and as he gazed through his binoculars, he was not too surprised to see the low, sinister profile of a submarine heading towards his ship at high speed.

That submarine proved to be the *Moncenigo*. Her attack on convoy OG 47 on the 21st had been a grave disappointment to her skipper, Alberto Agostini. With all the verve and daring of Italian submarine commanders of the time, he had succeeded in sinking the 1,250-ton Swedish vessel, *Mangen* but had then been unceremoniously chased off by the escorts, and promptly departed the area at a rate of knots in search of easier, less dangerous prey. As he gleefully studied the slow-moving freighter, clearly defined with the sun astern of him, Agostini's confidence returned with the knowledge that he had found what he had been looking for: a slow, virtually unarmed freighter alone and clearly in trouble.

Still unsure of the identity of the rapidly approaching submarine, Captain Herbert put his vessel stern-on to the U-boat, and ordered his guns' crews closed up on the antiquated 12-pounder mounted on the stern. In consideration of the superior fire-power of the enemy's deck guns, that was no more than a symbolic gesture of defiance but, being the kind of man he was, he was not prepared to take whatever was dished out without at least some resistance.

As the *Sarastone* responded to her helm, the first shell from the *Moncenigo* roared out across the few miles of ocean then separating the two vessels and fell short of its target, as did her second shot. Captain Herbert, well aware of the limitations of his pathetic 12-pounder, ordered his gun-layer to hold steady until the submarine had come within 2,000 yards (1,830 m). Quietly and patiently they waited, hands and foreheads clammy with sweat despite the cold December evening, until the *Moncenigo* came within range. As she did so, the *Sarastone*'s gun roared out its defiance, and the battle for survival had begun.

Agostini, confident that he was about to destroy his prey, was using just one of his two deck guns, and although it fired hesitantly, its shells were bursting uncomfortably close to the fleeing freighter. Whilst Captain Herbert concentrated on keeping his ship stern-on to the enemy, he unconsciously braced himself for the inevitable battering that his ship must endure. Then, as the *Moncenigo* rapidly overhauled the *Sarastone* and her shells crept ever closer, the impossible happened.

A man by the name of James O'Neil was the *Sarastone*'s gun-layer. A methodical sort of man who enjoyed doing everything he attempted correctly, in proportion and in sequence, he took careful aim with his 12-pounder and, with his fourth shot scored a direct hit on the *Moncenigo* just forward of her conning tower. Smoke and flames began billowing out of the small hole, shooting high into the still winter air even as the vessel slewed around until she was beam-on to the *Sarastone*. Then, to loud cheers and jeers, a second shell slammed into her pressure-hull.

As he studied the burning submarine through his binoculars, Captain Herbert could be forgiven the smile which creased his delighted features as he observed that she was attempting to dive, but without success. Scenting victory, he ordered the machine-guns which were mounted on the bridge wings to open fire. They were merely light Hotchkiss guns, however, and the range was far too great for such light weapons to be in any way effective. The 12-pounder, however, continued to fire its tiny shells, each one bursting closer to the vulnerable pressure-hull whilst the submarine was still making unsuccessful attempts to submerge. When the range had reached 4,000 yards (3,660 m), Captain Herbert ordered the 12-pounder to cease fire.

Wallowing sluggishly in the long Atlantic swells, the *Moncenigo* was rolling helplessly as her crew fought to stabilise her and gain some steerage way, but she remained stubbornly at a standstill on the heaving surface of the sea. Vast billows of yellow and black smoke were pouring through the holes in her hull, and men were seen stumbling up from her conning tower as though choking on the noxious smoke and fumes from the burning oil and rubber and chlorine gas from her ruptured batteries.

The *Sarastone* still had seven 12-pounder shells unfired, but Captain Herbert's natural caution prevailed over the urge to go after the enemy and finish her off. The *Moncenigo*'s deck guns were still intact, and he was unwilling to push his extraordinary luck too far. At 16.50 hours, he stood his guns' crew down and resumed his course for Lisbon, leaving the *Moncenigo* to whatever fate might befall her.

Still at her reduced speed of 5 knots (9 km) in a calm sea, the *Sarastone* entered

Lisbon during the night of 24 December, where Captain John Herbert and his jubi-
lant crew were able to spend a well-earned Christmas in port. Signals were sent to
the naval base at Gibraltar reporting their encounter with their Italian adversary,
and a few days later when repairs had been completed, the *Sarastone* continued her
delayed voyage to her original port of destination.

In Gibraltar, she was replenished with twenty-three 12-pounder shells to replace
those she had used in her extraordinary battle, but no cordite charges could be
supplied for them, simply because the Royal Navy had none. Such was the pathetic
state of Britannia's Navy at that time, courtesy of inept governments and high-
ranking naval, military and air force officers, all with over-inflated egos, who
wished only to bury their proverbial heads in the sand whilst Europe was going up
in Nazi flames and the flower of British youth was needlessly dying. Fortunately
however, the *Sarastone* did not meet with any hostile submarines on her homeward
voyage, and arrived safely in Swansea docks in early February 1941.

The *Moncenigo* did not sink, and she was eventually able to slink away to lick
her wounds and bury her dead, but she was not seen again for quite some time.
Under the command of a new skipper, she was next heard of in March 1942. Her
new career, however, proved to be as mediocre and ineffective as ever, accounting
for just one ship, a 1,500-ton French coastal vessel, before being destroyed in a raid
on Cagliari on 13 May 1943.

The *Sarastone*'s career was terminated some eighteen months earlier when, on
29 December 1941, she was bombed and sunk as she was leaving the Spanish port
of Huelva.

Bearing in mind the status of those two ships as ageing, overworked tramp steamers
with a motley collection of overworked, underpaid civilian seamen, the *Newton
Pine* and the *Sarastone*, armed with weapons which even the smallest ships of their
Royal Navy counterparts would have laughed at, not only broke every rule in the
book in their extraordinary adventures, but rewrote those rules. There is, of course,
ample evidence of other merchant ships engaging and sometimes sinking enemy
submarines by ramming them rather than engaging them with gunfire. German
submarine commanders were fully aware that merchant ships, even those ancient
tramps with their pathetic weapons, posed a dire threat to submarines on the surface,
and they were canny enough to stay submerged and do their clandestine work with
torpedoes.

These stories, however, only serve to underline that which is already well known
but never acknowledged: that the merchant navy, as well as keeping the population
of Britain and its armed services supplied and therefore playing a very significant
part in the defeat of the Axis forces, also took on the role of warships when neces-
sity decreed, with precious little to show for their efforts either in remuneration or
in accolades, which have been heaped upon our armed services although none of
them would have been able to function without those men. So let us from time to
time try, when we recall the incredible feats of courage and determination of the
armed services, also to remember the men of the merchant navy who, through their
own courage, tenacity and devotion to duty, made it all possible.

# 3 Fallen Stars

The Blue Star Line was founded by William, First Baron Vesty and Sir Edmund Vesty, in 1911 with just three ships. Midway through the First World War, the fleet had expanded to twelve ships, all of their names beginning with 'Brod'. It was not until 1920 that the now familiar 'Star' appeared in the form of the *Albion Star* and the *Royal Star* in a total fleet of fifteen ships.

At the time of its founding, as we have seen, British merchant seamen were being treated worse than medieval serfs at the hands of the more ruthless shipping companies. The Blue Star Line, however, was begun as one of the better companies, operating clean, safe and well-maintained ships aboard which the food was safe to eat and the water safe to drink. When certain members of my own family began sailing with them, the living and working conditions of the crews were far above those provided by many other shipping lines.

During its early years, the Blue Star fleet consisted exclusively of refrigerated cargo vessels on the China and South American runs. In 1926, however, the company began to take an interest in the lucrative passenger business and, by 1927, it had established a regular mail and passenger service to South America. That service began with four 15-knot (28 kph) refrigerated cargo ships of 11,000 tons each, and the five 'A' class passenger and passenger/cargo combinations with which this chapter is concerned.

By September 1939, the fleet had grown to a total of thirty-eight ships with a gross tonnage of some 381,000 tons. During the war, twenty-nine of these were lost, including all of its passenger vessels, and 646 crew lost their lives, including eleven captains, forty-seven navigating officers and eighty-eight engineers.

## The *Avelona Star*

All five 'A' class vessels that were built for the Blue Star Line between 1926 and 1927 were lost to German U-boats between June 1940 and October 1942. The first was the *Avelona Star*, a two-funnel refrigerated passenger/cargo combination, designed and built for the Argentine frozen meat and passenger trade.

The *Avelona*, as she was named at her launch, was built by the John Brown Shipbuilding Company of Clydebank. Her vital statistics were: length 535 feet (163 m); beam 63 feet (19.2 m), and draught 33 feet 9 inches 10.3 m). A twin-screw vessel, she was powered by four Parson's steam turbine engines with single-reduction gearing to two shafts, providing an output of 120 rpm, and producing 8,000 horsepower (6,000 kilowatts), giving her a top speed of 17 knots (31.4 kph). At 13,376 tons gross weight, she had a cargo capacity of 425,000 cubic feet (12,036 m³) in four hatches, two forward and two aft. She also had a first-class deluxe passenger capacity of 162.

She was launched on 6 December 1926, had completed her sea trials by early May of 1927, and began her maiden voyage on 20 May. In May 1929, she was renamed *Avelona Star* when her owners were restyled as the Blue Star Line Ltd. In 1931, with passenger overcapacity in shipping aggravated by a growing depression in worldwide trade, she was sent to Greenock and converted into a purely cargo-carrying vessel. All passenger accommodation was removed, her fore and aft well decks were closed in and her dummy aft funnel removed. Her bridge superstructure was lifted and moved bodily forward by 8 feet (2.4 m) so as to give her a vertical profile, and her cargo capacity increased to 647,000 cubic feet (18,300 m³) of refrigerated storage in eighty chambers. In 1934 she was again modified, increasing her cargo capacity yet again to give her a massive 699,000 cubic feet (19,800 m³), giving her the largest cubic capacity of any cargo vessel at that time.

On 3 September, when war was declared, she was in Dakar, Senegal. She received orders to sail, light-ship, for Buenos Aires, there to load a cargo of meat for London. Towards the end of May 1940, she sailed from Buenos Aires under the command of her skipper, Captain George Ernest Hooper, going by way of Santos, Brazil, and Freetown, Sierra Leone with an 8,800-ton cargo of frozen meat.

After an incident-free voyage across the South Atlantic, she reached Freetown on 15 June and sailed again the following day in company with the commodore vessel of a convoy which had already sailed. It was a thirty-four ship convoy, and the *Avelona Star* and her escort overhauled it on the 18th, finding it zigzagging over a broad expanse of ocean with escorting warships ahead, astern and on either flank.

After taking up their allotted positions within the convoy ranks, they steamed un-molested through the calm seas and energy-sapping tropical heat for the next twelve days.

At 10.00 hours on Sunday, 30 June, the convoy was approximately 200 miles (370 km) north-west of Cape Finisterre. At that point, all except ships bound for the Bristol Channel ports were changing course to the north-east and entering the Irish Sea when the first ship was torpedoed and sunk. The convoy commodore immediately hoisted his red and blue signal flag, indicating an emergency turn to starboard, and continued to zigzag for some time.

Throughout that day, the convoy was shadowed by several U-boats, but the escorts kept them successfully at bay until, at exactly 21.30 hours, the fate of the *Avelona Star* was sealed when she was hit by a torpedo fired by U-43 on her starboard side in her Number 2 hold, south-west of Land's End. A massive geyser of water, smoke and flame shot some 50 feet (15 m) into the air, lifting the vessel bodily as her hatch-cover burst open, throwing meat carcasses through the rent in her side and into the sea. She settled back with a 20-degree starboard list, and righted herself momentarily. Then, with the collapse of the aft bulkhead of Number 2 hold, water flooded into the stokehole and, with a tremendous roar and clouds of smoke, ash and superheated steam, her boilers exploded, almost hiding her from the view of other ships as her deck and hull plates were torn asunder and hurled upwards and outwards in all directions.

The order to abandon ship was given almost immediately and within minutes the entire crew, with the exception of four men who had been killed instantly when her boilers exploded, got safely away from the sinking ship. They were very quickly rescued by MV *Beignon* which, although steaming at her best speed after picking up the shipwrecked men, failed to catch up with the convoy.

At 03.00 hours, she had still not caught up with the convoy when a tremendous explosion and the usual geyser of water, smoke and flame heralded her own death. Hit on her starboard side, she took on an immediate starboard list and began sinking bows first. Fortunately, every man on board got away before the ship sank some twelve minutes later. She was a 5,000-ton motor vessel with a crew of just thirty men. At the time of her torpedoing however, there had been an additional eighty survivors from the *Avelona Star* and consequently there were insufficient boats to accommodate them all. Mr G.L. Evans, her chief officer, managed to get some of his men aboard a rather flimsy raft which had been rigged from old oil drums and timber, a common feature aboard all merchant ships throughout the war years. Twenty-five men sat on this rickety structure, which had become very unstable, up to their waists in very cold, oil-coated water. Despite the residual warmth of the summer's night, they were shivering uncontrollably with shock, and a terrible fear of the unknown. It was indeed fortunate that the weather was fair on that night as other sailors were fully immersed in the sea, some hanging onto lanyards around the few available boats, and others simply treading water in the hope that they could stay afloat long enough for rescue vessels to reach them.

In the vital minutes between the exploding torpedo and the vessel sinking beneath the waves, she managed to get out an SOS and, at about 05.00 hours, all were safely rescued by the destroyers HMS *Vesper* and HMS *Windsor*. All 110 survivors from both ships were eventually landed at Plymouth, the only casualties being the four men who had died in the *Avelona Star*'s boiler room.

## The *Arandora Star*

Of all the Blue Star Line ships which were sailing the seas in 1940, the *Arandora Star* must surely have been the pride of the fleet. Built as the SS *Arandora* by the Cammell Laird shipyard of Birkenhead and launched in January 1927, she was 12,838 tons gross, 7,818 tons net and 9,404 tons dead-weight. She was 512 feet (156 m) long, 63 feet (19.2 m) in the beam and had a 34 foot (10.4 m) draught. She was powered by four steam turbine engines with an output of 8,400 horsepower (6,300 kilowatts) and 120 rpm with a single-reduction gear to two shafts giving her a top speed of 15½ knots (28.7 kph). With 415,000 cubic feet (11,750 m³) of refrigerated cargo space in forty-nine chambers, she also had first-class accommodation for 162 passengers.

Entering service on 29 May 1927, she was the last of the five 'A' class ships to be built for the Blue Star Line, and the third to be built by Cammell Laird. In 1929 she was converted into a cruise liner at the Fairfield Shipbuilding and Engineering Co. Ltd of Glasgow and renamed *Arandora Star*, with a renewed passenger capacity of 400. Further modifications took place in 1935, and she emerged from the shipyard resplendent with white-painted hull which was enhanced by a distinctive red band like a blood-red gash painted around her hull just below her scuppers at main deck level.

From 1929, she undertook cruises to Norway, the northern capitals, the Mediterranean and the Caribbean. By that time, she had become an 18,300-ton vessel with a top speed of 16 knots (29.6 kph). She was nicknamed the Chocolate Box and the Wedding Cake, and was probably one of the best-known ships in the world at that time.

At the outbreak of war in September 1939 the *Arandora Star*, under the command of her skipper, Captain E.W. Moulton, was on passage to New York. Upon her arrival, she was recalled to Britain, where she was commandeered by the Admiralty and directed to Falmouth. There, she temporarily paid off and was later inspected by senior officers from the Admiralty and Ministry of War Transport for her suitability as an armed merchant cruiser. It was decided, however, that she carried too much top hamper (her superstructure was too high) for an effective warship and in mid-December 1939 she was directed to Avonmouth to be fitted with the experimental Admiralty net defences, and to undergo trials to determine whether or not they could be used by all large merchant ships at sea and what reduction in speed would be entailed.

The use of net defences was just one of the many suggestions submitted throughout the war years to combat the U-boat menace, usually comprising obstructions of one kind or another towed by ships on the flanks of convoys. The only one that proved to be of any practical use was a light wire net strong enough to catch speeding torpedoes before they hit the ship. Hanging from booms rigged in the bows, those nets would be slung outboard whenever the state of the sea permitted.

Having been fitted with these, the *Arandora Star* then proceeded to Portsmouth for nets of various sizes and meshes to be rigged.

Each dawn would see the *Arandora Star* steam out into the English Channel to run trials with the new defence system. Each evening she would return to her anchorage so that any alterations needed to either the booms or the nets could be completed before the next day's trials. The nets proved quite easy to handle and their crews were brought up to a fairly high standard of proficiency. Speed reduction was minimal and turning at full speed was also successful. Moreover, the nets themselves trapped all torpedoes during the trials.

Then, quite abruptly, and for reasons known only to themselves, the Admiralty abandoned these experiments and the ship was ordered into Davenport to have all her new gear removed. No sooner had she been stripped of her booms and nets than she was ordered to Liverpool to await orders. There she came to anchor off the landing stage next to the Cammell Laird shipyard at Birkenhead where Britain's newest and most prestigious battleship, HMS *Prince of Wales* was nearing completion. That night, a solitary German bomber flew over Liverpool's docklands and dropped a stick of HE bombs, giving the *Arandora Star* her first taste of a bombing raid.

Receiving new orders the following morning, she sailed to a rendezvous with the aircraft carrier HMS *Glorious* and the anti-aircraft cruiser HMS *Coventry* off Narvik, Norway. She entered the fjord on 4 June in company with several other vessels. That same day, she embarked 1,600 officers and men of the Royal Air Force, and an unspecified number of Polish and French troops. In total, some 25,000 men were taken out of Norway in various transport vessels and brought back to the UK, accompanied by the battleship HMS *Valiant* with her cruiser and destroyer escorts.

The *Arandora Star* stayed with the *Glorious* and the *Coventry* until 7 June. At that time, the German battleships *Scharnhorst* and *Gneisenau* were at sea, together with the heavy cruiser *Admiral Hipper* and two destroyers. The Admiralty and the Government had been warned by Bletchley Park that those ships were at sea and heading in the direction of Narvik, a warning that was ignored, with disastrous results. On the 8th, the day after the departure of the *Arandora Star* for Glasgow, the Germans sank the troopship *Orama*, the tanker *Oilpower* and their escorting trawler HMS *Jupiter*. That same afternoon, following a running battle, they sank the *Glorious* and her two escorting destroyers, HMS *Acosta* and HMS *Ardent*, a battle which left some 1,500 men in the water.

After discharging her human cargo of troops at Glasgow, the *Arandora Star* was next ordered to sail light-ship for Swansea, a regular destination for most Blue Star vessels, to await further orders. When those orders came, she was directed to Brest on the west coast of France to assist in the rescue of any troops and refugees that she safely could. German bombers were swarming all over the port and town when the *Arandora Star* arrived, however, so preventing anyone from escaping onto any of the vessels waiting to take them out. The *Arandora Star* had barely managed to embark between six and twelve people when she was forced to escape under a hail of bombs and heavy strafing. A British destroyer then went in to provide covering fire and she managed to clear the channel safely. All that could be seen of her saviour were geysers of water thrown up by the bomb blasts all around her and streams of tracer shells arching into the air from her anti-aircraft armaments.

Back at Falmouth, she disembarked her pathetically few survivors, refuelled and restocked and was then ordered to proceed to Quiberon Bay. The Germans were not as busy there as they had been at Brest, and she was able to embark about 300 refugees, landing them also at Falmouth. No sooner had she discharged her human cargo than she was ordered to Bayonne. Once again, the skies above were swarming with German bombers. She was met by dozens of small, overloaded craft of all descriptions adrift off the beach waiting for a ship, any ship, to pick them up. Unable to come to a complete stop because of the danger from falling bombs, she slowed to slow ahead and, despite the difficulty of embarking passengers from small boats onto the deck of a moving ship, the crew managed to take on an incredible 500 people and land them once more at Falmouth.

Their retreat down the French coast was by that time chaotic, and they were ordered to St-Jean-de-Luz, the last port from which there was any hope of rescuing survivors. All was quiet and serene when the *Arandora Star* arrived there, and the crew managed to embark some 1,700 troops and refugees including most of the Polish staff officers and their troops, all of whom had been fighting a rearguard action all the way down the coast. Her luck held firm and she cleared the coast just as a flight of German bombers appeared over the hills inland, and she was not molested in any way. She returned to Liverpool to discharge her passengers.

On 29 June, after having completed the most strenuous and frightening month of her career to date, she received orders to go alongside on the 30th to embark a large number of German and Italian prisoners of war and internees and proceed, together with their military guard, to St John's, Newfoundland. The Western Ocean in mid-1940 was a very dangerous place to be, and it was a prospect that few relished.

She sailed from Liverpool on 2 July packed with 1,673 people, made up of 174 officers and crew, 200 military guard, 479 German internees, 86 German prisoners and 734 Italian internees.

Steaming unescorted at 15 knots (27.8 kph) in fine weather, the *Arandora Star* was about 75 miles (139 km) west of the Bloody Foreland, County Donegal when, at about 18.15 hours, she was hit on the starboard side by a torpedo fired from U-47. On the bridge at the time was her First Officer, Mr F.B. Brown and her Third Mate, Mr W.H. Tulip. There were four lookouts posted, one up in the bows, one on the monkey island and one on each bridge wing; but even with those four sharp pairs of sailors' eyes, nothing was seen of U-47 until the side of their ship had been ripped open.

The torpedo exploded in the engine-room, which began flooding at once, killing everyone there, including two engineers who were on watch at the time and all the greasers, who were either killed outright by the exploding torpedo, scalded by high-pressure, superheated steam from ruptured pipes, or drowned as the sea poured into the fatal wound. With the turbines and main emergency generators completely wrecked, the ship was immediately plunged into complete darkness below decks, and all communications between the bridge, the engine room and the wireless shack were destroyed. One lifeboat on the starboard side directly above the blast zone was smashed to pieces whilst the davits and falls of another boat nearby were so badly damaged that the boat could not be lowered. As was standard practice at sea in those days, the ship's position was being meticulously plotted every thirty minutes and, as soon as the torpedo struck, Mr Brown sent their current position to the wireless shack with orders to transmit an immediate SOS which was picked up and answered by Malin Head.

Deck-hands who were busily engaged in lowering the lifeboats were hampered in their work when most of the Italians and some of the Germans rushed onto the boat deck, all scrambling to be first into the boats. They were quickly driven off by the military guard and a few dozen burly seamen, and stood around in agitated groups muttering curses and praying. About half of the ninety life-rafts which had been stowed on the upper deck were thrown over the side as the ship lost way, but none of the prisoners or internees could be persuaded to go over the side and get into them.

Once again, the panic-stricken Italians and Germans rushed the boats, only to be unceremoniously thrown back by the guards and seamen until finally, out of a total of twelve, ten boats were eventually successfully launched. No sooner had they reached the water than swarms of prisoners lowered themselves into them by means of the rope falls and Jacob's ladders, seriously overcrowding them in their haste to save themselves. The rest of the life-rafts were then safely launched, but still many Italians refused to leave the ship.

One hour after the torpedoing, the list increased rapidly and, at 19.15 hours, it was apparent that the ship was about to sink. Captain Moulton and his bridge officers calmly walked over the side, but even as the ship was sinking beneath them, the Italians who had earlier refused to leave could not be persuaded to get into the sea and make for the life-rafts, and all were drowned when the ship finally turned turtle and, flinging her bows vertically upwards, sank stern first into the murky depths. Captain Moulton and twelve other officers were killed when the vessel turned over on top of them.

An ever-widening slick of fuel oil coated the heaving surface of the ocean, its prism hues undulating on the swells, which were littered with rafts, broken spars and lifeboats, the pitiful evidence of personal belongings riding the waves amongst the heads of those in the water, desperately trying to stay alive as the thick, gluti- nous mass of fuel oil was ingested into stomachs and lungs, so leading to an agonising death by slow suffocation or drowning.

At 21.30 hours, the lonely drone of an RAF Sunderland flying-boat from Coastal Command was heard overhead, appearing as a small black dot on the horizon at first, then quickly materialising as it flew over the men and wreckage, dropping much-needed food, water, medical supplies and cigarettes in watertight bags, along with the welcome message that help was already speeding towards them in the shape of HMCS *St Laurent*. At approximately 13.00 hours on the following day, Commander H.G. De Wolf spotted the survivors as he arrived on the scene, steaming at full speed on his mission of mercy.

There then followed five gruelling hours of rescue work for the crew of the Canadian destroyer, all of whom displayed supreme courage and patience, not to mention good seamanship and judgement as they manoeuvred up to individual parties of men struggling desperately in the oil-coated water. Very few of the survivors were in a position to help themselves; they were not even able to grasp a rope because of the oil scum which covered them all. Nevertheless, the intrepid sailors of the *St Laurent* went into the thickly carpeted sea without a second thought and, with bowlines in hand, roped up the pathetic swimmers and hoisted them bodily into the rescue boats.

The British destroyer HMS *Walker* arrived on the scene some time later and scoured the area for some hours, but no other survivors were found. Approximately 868 survivors were eventually landed safely at Greenock but, in what must rank as one of the most distressing disasters of the entire war, Captain Moulton, twelve other officers and forty-two crew of the *Arandora Star* lost their lives. Of the rest, thirty-seven of the military guard were killed along with 470 Italians and 243 Germans, a total of 805 men out of 1,673 carried on board.

## The *Alemeda Star*

The *Alemeda Star* was the third vessel of the 'A' class ships to be lost to the German U-boats, sunk by just one torpedo fired from U-96 at 07.00 hours on 17 January 1941. If the sinking of the *Arandora Star* was amongst the most distressing of the war, then the loss of the *Alemeda Star* may be described as one of the most tragic.

Built by the Cammell Laird company of Birkenhead in 1926, the *Alemeda Star* was another passenger/cargo combination which, at 12,838 gross tons, was built for the passenger and refrigerated cargo service between the UK and South America.

Launched on 29 June 1926 as the *Alemeda*, she had an overall length of 535 feet (163 m), a 63-foot (19.2 m) beam and a 27-foot (8.2 m) draught. Powered by two Parson's turbine engines which, at 120 rpm transmitted some 8,000 horsepower (6,000 kilowatts) to her giant phosphor bronze screws, which pushed her through the water at 17 knots (31.4 kph). Her six hatches provided some 419,980 cubic feet (11,900 m³) of cargo space, whilst her first-class passenger accommodation provided for 180 people.

In 1929 she was renamed *Alemeda Star* and six years later she was lengthened by 65 feet 7 inches (20 m). With a new Maier bow then fitted, her tonnage had increased to 14,935 tons, whilst her passenger capacity had been slightly increased to just over 200 in first-class accommodation. With her twin funnels proudly sporting the distinctive blue star of the line, she was, like her sister ships, a beautiful vessel by any standards.

On 28 May 1937, she was run aground in thick fog just off Boulogne *en route* to Tilbury, but no damage was sustained and she was safely refloated the following day. She suffered more misfortune when, on 22 December 1940 she sustained some bomb damage whilst lying at anchor in the River Mersey. It was not serious, however and, after repairs had been carried out, she sailed upon her last fateful voyage from Liverpool on 15 January 1941 under the command of the Blue Star Line commodore, Captain H.C. Howard, with a crew of 166 officers and ratings and 194 passengers.

As the year 1940 had ended with some of the most tempestuous weather conditions imaginable in the Western Ocean, so 1941 opened with the same horrendous conditions as one storm succeeded another with dismal regularity. One deep depression followed hot the heels of another, creating storm force, and at times even hurricane force, winds in excess of 80 knots (148 kph) or more. To describe the boiling, leaden grey waters of the North Atlantic as a witch's cauldron would be a gross understatement. No sooner had the *Alemeda Star* cleared the sanctuary of the Mersey than she was swallowed up in the high winds and heavy seas of that accursed ocean, never to be seen again. Conditions on board can only be imagined as she rolled and pitched, twisting and yawing over the gigantic ocean rollers which travelled with incredible velocity across the sea.

She sailed as an independent, virtually unarmed and unescorted, and carrying nothing more lethal to Nazi Germany than her passengers and crew. At 07.45 hours on the morning of 17 January 1941, she was at 58°17'N, 13°40'W, approximately 35 miles (65 km) north of Rockall, and some 225 miles (417 km) west of St Kilda, the westernmost island in the Outer Hebrides, when a distress signal was picked up telling the world that she had been torpedoed.

That was the last that was ever heard from her, even though several destroyers amongst an assortment of other vessels were at once sent out in a vain rescue attempt. No trace of anything that could be connected with a shipwreck was ever found – no wreckage of any kind, not even a floating body, lifeboat or waterlogged raft was there to mark her passing. Nothing that could be traced back to her was ever washed up on any British coastline; it seemed as though she had simply been plucked from the sea and disappeared into thin air.

With the exception of that one solitary distress call giving her co-ordinates, nothing was known of her fate for quite some time after the event, not even from German sources. The skipper of U-96 later claimed that he had struck a vessel with just one torpedo in the co-ordinates given, but apart from that scant information, nothing is known of the eventual fate of either passengers or crew. The only thing that is stated in the official list is that she was torpedoed in the position given and that all hands were lost.

As I have said, weather conditions at the time were atrocious in the extreme and it would appear highly likely that, having been severely damaged by U-96's torpedo, the stricken ship was then, perhaps almost immediately, overwhelmed by the sheer ferocity of the storm, sinking into the Stygian depths some 200 fathoms below, 1,200 feet (360 m) of raging, storm-tossed ocean, taking all 360 souls down with her.

## The *Avila Star*

Launched on Clydebank from the John Brown shipyard on 22 September 1926, the *Avila Star* was built as a twin-funnel passenger/cargo combination and delivered to her owners in March 1927. At 12,872 gross tons she was, like the other four 'A' class vessels, lengthened in November 1934 at the Swan Hunter yard to 550 feet (167.6 m). That lengthening increased her gross weight to 14,443 gross tons. She had a 68-foot (20.7 m) beam and a 42-foot (12.8 m) draught, and was driven by four steam turbine engines and single-reduction geared to twin shafts, giving her a top speed of 16 knots (29.6 kph). She carried a crew of 166 officers and ratings, and had a first-class passenger capacity of 162.

On 12 June 1942, she sailed from Buenos Aires with a cargo of just over 6,000 tons of frozen meat and thirty passengers, including ten women. Seven days and 2,800 miles (5,190 km) later, she crossed the Equator. The terrible heat of the sun in those latitudes in mid-June can be mind-numbing at best, and at worst an agony of sun-scorched decks and bulkheads. At that point, they would have passed through the refreshing South-east Trade Winds and entered that area of the Atlantic known and dreaded by seamen the world over as the doldrum calms between 7°S and 5°N, a distance of some 500 miles (920 km) from north to south and 2,000 miles (3,700 km) from east to west. It is an area where there is very little wind.

She was then on a northerly heading designed to take her to a position some 300 miles (550 km) to the west of the Cape Verde Islands and 800 miles (1,480 km) west of Dakar, another favourite hunting ground for Doenitz's U-boats. From there, she had another 1,600 miles (2,960 km) to the Azores. For the following seven days she ploughed steadily northwards at her best speed of 16 knots (29.6 kph) under an azure sky and blazing, energy-sapping sun.

Her voyage from Buenos Aires had so far passed without incident, and by the time they reached a point 90 miles (167 km) east of San Miguel in the Azores, all the passengers were in a relaxed and happy frame of mind. Not so skipper and crew, however, because the Azores were at that time a hotbed of U-boat activity.

As a murky dusk heralded the onset of night on 5 July, the *Avila Star* was gently rolling in matronly fashion with a heavy but long swell passing under her port quarter as she zigzagged on a mean northerly heading, completely blacked-out. A multitude of winking stars shone down from a black velvet sky like chips of iridescent fire reflecting off the darkened ocean like fireflies in the night. Her course was straight up the moonpath in a calm sea. The phosphorescence was whisked away astern as light tendrils of mist hung upon the surface of the ocean like mysterious will-o'-the-wisps. The Chief Mate, Mr M.R. Tallack, was about to relieve the Second Mate as watch officer at 20.00 hours whilst the skipper, Captain John Fisher stood in one corner of the wheelhouse, the tension in his face clearly visible as he looked out over the dark, heaving sea.

Earlier in the day, Mae Wests had been issued to all passengers and crew, together with small battery-operated lights to clip onto them, as the ship rapidly approached the danger zone, with orders to wear them at all times until further notice. In the saloon, the passengers lingered over drinks and sandwiches as tension mounted, and in the various messes there were card games amidst a nervous chattering of subdued voices. Daily boat drills and action-stations had honed everyone on board to a high degree of readiness for all emergencies until there was nothing left to do but wait and hope.

The ship's surgeon, Dr Maynard Crawford, had prudently filled a haversack with brandy, sal volatile, iodine, dressings, morphine and a hypodermic syringe, as well as various other drugs, just in case they were forced to abandon ship. He had served some time with the Army Medical Corps before going into the merchant navy, and was therefore well schooled to react quickly to any and all emergencies. Not even he was prepared for the tremendous explosion which rocked the *Avila Star* at precisely 21.05 hours on that fateful evening, however. He was sitting quietly in his cabin at the time, typing out his medical report for the voyage, when a single torpedo fired from the tubes of U-201 ripped into the starboard side of the ship, exploding in her boiler room and instantly killing every man on watch there at the time. With the tremendous pressure of cold, inrushing sea, the boilers burst in a massive explosion, sealing her fate once and for all.

With a mighty heave, the ship lurched heavily over onto her port side as the torpedo exploded and the lights began flickering before going out altogether, plunging the vessel into complete darkness. In the blackness before the emergency lighting tripped in, children began crying hysterically and women screamed in terror, the noise adding to the banshee wailing of a screaming klaxon, the dreaded signal for abandoning ship, and the awful hiss of escaping high-pressure steam from ruptured pipes and wrecked boilers. After the initial shock, however, there was no panic, not even amongst the children, and with controlled haste passengers and crew walked to their allotted boat stations, stumbling in the darkness as they went. Then on that quiet July evening the *Avila Star* went to the bottom of the sea.

The Number 5 lifeboat on the starboard side came to grief as it was being lowered, when its aft fall took charge, leaving the flimsy craft hanging suspended by the bows, tipping its occupants and emergency supplies into the sea. The Number 7 boat immediately abaft it was lowered successfully with a full complement of passengers and crew. Also in that boat was Mr Weston, the ship's purser, and Dr Crawford. As their boat hit the water, a sailor skilfully unhooked the huge block, shouting as he did so, 'Mind the blocks.'

The Number 7 boat lay alongside after swinging free of her tackle, taking on more survivors who were sliding down the rope falls as Dr Crawford kept his flashlight on them. Eventually, with the boat carrying its full capacity, they floated free.

As they were about to unship the oars, another violent shock occurred. Without warning, a second torpedo slammed into the ship directly under the doctor's boat and exploded the instant it struck. The frail craft was lifted bodily out of the water by the violent blast and the subsequent upheaval of the sea. As it rose high on the massive geyser it disintegrated and the occupants were thrown unceremoniously into the sea.

After what seemed to be an eternity of sinking, Dr Crawford finally rose to the surface, gasping desperately for air and covered with a thick, glutinous mess of fuel oil. He neither saw nor heard anyone else from the Number 7 boat, indeed, he mysteriously found himself floating some way from where its pitiful remains lay, broken and wrecked, kept afloat only by its flotation tanks. Later, he described the terrible loneliness which suddenly gripped him before being replaced by a crushing fear of being sucked under when the ship took her final plunge. In a panic, he swam as hard as he could into the moonlight and suddenly found himself right under the ship's bows. Looking frantically around, he spotted one of the rafts which had been thrown over the port side and, almost exhausted, he feverishly tried to haul himself aboard. The oil covering his body prevented him doing so, however. Here and there on the dark swells he could see the little flickering red lights from the lifejackets of other survivors in the water. He listened with an aching heart to their pathetic cries for help as they drifted at the whims and fancies of the oil-coated sea, but they were too far away for him to be able to get to them.

Being at somewhat of a loss as to what to do next, he simply lay back in the cradle of the sea and floated for awhile looking languidly up at the stars, which seemed almost to mock at him with their flickering light. For some reason he seemed not to feel the cold as he floated there, but slowly he became aware that one of his eyes was half closed whilst his right foot began stiffening, both throbbing with pain. He was injured and alone, floating free in a hostile ocean. He looked up at the ship from time to time, noticing that she was a little lower in the water with every glance. He knew that her emergency dynamos were still turning because there were lights on deck; but she was sinking fast by then, her forecastle dipping beneath the sea and the water rising up to the base of her funnels.

Suddenly he dropped into a deep trough. He seemed to be there for quite a long time, and when he rose again on the next swell, the *Avila Star* had disappeared. He could feel himself being drawn towards the violent turbulence as the ship went down, and a terrible fear gripped him as he realised that the sinking ship was about to drag him down. Then, as though some divine hand had taken hold of him, he heard and felt a violent shock which drove him away. He did not know what caused that sudden, violent underwater explosion, but whatever it was, it saved his life. The time was exactly 22.10 hours, one hour and five minutes after the initial torpedoing.

Seeing some red lights directly ahead of him, the doctor swam towards them, still with his precious haversack slung around his neck. That extra burden finally proved to be too much for him in his weakened state, however, and with great reluctance he let it slip away and took off his outer clothing. Feeling a lot lighter then, he set off at a slow crawl, stopping every so often to rest and blowing upon his whistle as he floated on the swells. Finally, with his right foot a mass of agony, a boat appeared out of the darkness. Blowing his whistle once again, he recognised the voice of the Chief Officer, who asked, 'Who's that?'

'Surgeon,' he replied.

'Haul yourself aft by the safety lines and we'll pull you aboard.'

His body wracked with pain, Dr Crawford could do no more than fall lifelessly onto the aft thwart, where he lay as though dead. He had been alone in the water for a little over an hour. When he was examined, it was found that his injuries consisted of a broken right foot, a badly lacerated left leg, one eye almost closed, a badly cut lip and several teeth missing. He was very fortunate to have survived at all.

In total, seven boats had been successfully launched. The Number 7 boat had been blown up when that second torpedo had exploded, however, the Number 5 boat was leaking so badly that she had to be abandoned, and the Number 8 boat, which was the only one with a motor, was full of water and needed baling out before the engine could be started. In his report, Second Mate Anson wrote: 'There was no doubt that most of the casualties occurred at the time of the second explosion, the torpedo striking immediately under the number seven boat, blowing its occupants into the sea.'

After all the boats had left the scene of devastation, the Chief Mate, Mr Tallack, found himself still aboard the foundering vessel in the company of Captain Fisher, the Fourth Engineer, Mr H. Massouda, and a quartermaster, Able Seaman J. Campbell. They tried to launch the one remaining raft on board, but the lashings were soaked and they had no knife with which to cut the ropes securing it. They therefore threw lifebuoys, oars and any other materials which would float into the sea and jumped over the side after them.

When they hit the water, Mr Tallack at first drifted away from the ship but then, after a minute or two, found himself being gradually pulled back alongside with the force of the suction caused by the inrushing sea. Drifting in towards the bows, he became tangled up in the paravane A-frame gear but fortunately managed to extricate himself after a struggle. He then drifted away to the other side of the ship. He must have been caught up in some kind of current at that point because, looking back, he suddenly realised that he was far enough away from the wreck to be safe from being pulled under with her, and trod water as he watched her go down by the head, almost on an even keel except for her bow trim.

Looking around him then, he began to locate the others and soon heard Mr Massouda calling for help whilst in the background he could also hear Captain Fisher calling his name. From Able Seaman Campbell he heard nothing, but very soon contacted the skipper. They stayed together for thirty minutes, supported by an oar and a lifebuoy. At the end of that time, both were exhausted and desperately trying to cling to their precarious flotation pieces whilst their oil-coated bodies caused them constantly to slip away. Captain Fisher then began mumbling, saying that he could not hold on for very much longer because the intense cold was causing him stomach cramps. With agonising slowness, he gradually lost his strength until he eventually simply let go of his spar and drifted away into the night. Exhausted and rapidly losing strength himself, and almost numb with cold, Tallack could do nothing to help as he lost sight of his captain between two swells.

He drifted around aimlessly for some time longer with no conception of time, shouting for help from time to time whenever he saw a light from one of the boats. He was eventually picked up by the Number 4 boat at 02.00 hours.

Dawn came agonisingly slowly, and with the advent of full daylight, they made contact with other boats. Mr Tallack transferred to the Number 8 boat and assumed command. From the remains of the Number 7 boat he picked up a further five people, three of whom were very badly injured. One other was almost paralysed with shock whilst the fifth was exhausted but otherwise uninjured. The man who was in shock, a Mr F. Walton, died later that day and his remains were committed to the sea.

On 39°N in July, the weather is quite calm and sunny with the warm, westerly breezes bringing welcome relief from what could otherwise be a burning sun. In open boats after the severe shock of leaving a torpedoed ship more than 600 miles (1,100 km) from the nearest land, however, the situation can very quickly become critical even for seasoned seamen. For passengers whose only experience of the sea is the time spent in pampered isolation aboard a large vessel, such a situation can very quickly become dangerous, and in this instance it very quickly did. Full daylight brought with it a calm sea with a heavy swell from out of the south-west and a south-westerly breeze of force three.

Mr Tallack quickly gathered together all the boats, sorting and transferring crews as necessary. The Number 5 boat, however, was found to be making water and had to be abandoned. The Bosun, Mr A.J. Grey, was placed in command of the Number 1 boat and the Second Mate, Mr Anson, put in command of Number 2. With him was the Third Mate, Mr R.T. Clarke, Mr Brandie, the Chief Refrigeration Engineer, the three assistant engineers, Girdler, Ginn and Turner, two female passengers, Miss Traunter and Miss Ferguson, and a total of twenty-eight crew members.

Lifeboat Number 4 was commanded by Mr E.R. Pierce, whilst Number 6 was under the command of Mr R. Reid, former Chief Officer of the *Lyle Park*, on passage aboard the *Avila Star* after his own vessel had been torpedoed and sunk by a German armed raider in the South Atlantic on 11 June. The motor boat, Number 8, was under the command of Mr Tallack. When all boats and crews had been organised, masts were stepped and sails set, and they began to steer an easterly course towards what they believed was neutral Portugal. The sailing capabilities of those boats, however, varied quite dramatically and they were unable to keep adequate contact. That was the beginning of their problems.

At 18.30 hours, the fair breeze which they had been enjoying throughout the day began to wane, and Mr Tallack started his engine. Contacting boats Number 2 and 6 he suggested that, because everyone was exhausted, it might be advisable if they were to lay to their sea anchors throughout the night. Mr Anson and Mr Reid disagreed with that suggestion, preferring instead to remain under way. They did ask that the three boats should remain in company, but Tallack was unable to contact the other two until after dark, and by that time that breeze had almost died away, becoming very fitful and intermittent. The motorboat turned out to be a very bad sailer, and the Chief Mate was aware that his fuel supply was not going to last for very long and needed to be strictly controlled. His main concern at that time was for the thirty-nine people he had on board, for whom he was solely responsible. All of them were covered with a thick layer of gelatinous fuel oil, and were very ill because of it, with stomach cramps and vomiting. Three had been seriously injured, and a further six had received some minor injuries, all of which required medical attention. Add to that an almost total exhaustion, and Tallack's decision that the sails should be furled and sea-anchors run out was absolutely right.

As the dawn crept over the horizon on the 7th, there were no other boats in sight of Tallack's. He therefore started his engine and proceeded to look for them. About two hours later, he had found Numbers 2 and 4. Once again stepping their masts, they remained within sight of each other for the remainder of that day, sailing slowly eastwards with a light breeze at their sterns. All through the night of the 7th/8th those three frail crafts kept in contact, but by dawn on the 8th, Mr Tallack was becoming seriously concerned about the deteriorating condition of the sick and wounded in his boat. With that thought uppermost in his mind, he took a careful inventory of his reserves of fuel, water and provisions before deciding to leave the other two boats and forge ahead as best he could and close the Portuguese coast, at that time nearly 600 miles (1,100 km) distant, as quickly as possible. Prudently, he remained under sail for the rest of that day then, at 20.30 hours, just as dusk was spreading its impenetrable blanket over the sea, he started his engine.

After about one hour's motoring, lights were sighted off the port beam, and with no little excitement rippling through the boat, Tallack changed course towards them. Lights at sea in those days could only mean that the unknown vessel was neutral and, safe in that knowledge, SOS messages were flashed with a torch and flares burnt. Then without warning, the survivors in the boat were blinded by a powerful searchlight.

The ship turned out to be the Portuguese destroyer *Lima*, on passage from Lisbon to Ponta Delgada in the Azores. Taking his boat skilfully alongside the destroyer, Tallack went aboard, where the skipper, Captain Rodriguez, gave him the option of going to Ponta Delgada. With joyous heart, Tallack accepted. His charges were transferred to the destroyer and the boat sank.

Before leaving the area, Captain Rodriguez asked if there were any more boats in the area. Tallack suggested that, if he were to steer west about 30 miles he would, in all probability, find another two boats. Before long, Numbers 1 and 4 boats were found. That left two other boats still unaccounted for, Number 2 under the command of Mr Anson, and Number 6 commanded by Mr Reid, late of the *Lyle Park*. For the next twenty-four hours, Captain Rodriguez searched for them but, being short of fuel by that time, he was forced to abandon the hunt and continue his voyage.

If the fate of the *Arandora Star* was distressing and that of the *Alemeda Star* tragic, then what happened to the occupants of boats Numbers 2 and 6 of the *Avila Star* were truly horrendous. They parted company from Mr Tallack on the evening of 6 July.

Mr Anson in Number 2 boat had problems as soon as he parted company with Mr Tallack. More than half the complement of his boat were coated with a thick, viscous layer of oil. One was in an agony from a badly smashed hand, which was bleeding copiously, and a badly swollen and horribly discoloured ankle. Another had sustained a very deep gash across one eyebrow, and a third appeared to have at least one broken rib. Some were suffering quite badly with dysentery and an assortment of injuries and, although those who were in a relatively fair condition cared for the sick and injured as well as could be expected under such harrowing circumstances, it was never enough. The lack of adequate clothing coupled with the fuel oil that covered not just the survivors themselves, but everything they touched, and serious shortages of food and water, made it very difficult for them to render any beneficial aid at all.

After leaving Mr Tallack, the two boats managed to keep contact with each other as they steered an easterly course with a light north-westerly breeze of 4–6 knots (7.4–11.1 kph), a calm sea and long, lazy following swell. With no navigational instruments except for a small compass and very little in the way of charts, course-keeping had become a nightmare. Moreover, with no sextant by which they could fix their line of latitude, no chronometer to determine their line of longitude and no log-line to determine their speed, dead-reckoning had become next to impossible. In the swell which was running at the time and which is always in evidence in that area, the small boats were yawing and rolling quite badly as they breasted each successive sea, and both passengers and crew succumbed to seasickness, much of which was caused by the foul stench and taste of the omnipresent fuel-oil.

Sometime during the daylight hours of 8 July, both boats hove to in order to compare notes and examine whatever charts they possessed. After some consultation and dead-reckoning based mainly upon guesswork, they concluded that they had made approximately 100 miles (185 km) since leaving the scene of the wreck, and assumed that they had a further 500 or so miles (900 km) of sailing before closing the Portuguese coast. They rigged sail and set off once more upon their wearisome way.

The following morning, the light breeze which they had been experiencing had lifted to a 24-knot (44 kph) fresh breeze. There was a moderate sea running with a corresponding swell, longer and higher by then, with whitecaps beginning to curl at their crests and sea spray stinging exposed flesh. An ominous-looking sky building up on the western horizon gave the promise of bad weather to come and already rain squalls were sweeping over them, making their lives an even greater misery. Nevertheless they sailed steadily on before the rising wind. All through that night, the frail boats scudded along before wind and sea under a canopy of black, moonless sky and driving rain squalls which, added to the spray then coming inboard with relentless monotony, kept them all permanently soaked through and so cold from the effects of sea and wind-chill that they were almost numb.

A weak, watery sun rose over a storm-tossed horizon on the morning of the 10th, and throughout that dreadfully cold day, weather conditions deteriorated to a moderate gale of force 7, with a wind speed of between 32 and 38 knots (59–70 kph). The seas were heaped up with white foam being whipped away from their crests whilst the shorter, steeper seas were blown into well-marked streaks. On the darkening western horizon, a solid mass of nimbostratus was rapidly building up and bearing down upon the boats as they wallowed in the steepening seas, the grey, dark masses of cloud rendered diffuse by the densely falling rain. The temperature had dropped dramatically to −2 centigrade. Both boats were then making a south-easterly course, pitching and rolling sickeningly as they breasted each successive sea, shipping heavy spray. By that evening, everyone was in a state of dangerous exhaustion as they streamed their sea-anchors in order that they could ride out the gale throughout the storm-filled night. Very little could be done for the sick and injured.

At 04.30 hours on the morning of the 11th, they once more hove their sea-anchors and, setting sail, they again steered an easterly course before a following wind and sea. The leaden grey ocean had become very rough by that time as the wind veered around to the north-north-east. At midday Mr Anson estimated that the Portuguese coast was some 370 miles (685 km) distant. By 20.00 hours that evening, the wind had risen to gale force 8 with a wind speed of between 34 and 40 knots (63–74 kph). There was a much greater distance between each successive sea as their crests broke up into spindrift and well-marked streaks of foam cutting downwind like flocks of storm-tossed seabirds. Conditions had become very confused and extremely uncomfortable for the wretched survivors as they fought wind and sea, and Mr Anson prudently decided to stream his sea-anchor. For some reason Mr Reid was unable to stream his own sea-anchor, and it was at that point that the two boats parted company. Number 6 was never seen again.

The situation in Mr Anson's Number 2 boat was reaching the critical stage as the sick and injured became worse and those who were still relatively fit began to sicken. Salt-water boils and open, suppurating sores were very much in evidence and, with no medical supplies and a starvation diet, they quickly became worse.

Tongues were beginning to swell through a serious shortage of water, and at least one passenger began showing signs of delirious hallucination.

By 04.00 hours on the 12th, the gale had moderated to a fresh breeze of force 5, with a wind speed of about 20 knots (37 kph) and had once again veered to the north-north-east. The swells had also lengthened but the sea was still rough, with whitecaps turning to stinging spray. The boat's motion had eased a little by then, and at 04.30 hours their sea-anchor was hove in and they once again got under way at an estimated speed of 3 knots (5.5 kph).

Throughout the day and night of 12/13 July they sailed on, making little headway in the still-rough seas, with the delirious passenger still hallucinating. Everyone did what they could to keep him under control, but a little after 04.00 hours on the 13th, he suddenly leaped over the side of the boat. Mr Anson brought the boat up into the wind, furled sail and tried to reach him, but he was swept away. For the following fifty minutes, all those who could rowed frantically against the heavy swell, but finally lost sight of him altogether. By that time, they were all thoroughly exhausted and were forced to abandon their search. That was the first death on that nightmare voyage.

The evening of 13 July saw the weather deteriorate yet again as another area of low pressure swept in from the west and very quickly built up into a fresh gale of force 8 with a corresponding wind-speed of between 34 and 40 knots (63–74 kph), forcing them to stream their sea-anchor once more. They rode throughout the night to their sea-anchor, with everyone spending a desolate, cramped night of numbing cold and continuous soaking by rain and spray. Their precarious situation was taking its toll. Tempers would suddenly flare over the least little incident, and there were times when Mr Anson was hard pressed to maintain discipline.

At 04.00 hours on the 14th, the sea-anchor was once again hove and the boat got under way. The man with the injured foot was in excruciating pain by that time: his injury needed constant redressing, but there seemed very little hope of saving him because it was thought that gangrene had set in. At noon on that day, Mr Anson noted in his log: 'Portugal appears to be out of the question now owing to adverse NNE winds and sea. Distance to Spanish coast, two hundred and twenty-five miles.' In fact, by that time they had inadvertently drifted into the path of the North-east Trades and were drifting towards the coast of West Africa.

One crew member, almost insane with thirst, had drunk sea-water, which only exacerbated his thirst, putting him on a suicidal spiral towards eventual madness and excruciating death as his tongue became swollen to three times its original size, forcing it grotesquely through his lips and eventually choking him. One of the passengers who was suffering from dysentery had become very weak, whilst others had become so dehydrated that it was impossible for them to chew their meagre food ration.

The severe shortage of food was bad enough, but it was the dwindling water supplies which gave rise to Anson's gravest concerns. It had been rigorously rationed right from the start, with a ration of just 7 ounces (198 g) per day, and, by the morning of the 15th, it had become very scarce indeed. The ration had been cut to just 1½ ounces (42.5 g) – just about 1 inch (2.5 cm) in the bottom of an ordinary tumbler – three times per day. That daily total of 4½ ounces (127.5 g) very soon needed to be cut yet again to just 3 ounces (85 g) per day. At 08.00 hours, each person was issued with one biscuit, a little pemmican and two Horlicks tablets. At 11.00 hours, they received one chocolate. At 12.30 hours it was two Horlicks tablets and two chocolates, and at 18.00 hours, one biscuit and two Horlicks tablets, which was all they got until the following day. It was meagre fare indeed, but with all of them being constantly soaked with brine, it was the excruciating thirst that became their principal source of distress.

Throughout the long, bitterly cold night of 16/17 July they continued under sail in that savage, uncompromising environment, with the boat rolling, pitching, twisting and yawing, spreading seasickness and misery. Although the weather had moderated slightly, they still had the torment of breaking seas and cold rain squalls to contend with. At noon on the 16th, Anson had calculated that they had about another 45 miles (83 km) to the Spanish coast. What he did not know, however was that, not only had he overestimated the speed of the boat under sail throughout, but they had also drifted some 250 miles (460 km) south, placing them not just off the coast of Spain, but a long way off Morocco.

The sick and injured now began dying as their condition deteriorated, and every mind-numbing day became worse than the day before. Each dawn revealed another corpse to be thrown unceremoniously over the side. There was no time, strength or energy left for ceremonious burial or words of salvation for the dead. The only laws to be observed by that time were those of survival of the fittest. The days and nights of 17 and 18 July were nothing more than variations on a theme as pain, cold, hunger, thirst, misery and death engulfed them all. For those who still lived, there was only deteriorating sickness and a deep despondency that produced an awful sense of creeping finality.

Throughout those days and nights, the bad weather continued unabated, causing the weary, seriously weakened bodies in the violently moving boat to heave with nausea. Within their rime-sore eyes, there was nothing except an opaque dullness, and their faces had taken on a sick, greenish hue under rivulets of sea and rain water. With a superhuman effort of will and extreme courage, Mr Anson tried desperately to force his numbed mind to function clearly, but it was all somehow dreamlike and unreal as he pushed himself to the limit of insanity and death. During the early hours of 20 July, one of the passengers succumbed to the final oblivion, and several crew members died during that night. On the 22nd, another passenger died, along with several more crew members as the cruel wind and sea cut through their thin summer clothing, chilling them all to the bone.

Dark, baleful storm clouds, heavily pregnant with stinging rain, crouched menacingly over the pathetic wretches upon the darkened ocean in the early dawn of the 23rd. Then at 05.30 hours, an able seaman reported that he thought he had seen the navigation lights of an aircraft. No engine noises were heard, however, and nothing further was seen. Their hopes of rescue, so suddenly raised, were dashed and their tenuous hold on life seemed to have been reduced to a gossamer thread. Amidst heart-rending scenes of human despair, the survivors drifted on like unearthly spectres in the misty twilight of early morning.

It is said that the bravest of men undergo the hardest of tests, and the determined will to survive shown by those human wrecks under the most harrowing conditions is one of the enigmas of the human spirit. Half dead with exhaustion, hunger, thirst, malnutrition, exposure and sickness, they put aside their disappointment and sailed on as a grey sun rose over the storm-tossed horizon, silvering the ragged edges of the dark, ominous rain-clouds. Then, at 10.30 hours, the aching void in their hearts suddenly turned to an intoxicating euphoria as two seaplanes bearing Portuguese markings appeared and, spotting the tiny boat, circled for several minutes before ejecting three objects from their underbellies. They were lifejackets to which had been attached several bottles of water and tins of biscuits. Two were quickly re-covered and the survivors' spirits rose to unprecedented heights. Fifteen minutes later, one of the planes dropped a cylinder containing part of a chart of the West African coast, giving the position of the boat as 34°N 11°45'W, and a message that help was on its way. Those co-ordinates placed them some 300 miles west of Casablanca; they were very fortunate indeed to have been spotted at all in such a rough sea.

Their euphoria was short-lived, however, because they were destined to spend a further five gruelling days in that lifeboat. That afternoon, as though, with the coming of the planes, the hand of providence had touched them, the weather cleared and they steered a course due east-south-east with a gentle breeze filling their sail, a slight sea and a fine clear day under the yellow orb of a warming sun. The water and biscuits provided for them had lifted their spirits quite considerably, but they were soon to fall again as the deaths continued. By the early dawn of the 25th, yet more corpses lay on the duckboards of the boat and were committed to the deep without preamble or very much in the way of ceremony.

At 10.00 hours on that day, however, their depression turned once more to euphoria as Able Seaman Robinson sighted the masts of a vessel heading towards them. Flares and items of clothing were quickly burned to attract its attention, and by noon they were picked up by the Portuguese sloop *Pedro Nunes*. They were cared for with meticulous efficiency, but one other man died shortly after being taken on board.

They had eventually been picked up about 100 miles (185 km) west of Casablanca twenty days after escaping from the torpedoed *Avila Star*. Twenty-eight people out of an original forty reached safety after the most harrowing ordeal imag-inable. Sadly, however, a further two people died two days after reaching hospital in Lisbon.

As I have said, Mr Reid's Number 6 boat was never heard of again. Out of a total of 199 people on board the *Avila Star* at the time of her sinking, seventy-three had perished in circumstances too horrible to contemplate. Many of the crewmen were later awarded various citations for extreme courage, and many praises were heaped upon them all by the *London Gazette* of 24 November 1942. So ended the career of the *Avila Star*.

## The *Andalucia Star*

The last 'A' class ship to be lost to German torpedoes was the 12,846-ton *Andalucia Star*. With an overall length, beam and draught similar to that of the *Alemeda Star* and built by the same company, she was launched on 21 September 1926 as the *Andalucia* and renamed *Andalucia Star* in May 1929. With a top speed of 17 knots (31.5 kph), she entered service on the South American passenger and frozen meat run in March 1927. She served on a continuous basis until 1935 when, like the other four 'A' class vessels, she underwent alterations and modifications, being lengthened and refitted similarly to the *Alemeda Star*, and with an increased tonnage to 14,934 gross tons.

With her skipper, Captain James Bennett Hall, in command, she sailed from Buenos Aires on 27 September 1942 bound for the UK by way of Freetown, Sierra Leone. In her cavernous holds, she carried her usual cargo of frozen meat, corned beef, butter and a variety of other chilled foodstuffs for a beleaguered Britain. Expertly handled by a crew of 170 men, she also carried eighty-three passengers, most of them British expatriates from Argentina who had volunteered to return to Britain in order to play whatever part they could in the war effort. Included amongst their number were twenty-two women and three children.

Over the course of the following ten days, the *Andalucia Star* and her complement endured the searing daytime heat and freezing, star-studded nights of the tropical South Atlantic as she ploughed through the Southern Ocean in an incident-free voyage. As she crossed the southern latitudes and the bright, guiding light of the Southern Cross slowly sank beneath the horizon, the savage war then raging in the northern hemisphere might have been a million miles away. Passengers and crew alike had become relaxed, almost lethargic as the tremendous heat sapped their strength and energy, lulling them all into a false sense of security as the ship zigzagged its way towards Freetown.

She finally crossed the Equator at approximately 10.00 hours on the morning of 5 October 1942 and, at her top speed of 17 knots (31.5 kph), she was some forty-eight hours' steaming time on a straight course from Freetown. Thirty-six hours later, at 22.00 hours on the 6th, she sailed into the cross-hairs of U-107. Even without lights, she was an easy target as she became silhouetted against the vast red ball of the setting sun. Her position was 6°38'N, 15°46'W, almost yards from where two ships of the Blue Star Line, the *Viking Star* and the *Tuscan Star*, had been delivered of their own death blows on 25 August and 6 September respectively.

Passengers still strolled the darkened decks in the swiftly gathering gloom of approaching night, taking a final breath of cold, clear air before retiring for the night. The watch on deck went about their various duties in the time-honoured way with lookouts posted on each bridge wing, one on the foremast cross-tree and one on the monkey island. A long, low swell from the south-west raised her stern to the scend of the ocean as each gentle sea passed beneath her keel, and a bright yellow tropical moon turned the surface of the black water to liquid gold as the reflection danced across its heaving surface.

At 22.00 hours precisely, the peace and tranquility of that star-studded night was rent asunder when two massive explosions rocked the *Andalucia Star* as though she had suddenly been engulfed by a tremendous upheaval of the ocean, rolling her first over onto her port side and then to starboard as two torpedoes from U-107 ripped into her side, exploding in her Numbers 5 and 6 holds on her starboard side. Mortally wounded, Captain Hall immediately gave orders to abandon ship, and passengers and crew began to muster at their allotted boat stations. Even as they were hurrying to their places, Captain Hall took a message from the engine-room, telling him that it was flooding fast as the bulkhead separating the stokehole from the Number 5 hold had collapsed. Realising then that there was no earthly hope of saving his ship, he gave the order to lower away.

There was no panic amongst either passengers or crew. Not even the children showed any sign of distress as the well-drilled and highly efficient seamen ushered the passengers and those crew members who would man them, into the boats and began lowering away. There was just one unfortunate incident as the boats were being launched; the Number 2 boat came to grief when it was just halfway to the water. Full of people at the time, the easy flow of its drop was suddenly interrupted when the after fall took charge, leaving the boat suspended by its aft fall and precipitating most of its occupants and all of its gear and supplies into the sea. Fortunately, all except two of the occupants, a steward and stewardess, were safely picked up by other lifeboats.

The stewardess was Mrs L.A. Green. Just before the incident she had displayed extreme devotion to duty, level-headed efficiency and foresight in caring for the women and children in her care. Her final act of selflessness was to attach and switch on the red waistcoat light of a little 4-year-old girl, and it was that small, red light which ensured that she was rescued after she was thrown out of the Number 2 boat. She was seen momentarily by one of the crew members, but drifted away into the night before she could be reached. After a frantic search, however, her little red light was spotted by the eagle-eyed lamp-trimmer, William Steward Wheeler, who without hesitation dived into the oil-coated sea and swam 600 yards (550 m) to rescue her. For that courageous act, he was later awarded the Bronze Medal for Gallantry. Mrs Green was later awarded a posthumous commendation for her act of mercy, the merchant navy's equivalent of a Mention in Dispatches.

For the remainder of the boats, all went well as they hit the water and their crews began pulling hard on the oars to get away from the sinking ship. As they began to organise themselves into some semblance of order, they rested on their oars, wanting to see the last of their ship before she slipped beneath the waves. They did not have long to wait. Two of the lifeboats had lingered for too long near the starboard side of the vessel, and U-107, slinking beneath the sea, crept around to the port side and stove in the hull just abreast of the Number 1 hold. With a 60-foot (18 m) rent already torn in her starboard side, the third torpedo was unnecessary, but it blew a massive hole of some 40 × 30 feet (12 × 9 m) in her port side whilst at the same time blowing out the whole length of what remained of her starboard side. Some divine intervention must have been protecting the occupants of the two boats which were still alongside as the third torpedo exploded. As the starboard side disintegrated, showering them all with a deadly hail of razor-sharp debris, the boats were thrown unceremoniously about, but everyone on board was spared even slight injury as the crews pulled rapidly away.

The sea all around the bows of the stricken vessel had become covered with a thick mass of fuel-oil which gave off a most foul stench as its prism hues reflected in the eerie light of the tropical moon. On the foredeck of the rapidly sinking ship, Captain Hall stood with four other men, the last to leave the vessel. Having missed the boats, the skipper pondered their situation, and decided that they might stand a better chance aft where he hoped that the water would be relatively free of the cloying, viscous oil.

Upon reaching the poop deck they were amazed to see a lone passenger standing there as though hypnotised. Managing to launch a raft which had been stowed there, they threw it into the sea and jumped overboard after it. Despite much cajoling, threats and coaxing, Captain Hall could not convince the passenger to leave the ship, so they simply threw him overboard and he surfaced quite close to the raft. Unfortunately, however, he was lost to sight almost immediately he surfaced and was not seen again. Even more unfortunate was the crew-member who suffered a heart attack and died before he could reach the relative safety of the boats.

No sooner had they safely cleared the foundering vessel than, at 22.25 hours, the *Andalucia Star* took her final death plunge. Her bows rose vertically into the air and, with an explosion of smoke and steam and compressed air gushing up through her funnel and engineroom skylights and bursting through doors, deadlights and portholes, she plunged some 30,000 feet (9,000 m) to the ocean floor. U-107 was not seen throughout that incident, and without surfacing to find out whether or not she could be of any assistance to the survivors, she slunk away to find her next victim.

With a raft supporting them, Captain Hall and the other men who had left the sinking ship with him finally found the lifeboats. He took charge and decided that they should all remain together throughout the rest of that night, then set about lashing all the boats and rafts together. Fortunately the weather remained calm, with the same slight swell from the south-west under a canopy of glittering stars and bright yellow moon. Even with the very real threat of a slow, agonising death under a blazing tropical sun by day and freezing temperature by night, there was no panic among the survivors.

The dawn finally crept over the eastern horizon in a blaze of crimson glory under an azure sky, heralding the start of another scorching day. They swept the horizon, looking for any sign of ship or aircraft, but there was nothing, not even a seabird to break the monotony, just a flat, featureless, empty sea. Freetown was approximately 180 miles (330 km) to the north-east and, as the Captain and the Mate, in separate boats, began plotting their position by dead-reckoning, a light breeze began to ruffle the oily calm surface. Masts were very quickly stepped and sails bent on as, with the First Mate navigating, the boats turned their sterns to the breeze and began moving toward their destination.

The light breeze rose steadily throughout the morning until, still lashed together, the boats were scudding across the sea at a steady 5 knots (9.2 kph), with a fair wind at their sterns. In the afternoon, the sky became overcast and darkened perceptibly as a light rain began to fall, cooling the people in the boats and refreshing them after the blistering heat of the morning. But as the darkness covered the ocean once more, the deadly tropical cold began eating into scantily clad flesh, and the sense of well-being that the rain had brought quickly turned to a misery of intense cold as it continued to fall, becoming a malignant enemy rather than the friend it had been just hours before.

At about 02.00 hours, they sighted a ship cleaving through the water at high speed from the north-east. It turned out to be the British flower class corvette, HMS *Petunia*. A great cheer went up as people realised that they had been spotted, and by 04.00 hours, all were safely aboard enjoying hot drinks, with the aroma of frying bacon and eggs strong in their nostrils.

Although by no means taciturn, Captain Hall was a man of few words. Consequently, when he had completed his report of the sinking it was rather terse and restrained, containing very little other than the bare facts of the incident. At the end of that narrative, however, he added this anecdote: 'I would like to mention here that W.S. Wheeler, Lamp Trimmer, dived into the water from his boat and rescued a little girl passenger, bringing her safely to the boat. Also N. Bennett, who volunteered to take over the wheel in place of Williams, who was a married man. This request I granted, and he was one of the last men to leave the ship with me.'

Captain Hall died later of his wounds.

That was the last of five of the finest vessels ever to have put to sea in the service of the Mercantile Marine. It was by no means the end of the story, however, because, in the years of savage war yet to come, many more fine ships, together with their gallant crews, were to be lost to German bombs, mines, shells and torpedoes.

# 4   The American Turkey Shoot

As we have seen the Second World War was just twelve hours hold when Admiral Karl Doenitz unleashed his U-boats against British shipping in the South and North-western Approaches with the sinking of the *Athenia* on 3 September 1939. For many months before war was declared, it had been assumed by both Britain and Germany that it would be Germany's larger, faster and better-armed capital ships from which British shipping would have most to fear. The very small U-boat fleet had been designed solely to engage in the destruction of coastal shipping and to mop up anything which the heavy units might have missed in the deep oceans. In that assumption both countries were wrong as, beginning with the *Graf Spee* in December 1939, all of Germany's heavy units were systematically destroyed or kept bottled up in various ports or anchorages by the British blockade for most of their time. The last of those battleships, *Scharnhorst*, was destroyed in December 1943 by Admiral Fraser in the *Duke of York* in the Battle of the North Cape, without making very much of an impact on Allied ship losses.

Early in 1942 as Britain, under the direction of the Royal Navy, improved its convoy system and began routeing convoys further north, Doenitz directed his submarine captains to patrol the Denmark Straits between Iceland and Greenland, the Davis Straits between Greenland and the eastern coast of Canada, and south along Canada's eastern seaboard. However, the growing expertise of the Royal Canadian Navy in convoy protection, coupled with America's entry into the war in December 1941, prompted him to direct them further south, to the eastern seaboard of the United States.

All along that deadly shore, with the peacetime lights of America still burning like a welcoming beacon in the background, U-boat commanders reaped a rich harvest of Allied shipping until the Americans finally established an effective convoy system to provide adequate protection for merchant ships along its entire eastern seaboard. That system, however, was not forthcoming for many months after Germany declared war on the United States, and only then at the insistence of the British government and with the expertise of the Royal Navy. After that development, Doenitz moved his U-boats even further south, to the Caribbean and the Gulf of Mexico where ships were still sailing independently without the benefit of convoy protection.

That move caused heavy losses in that area, with 750,000 tons of shipping, representing nearly 600 ships of the Allied nations, sent to the bottom in just three months. In response to that devastating toll, the Allied navies had sunk just eighty-seven U-boats during the whole of 1942, and although that was a higher total than in the previous year, it still averaged only eight per month. By the end of July 1942, the U-boats had accounted for nearly 17 million tons of Allied shipping.

Early in January 1942 in the states along America's eastern and southern shores, the living was easy and unrestrained for locals, vacationers, casual workers and military and naval personnel. The war then raging in Europe, which America had entered just three weeks earlier, seemed so far away as not to exist at all. At night, the coastal neon of night clubs, bars and shops, street lighting and the domestic lights of large stores, apartment blocks, houses and offices, burned as brightly as ever from New York to Florida and down into the Gulf of Mexico from Miami on the west coast of Florida to Brownsville on the border between Texas and Mexico. People there were blissfully unaware that just a few short miles off their coast lurked one of the world's most potent military forces, poised to strike at their country. Doenitz's U-boats had arrived off America's southern coastal waters, ready to cause the greatest naval disaster suffered by the United States Navy in the Second World War.

In company with four other U-boats, Reinhard Hartegan, commanding Type 9, U-123, left Hamburg on 23 December 1941, bound for the Gulf of Mexico, there to be joined by two other U-boats which had been driven out of Canadian waters by the Royal Canadian Navy. Unknown to Hartegan, however, the British Admiralty, by making good use of the recently captured and deciphered Enigma machine, was tracking the position, course and speed of that flotilla day by day, and supplying the US government with all the information they could ever need on its progress, destination and intent.

Archive documents and situation maps of the US Navy show just how detailed their knowledge of the approach of that fleet was, yet with twenty-one destroyers penned up in harbour on the orders of Admiral King, chief of the US Navy, for the very purpose of resisting any German U-boat fleet in US waters, they did nothing, and those vital ships were never sent to sea. Shore lights, lighthouses and the lights of mooring buoys were all left blazing, enabling U-boat commanders to pick out their targets with ease. Even American merchant ships sailed those treacherous waters with all navigation lights showing, as though the war did not exist.

On 14 February 1942, the flotilla of seven boats gathered off the Florida coast and there, within sight of homes along the shoreline, their *Paukenschlag* offensive began. Two days later, on the 16th, Operation Neuland was launched with a series of carefully planned attacks against tankers and local oil industries along the Caribbean coast. The U-boats of the *Paukenschlag* and Neuland did not operate in packs, but as individual lone wolves against targets of opportunity. There were more than enough.

Theoretically, under the rules of submarine warfare as laid down in the London Submarine Agreement of 1936, any U-boat sighting a lone enemy merchantman was required to surface, stop the ship in question so as to ascertain her country of origin, cargo and destination, then give her crew time enough to abandon ship and pull well clear before sinking the ship. German submarine commanders, however, under the direction of their supreme commander, Karl Doenitz, were not known for observing the rules of conduct. To give some insight into their approach, and to emphasise the terrible ordeals that merchantmen faced during the war at sea, one need only consider the sinking of the British tanker *San Emiliano*.

The *San Emiliano* was a 16,000-ton British tanker which, some time in early February 1942, was sailing independently some 300 miles (550 km) to the east of Caracas, *en route* to the UK and loaded to her marks with Venezuelan crude. Grenada and the Windward Islands were approximately 100 miles (185 km) off her port bow and Trinidad about the same distance off her starboard bow. An overcast, incredibly hot and humid day had given way to a cold, almost frosty night, dark and starless under a dense blanket of stratocumulus.

Midway through the first watch, at about 02.00 hours, without any warning, she was suddenly ripped apart by three torpedoes which exploded along her port side. Those three tremendous explosions almost lifted the deeply laden vessel out of the water as her full tanks erupted into a raging inferno of blazing oil, which lit up the darkness of the night like a monstrous beacon. The doomed ship was ablaze from stem to stern and from truk to keel within seconds. Her Chief Mate managed to get just one lifeboat cleared away and laid alongside, together with nine other crew members who had managed to escape the massive conflagration. Within a few minutes her hull, decks and superstructure began to glow crimson and her half-inch thick steel plates began buckling under the fierce heat. Realising that no one else could possibly get off that ship alive, in immediate danger of becoming engulfed in the blazing oil which was even then rapidly spreading around them, and in very real danger of being hit by the bursting rivets which had begun flying through the rolling black smoke and blood-red flames with the velocity of rifle bullets, the Chief Officer gave the order to unship oars and pull clear.

When they were far enough away from the blazing wreck to be safe from being pulled under when she went down, they rested on their oars to take one final look back at the ship which had been their home. Apart from the mate, all of those men were very young, ranging in age from sixteen to nineteen, and as they watched their vessel burning and glowing in the night they could see, vividly outlined against the leaping flames, the figures of their shipmates burning as they ran around the melting decks like out-of-control puppets and flinging themselves from the still-erupting ship into the sea of burning oil to a certain death. A pitiful cry for help near the lifeboat prompted the mate to look around, and he was astonished to see a greaser who was kept afloat only by the lifejacket that he wore. Pulling the unfortunate man inboard, they were devastated when they saw how badly burned he was, and even more so when the skin of his arms and body peeled away in their hands like rubber gloves as they pulled him aboard.

For the following three hours, his groans of agony were terrible to hear as he lay helpless on the duckboards at the bottom of the boat covered with a thick woollen blanket, his body and clothes shining beneath a thick coating of crude. A little later there was nothing to be heard; the man had died. As they laid him gently across one of the thwarts, the mate was advised that the second steward had also died. They uncovered him to discover the most horrific stomach wound through which the contents of his stomach and chest cavity were still pouring, interlaced with a thick oozing of blood and gore, most of which had, by that time, congealed into a thick, viscous pool in the bottom of the boat, mingled with a layer of syrupy oil. He too was laid across a thwart just prior to burial. The only thing that young steward had complained of throughout that hideous night was the penetrating cold.

Those pathetic wretches hoisted their single sail and made their slow way through the shark-infested waters of the southern Caribbean. They finally made landfall in Trinidad after enduring three days of baking sun and nights which were cold and wretched. Just eight men out of a crew of forty had survived.

Curaçao's harbour on Oraniestad was defended by just one converted Dutch whale-boat on the night of 16 February when *Kapitän-Leutnant* Hartenstein nudged his U-156 into the port under cover of darkness and attacked its oil storage tanks and refinery and two tankers which were tied up at the wharf. A captain of the US Army witnessed the destruction that Hartenstein wrought, which heralded the opening salvos of Operation Neuland. What he reported was a curtain of flaming oil spreading like wildfire over a very wide area of the harbour, and fanned into an uncontrollable conflagration by a stiff breeze from the north-west. A steady stream of white-hot tracer bullets arced into the heart of the refinery from the dark ocean, puncturing tanks and pipes which immediately burst into flames, sending large globules of burning oil high into the night sky. These fell onto the roofs of houses, warehouses and other ships, and ensuing fires caused panic and chaos in the streets and all around the harbour in a thundering cacophony of noise from guns and ships' sirens and the screams of people running in all directions. Cries of agony could be heard above the roaring flames as men struggled in the burning, shark- and barracuda-infested water, burning even as they struggled to stay afloat. The first night of Operation Neuland had been a complete success as three other U-boats which had joined the beano sank a further seven tankers. By the end of February, that number had risen to seventeen.

Admiral Hoover's Caribbean Sea Frontier Force, with its headquarters in San

Juan, Puerto Rico, was powerless to stop the carnage. The only vessels available for deployment were two ancient destroyers and two equally ancient patrol boats, which had to defend the vast stretch of ocean from Key West to Trinidad. Even that pathetic force was more than the strength of the Gulf Sea Frontier Force, which possessed just three coastguard cutters and a motor yacht with which to patrol the whole of the Gulf of Mexico, the Yucatan Channel, Cuba and the west coast of Florida.

Quickly realising the severe weakness of the American defences, the U-boat captains roamed free and without challenge, increasing the tempo of their *blitzkrieg* in the Caribbean. The details of ship sinkings in the Caribbean and the Gulf of Mexico are quite horrendous to relate, especially those of tankers. Tankers, and the men who sailed in them, died hard, quickly if they were fortunate enough to have their ship explode on impact, but more often than not slowly and hideously in a sea of burning oil from which there was no escape. The tanker *O. A. Knudsen*, for example, was attacked three times in twelve hours off Hole-in-the-Wall, Bahamas, before finally being sunk by two U-boats in a simultaneous attack which blew the ship apart. Her wireless distress signals did not attract even one rescue vessel or aeroplane. There were no survivors. One unidentified U-boat captain even had the effrontery to sink the deeply laden tanker *Gulftrade* just 500 yards (450 m) from an impotent coastguard cutter. The Chilean freighter *Tolten* was torpedoed and sunk 30 miles (55 km) off the Ambrose Channel, New York, taking all but one of her crew down with her. The tanker *Tiger* was torpedoed and sunk off Cape Henry whilst taking a pilot on board. The following night, the unarmed collier *David H. Atwater* was sunk by gunfire from a range of just 600 yards (550 m) between Cape Charles and Cape Henlopen by an unidentified submarine. Her crew of twenty-seven men were given no opportunity to abandon ship, but instead were riddled with machine-gun fire, even as they were attempting to lower the lifeboats. Just three men survived, but no one was ever tried for that atrocity.

Before the war, *Kapitän-Leutnant* Achilles had been a merchant captain, and being employed on a regular service to the Caribbean, knew the area intimately. On the night of 18 February, unobserved by the complacent population and defenders, such as they were, he nosed his U-161 into Port of Spain harbour, a haven he knew well. Taking all the time he needed to have a good look around through his periscope, he finally decided on a tanker and a freighter.

The tanker went first, exploding in a vast fireball of billowing smoke and flames which soared hundreds of feet into the still night air before mushrooming outwards and showering the port, other ships and surrounding homes with fiery liquid. Achilles then carefully and very deliberately turned the bow of his vessel towards a deeply laden freighter and, with two well-aimed torpedoes which exploded in the engine-room and Number 2 hold, the vessel sank in less than twenty minutes. A month later, he repeated his bold operation with a night attack on St Lucia, sinking two fully laden freighters riding at anchor there. Within a very short space of time, *Kapitän-Leutnant* Bauer arrived on the scene in U-50, and in just two weeks in the Windward Passage and the Old Bahamas Channel, he sunk nine ships before running out of torpedoes.

After hearing reports of his U-boat captain's exploits, a delighted Hitler telephoned Doenitz to congratulate him. Their morale boosted by the easy successes they had achieved in the warm, tropical waters of the Gulf of Mexico and the Caribbean, the U-boat crews referred to that period as the 'American turkey shoot'. However, despite these successes, Doenitz failed to exploit a situation which was crippling Allied merchant shipping in that area because Hitler insisted on keeping twenty boats in Norway, leaving him with just six boats to deploy in American waters.

By late April, however, Doenitz had somehow managed to persuade Hitler of the advantages of exploiting the situation in the Caribbean and the Gulf of Mexico and he was consequently able to marshal eighteen boats for an all-out assault on shipping sailing independently off the Florida coast, whilst a further nine Type IXs were ordered into the Caribbean, there to stalk and dispatch merchant ships in the warm, shark-infested waters between the Bahamas and Trinidad. That offensive was sustained by 1,700-ton milk-cow U-boats, three of which were immediately dispatched. Each was capable of carrying 700 tons of spare fuel and sufficient torpedoes to keep a dozen U-boats operating deep into the Caribbean as far west as the Panama Canal.

The first of these vessels arrived on 22 April, refuelling its first boat, U-108, 500 miles (900 km) off Bermuda. During the following two weeks, she had topped up the tanks and replenished the supplies of torpedoes of twelve Type VII boats and two Type IXs. This was a nerve-shattering period for Admiral Hoover, commander of the Caribbean Sea Frontier Force; in May and June 1942, sinkings rose by 148 in just five months in that one sea area alone. Yet the US Navy still did nothing.

Encouraged by the success of *Paukenschlag*, and not content with the long-range strikes deep into the Gulf of Mexico, Doenitz confidently ordered his U-boats to head for the Mississippi Delta ports of New Orleans, Jacksonville, Pensacola and Mobile, ranging as far west as Galveston. Fifty per cent of all American oil came from the Texas oilfields, and off the coast of that area could be found a rich traffic of tankers and bauxite carriers ferrying supplies to this extensive concentration of refineries and aluminium smelters. These industries were crucial to the US, and by association the British, war effort.

The first blow was struck on 6 May when *Kapitän-Leutnant* Schacht in U-507 sank the 8,000-ton bauxite carrier *Alcoa Puritan* 100 miles (185 km) south of Mobile, causing heavy loss of life when crew members were dragged down as the ship sank. On the following day, Reinhart Hartegan in U-123 was patrolling off the coast of Jacksonville and manoeuvred his boat between a crowded holiday beach and the American tanker *Gulf America*. Surfacing in order to save his supplies of torpedoes, he used his deck gun, causing incredible carnage amongst the crew as he shelled and sank that vessel. Half of the thirty-eight crewmen died in the ensuing inferno. The only answer that Admiral King could find to that incident was to halt all tanker traffic for a month, which might well have saved a few ships from being sunk, but certainly did nothing for either the American or British war effort.

With just two destroyers, a few smaller vessels and a dozen aircraft available to protect shipping in the Gulf of Mexico, U-507 and 506 were very soon sinking a ship a day each, and although the total number of U-boats operating in the Gulf never rose above six at any one time, forty-one ships were sunk during the month of May alone, half of which were vitally needed tankers. That was double the casualty rate of any month on the Eastern Sea Frontier, and was felt to such an extent in the United States that petrol rationing had to be introduced on 15 May 1942, limiting drivers to just 3 gallons (13.6 l) per week.

This savage *blitzkrieg* raged on unchecked for close to six months. During that time, not one U-boat was accounted for, and well over 1 million tons of shipping, together with their vital cargoes and most of their crews, had been sent to the bottom. Those severe losses in the Caribbean and Gulf of Mexico began to threaten the entire American war effort, and General Marshall, unable to contain himself any longer, sent a letter on 19 June saying as much to Admiral King, Commander-in-Chief, US Atlantic Fleet, and effectively criticising him for his lack of response to appeals for a convoy system to be introduced.

In a cold letter of reply, Admiral King bemoaned the shortage of submarine chasers and escorts which had, 'forced the Navy to rapidly improvise on a vast scale. Only recently,' he wrote, 'had the Sea Frontier Force possessed sufficient escorts for convoy work and, since May, our east coastal waters have experienced a high degree of security.' Admiral King then went on to say that, 'losses outside the east coast zone would be reduced as more air cover became available'. And in his final paragraph he revealed his complete about-face on the need for convoys. 'I might say in this connection that escort is not just one way of handling the submarine menace; it is the *only* way that gives any promise of success. The so-called patrol and hunting operations have time and again proved futile.'

That last sentence refers to Admiral King's earlier response to the U-boat menace when he requisitioned hundreds of small boats to patrol the southern waters. Schooners, shrimps and even private yachts were called upon to hunt and destroy enemy submarines. To man those ludicrous and totally inadequate vessels, the Coastguard Auxiliary was formed. No physical examination or seafaring or navigational skills were required to join; if a man was capable of breathing and walking, he was in. No navigational equipment was made available, and when they were at sea, no one who manned those vessels knew where they actually were. In fact, even had such navigational equipment been available, that force did not possess anyone capable of navigating a ship at sea. To give some insight as to the kind of armaments available to those vessels, a two-masted schooner equipped with sails and a small diesel engine designed solely to manoeuvre in and out of harbour, would usually have a 50-calibre machine-gun on the bows and three depth-charges aft. It can be imagined what would have happened if any of those small craft had actually found a submarine and dropped those depth-charges.

It is pretty certain that the disaster in the Caribbean and Gulf of Mexico during the first six months of 1942 could have been avoided if Admiral King, who possessed all the authority needed for organising anti-submarine warfare, had done a number of things.

If he had heeded the U-boat intelligence which was reaching him every day from the British Admiralty in London, and if he had heeded the British tactical doctrine for combating U-boats, hard-earned knowledge that Britain gave to Admiral King and his subordinates, the situation could very well have turned out very differently; but he did not. In fact, he pointedly ignored all of that information simply because he detested the Royal Navy, and in particular, its intelligence. He categorically refused to accept the idea of convoy on the ridiculous grounds that it was, in his opinion, purely defensive warfare. The British, however, had learned the hard way that it was in fact *offensive*, as the U-boats were forced to go to the convoys where escorts stood a much better chance of finding and sinking them.

The second thing he could have done was to switch off the lights. Instead, he ordered that the lights be dimmed but not blacked out, and so the massacre was able to continue unabated because, even with the shore lights dimmed, the U-boat crews could see the silhouettes of vessels quite clearly against them.

That slaughter was not only threatening to undermine Allied strategy, but its effects were also being acutely felt by US citizens as coffee, sugar and petrol became increasingly scarce. President Roosevelt's broadcast appeal for everyone to cut their driving habits in half were very soon echoed in Britain, where the loss of ¼ million tons of tanker transport, courtesy of Admiral King's intransigence, had created a desperate fuel shortage. That shortage prompted the First Sea Lord, Admiral Pounds, to fly to Washington to try and persuade Admiral King to agree to several emergency tanker convoys from the Caribbean. In fact, at that particular time, Britain's total fuel reserves amounted to just three weeks' supply.

The situation was so serious that Admiral Pounds even offered to provide any escorts by reducing the number of Royal Navy escort groups in the North Atlantic to ten, the barest possible minimum for safety, especially as the U-boats were rampaging over the entire length and breadth of the Atlantic Ocean from the Barents Sea in the north to the Cape of Good Hope in the south, and from Greece in the east to the Panama Canal in the west. The situation was particularly galling for the Royal Navy, as they had gone to all the trouble of providing accurate information about the U-boats, only to have it ignored by Admiral King and his staff. Cape Hatteras became known amongst merchant crews as Torpedo Alley.

Whilst this was going on, the FBI had become paranoid with the fear of the possibility of German saboteurs being put ashore from the U-boats to sabotage the refineries and petrochemical plants in the area. To aid them in their quest for these operatives they encouraged the people of Galveston to spy on each other and report who went into certain houses. Because no one could understand how the Germans knew when and where to intercept the ships they were sinking, the FBI had become obsessed with the idea that certain people were relaying messages to the U-boats. It never seemed to occur to them that all the U-boats had to do in order to find all the targets they could handle was to patrol the coast. So, even though what they were suggesting was utter rubbish, it was all so very mysterious to them that they became convinced that there were spies in their midst. People began looking for Germans coming ashore in dinghies and suspecting friends whom they had known for years, and even relatives. It was a fear of the unknown generated by paranoid incompetence.

To aid them in their hunt for saboteurs, the FBI provided horses for the Coastguard to patrol the beaches, riding back and forth across the sand and scanning the sea for U-boats and possible infiltrators. To repel any invaders they encountered, they were issued with shotguns. What they thought such pathetic weapons could achieve against submachine-guns and automatic rifles is difficult to imagine, but that is how it was. If nothing else, it must have kept them all from being bored.

To a certain extent, however, that paranoia was justified. In the early summer of 1942 the FBI's nightmare became a frightening reality when, under the cover of darkness on a moonless night, four German saboteurs were put ashore from an unidentified U-boat off the Florida coast. Their instructions were to rendezvous with four other saboteurs whom had been put ashore at Abaganze, Long Island. That was called Operation Astorious, and was a German plot to blow up industrial installations, destroy war production and achieve a devastating propaganda coup all in one fell swoop. Secreted away amongst the dunes of the Florida beaches, the saboteurs had buried cases of explosives and detonators before heading inland for their rendezvous with their colleagues in the north.

The plot was very soon betrayed by two members of the gang who were American citizens, but desperately in need of an ego-boost, the chief of the FBI, J. Edgar Hoover, claimed the credit for their detection and subsequent capture. With the aid of the two American traitors, the hidden cache of explosives was very soon found and retrieved, and the conspirators were tried by a hastily convened commission in Washington. Within a very few weeks, the two informants received long jail sentences because they had informed the authorities about the plot, whilst their six fellow conspirators were all executed at fourteen-minute intervals – the fastest multiple executions in American history.

It was not until 10 June 1942 that Admiral King, under pressure from the Royal Navy and high-ranking American officers, finally accepted the need for a full convoy system throughout the Caribbean and Gulf of Mexico. Apart from the fact that American naval officers considered escort work beneath their dignity, however, the US Navy was virtually impotent to provide escort cover, and it was therefore agreed that it would be organised with the assistance of British escort groups taken from the Western Ocean and a squadron of RAF Hudsons operating out of Trinidad. It came too late, however, for the hundreds of ships and the thousands of merchant seamen needlessly lost. On 15 June, the urgent need for a convoy system was savagely underlined when, to the horrified amazement of thousands of sun-worshipping holidaymakers thronging Florida's Virginia Beach resort, two large freighters were torpedoed and sunk almost within hailing distance of the beach, again, with a great loss of life. As escorted convoys became ever more numerous, however, and antisubmarine patrols began to take a rising toll of the U-boats, Operation Neuland began to peter out in the late summer of 1942.

The heavy losses I have described might well have been far greater had the Germans sent their heavy surface units into the Atlantic in support of the U-boats. Hitler, however, had become obsessed with the idea that Britain intended to invade Norway at the earliest opportunity. This obscured all other considerations, and threw away the glittering opportunities which were available in the Atlantic, instead concentrating every available surface unit and many of Doenitz's vital U-boats in Norwegian waters. 'Norway,' he said in one of his speeches, 'is the zone of destiny in this war.' Norway was, of course, a most important theatre at that time, it was in the Atlantic that Germany's greatest opportunity lay.

The stress of operating more than 4,000 miles (7,400 km) from their bases was beginning to take a heavy toll on the U-boat crews. Many weeks of uninterrupted patrolling in the energy-sapping heat of the Caribbean, the claustrophobic atmosphere of a cramped U-boat and the nauseating stench of human sweat and waste became difficult for the submarine crews to endure. The principal concern of a U-boat commander was food reserves. *Kapitän-Leutnant* Reinhard Suhren, commanding U-564 in the Caribbean, wrote:

> The diet for the first eight days was quite good, we always left our base with a lot of fresh fruit, vegetables and meat. The second lavatory was used as a larder, but there were disadvantages. Forty-six men to one lavatory is not really adequate. When all the fresh food was used up, we turned to our supplies of tinned food; but no matter whether it was fresh or tinned, it always tasted of diesel oil. The biggest problem was the bread, in the damp and sweaty atmosphere it rapidly went stale. The loaves would soon look like rabbits, covered in fluffy mildew. We just removed as much of it as possible before eating it.

Moreover, merchant ship sinkings were becoming fewer and fewer, and U-boats were beginning to be lost. But even so, they continued their campaign of terror to the bitter end.

For the men of the Royal Navy's BS Escort Group assigned to operate with the US Navy in the Caribbean, their duties became more like a holiday cruise after the freezing temperatures of the bleak and stormy North Atlantic. It was only when the U-boats attacked or when survivors were plucked from the shark-infested waters that the naval crews were brought face to face with the unique horrors of the sea war in those far-off tropical seas.

Those horrors were brought savagely home to the naval crews when, on the night of 18 August, convoy AW 13 was attacked off Trinidad. Two freighters and a tanker, all laden to their marks with vital war supplies, were lost. Quite a large proportion of the freighter crews were plucked from the water which, by the time HMS *Pimpernel* arrived on the scene, was alive with sharks of every size and description; but there were no survivors from the tanker. She had been struck by just one torpedo amidships and, as is the way with tankers, immediately burst into an uncontrollable conflagration. Within seconds, she was a raging inferno from stem to stern, listing badly and settling fast in the water. With the whole ship a mass of blood-red flames and black, oily smoke curling evilly for hundreds of feet into the air and her hull glowing almost white from the intense heat, her crew stood no chance of escape and, sadly, the *Pimpernel* turned away to catch up with the convoy, leaving the burning tanker and its pathetic crew to their ultimate fate.

The increasing tempo of the U-boat war around Trinidad during the months of July and August was endangering coastal traffic trading along the Brazilian coast. Such a threat to vital supplies of minerals and coffee prompted the Americans, with the permission of the Brazilian government, to despatch US Marines to construct a series of airstrips on the undefended stretch of coast. There was a very real threat of the Germans building secret supply depots in any number of the isolated coves there in support of the U-boat offensive in the Atlantic. Hitler had already offered the Brazilian government many millions of captured US dollars for such depots, but then discovered that, on the advice of the American government, all Axis sympathisers had been rounded up and jailed.

Hitler then agreed to Admiral Raeder's proposal to extend the U-boat operations down the coast of Brazil. It was to prove a serious mistake. Following the sinking of three Brazilian merchant ships within the space of three days, Brazil declared war on Germany and Italy on 22 August 1942. Taking immediate advantage of that new development, Admiral J.H. Ingram's South Atlantic Force was quickly moved into the invaluable Brazilian bases in order to control the vital Mid-Atlantic Narrows. The US Navy's protection of the coastal shipping off South America proved to be the final link in the comprehensive Allied convoy network.

After August 1942, the curtain abruptly fell on the 'American turkey shoot', and the merchant ships which plied the Caribbean and the Gulf of Mexico were again reasonably safe from U-boat attack. In the succeeding months, 1,400 merchant ships were convoyed through the interlocking system, and only eleven of those were sunk. Admiral King and the US Navy had paid a high price to learn the hard way what British Intelligence had been telling them since the beginning of that year, that it was the well-escorted convoy that would defeat the U-boat menace.

# 5    A Regrettable Error?

In times of total war, it unfortunately becomes necessary to paint one's friends and enemies in monochrome black and white. Enemies must always be wrong. God is always on the side of the righteous, the 'righteous' being whichever side one happens to be on. So all negative images which could be evoked against the Axis forces were used by the Allied propaganda machine to promote a hatred among civilian merchant seamen and Royal Navy personnel of the German U-boat crews.

There was a perception of a brutal, unremitting enemy committing barbaric acts of violence against survivors in lifeboats, and there have in fact been several oral reports of such atrocities from survivors, but the only proven case of the machine-gunning of survivors in the water was committed by *Kapitän-Leutnant* Eck, who was commanding U-852 at the time. Together with his officers, he was tried and convicted after the war by an Allied court of deliberately killing survivors in the water when he torpedoed and sank the Greek ship *Peleus*, and was executed for acts of extreme barbarism. So although the work of submarine crews was considered by merchant seamen as dirty and murderous work, very few of Germany's *Kriegsmarine* commanders indulged in deliberate acts of barbarism.

Allied propaganda created a fearsome image of German submariners, with horrendous tales of cowardly attacks against merchant shipping, implying that they were nothing short of cold-blooded killers, predatory wolves of the sea who killed and maimed indiscriminately from beneath the waves without thought or feeling for those they destroyed. Although there was some truth in that picture, but it must be borne in mind that merchant ships were fitted with both high-angle (HA) and low-angle (LA) naval guns, albeit small or antiquated, and therefore posed a very real threat to U-boats on the surface. It was not a very good idea for U-boats to surface and stop merchant ships before sinking them whilst they were sailing in convoy, as required by the London Submarine Agreement of 1936. Moreover, what the Allied propaganda machine did not say was that Allied submarines were doing exactly the same thing to Axis surface shipping.

It must also be said that there were many U-boat skippers who were impeccably correct in their behaviour towards shipwrecked mariners. There are countless examples of submarines surfacing after a successful attack to offer whatever aid they could to survivors in lifeboats – after doing their damnedest to destroy them in the first place of course.

One example of this behaviour involved *Kapitän-Leutnant* Schultz of U-48, who sent radio messages to the British Admiralty requesting that a ship be sent to pick up survivors of a British merchant ship he had torpedoed and sunk. Another involved U-125, which surfaced after sinking the British freighter *Tweed* in the South Atlantic in April 1941, and took on board survivors who had been clinging precariously to a capsized lifeboat, which they then repaired and provisioned. After ensuring that those survivors were in reasonably good condition, the German sailors then gave them a course to steer for the nearest land and freedom.

Karl Doenitz was very much aware of these acts of mercy, but he was always uneasy about it because of the danger posed to U-boats on the surface. This view is supported by documentary and oral evidence from survivors themselves, two of the most significant cases being those of the Egyptian liner *Zamzan* which succumbed to the guns of the German surface raider *Atlantis* in April 1941, and the British troopship *Laconia*, torpedoed and sunk by U-156 in September 1942, which is the subject of this story.

The 19,695-ton SS *Laconia* was built for the Cunard company by Swan Hunter and Wigham Richardson of Wallsend, and launched on 9 April 1921. She was the last of a trio of similar ships built for the Cunard Line especially for the New York service, and on 25 May 1922, having satisfactorily completed her sea trials, she was moved to Southampton. From there, she made her maiden voyage to New York, then back to Liverpool.

Between 1923 and 1928, she made a number of summer voyages from Hamburg to New York, being refitted in 1928 for cabin, tourist and third class passenger service. Between 1930 and 1939 she was frequently used as a cruise liner out of New York and the UK. On the outbreak of the Second World War in September 1939, she was requisitioned by the Royal Navy and converted at Southampton into an armed merchant cruiser. In 1941 she was reclassified as a troopship and served in that capacity until her fateful encounter with U-156 in September 1942.

The *Laconia* Incident, as it later became known, took place at 08.00 hours on

12 September 1942 after she had been torpedoed and sunk by U-156 some 360 miles (660 km) north of Ascension Island. After the sinking, the captain of U-156, *Kapitän-Leutnant* Werner Hartenstein, discovered that, out of the 2,562 passengers the *Laconia* had been transporting, 1,793 were Italian prisoners of war who had been captured in the Western Desert. Along with a mixture of civilian and military personnel, they were being transported from Suez via the Red Sea, the Indian Ocean and the Cape of Good Hope to Britain where they were to be interned for the duration. Whether or not it was the Italian prisoners who influenced Hartenstein's decision will never be known for certain, but after the sinking, he became the first submarine commander to undertake a rescue operation of all the survivors from a ship he had torpedoed.

For the first time ever in the Second World War, a German U-boat sent an open message across the airwaves, asking for immediate help. He radioed his intention to mount a rescue operation to Karl Doenitz in Paris. Doenitz agreed, albeit reluctantly, to send U-506 (*Kapitän-Leutnant* Wurdemann), and U-507 (*Kapitän-Leutnant* Ekkehard Schacht), to assist. As though that were not enough in time of total and unrestricted warfare, Doenitz also requested assistance from the Vichy French at Casablanca. They immediately responded by sending the cruiser *Gloire* and the two sloops *Dumont d'Urville* and *Annamite* from their base at Dakar, approximately 1,400 miles (2,600 km) away to the north of the *Laconia*'s last known position. Those three ships had been laid up for over a year and carried no guns' crews or working anti-aircraft systems; they therefore posed no threat to Allied shipping. The signals, sent out in plain language across the airwaves, could not have failed to be picked up by listening stations ashore, nor by ships at sea. Moreover, the fact that three Vichy French warships were putting to sea unarmed would surely have been known to the Allied naval and air force intelligence authorities.

On the 16th, after wireless messages had been exchanged and all arrangements completed between Germany, Vichy France and the International Red Cross in Geneva, Hartenstein, together with U-506 and U-507 which had been following some way astern, proceeded to take as many of the survivors as possible onto their decks. After issuing fresh water, food and cigarettes to the dazed and exhausted survivors, most of whom had not slept for the four days after the sinking, they took four lifeboats full of distressed survivors in tow with the intention of ferrying them to the rapidly approaching Vichy French warships.

In case they were spotted by enemy aeroplanes or warships, Hartenstein had covered his deck guns with white sheets on which he had painted a massive red cross so that his peaceful and humanitarian intentions could not possibly be mistaken. Having said that, it is illegal under international law for combat ships to display a Red Cross flag, so those flags could have been mistaken for a bluff to lure unsuspecting enemy ships into a lethal trap, as was later claimed by the Americans. That sort of bluff had indeed been used on numerous occasions by German surface raiders who had developed the habit of disguising themselves as hospital ships, ships of neutral nations or ships in distress, and using the international distress call to attract merchant ships to their hidden guns. That notwithstanding, however, it is difficult to imagine how anyone could have considered that he was bluffing, with so many survivors on the decks of those U-boats and in the lifeboats being towed astern.

Karl Doenitz's memoirs reproduce an extract from the log of U-156 which reads:

> ... shortly before the arrival of another two boats [U-506 and U-507] a four-engined aircraft with American markings bearing 70. As proof of my peaceful intentions, [I] displayed large Red Cross flag four yards square on bridge facing line of flight. Aircraft flew over once and then cruised in vicinity for some time. Made Morse signals, 'Who are you?' and 'Are there any ships in sight?' No response. Aircraft flew off in SW direction.

At approximately 11.00 hours on that day, a raft was sighted by a sharp-eyed lookout on board U-156. It held just one female survivor, who appeared to be in some considerable distress and in very poor shape. Without hesitation or regard for their own safety in those shark-infested seas, two German submariners leaped overboard and swam to her rescue. She was found to be several months pregnant.

At 07.00 hours on that same day at Wide-awake Field on Ascension Island, a certain Captain Richardson of the US Air Force cleared a B-24 Liberator bomber for takeoff. Loaded to capacity with bombs and depth-charges its pilot, Lieutenant Harden, headed north-east into a clear, powder-blue sky for the last known position of the *Laconia*.

On board U-156, Hartenstein received the news from Doenitz that the Vichy French warships were scheduled to rendezvous with him the following day. At that time, he had approximately 200 survivors crowding his decks and more than 200 more huddled in the lifeboats being towed astern. Inside the cramped hull of the U-boat there were several more men, women and children, amongst whom were the *Laconia*'s Senior Third Mate, Thomas Buckingham, one of only four bridge officers who had survived the sinking. Four others, including her skipper, Captain Randolph Sharp, went down with the ship.

At 09.30 hours, Harden sighted a U-boat on the surface, its decks covered with a mass of people and towing four lifeboats, also full of people. From his position, and with a far wider horizon than the U-boat he had spotted, Harden also saw U-506 and U-507 travelling on the surface at high speed in the direction of the *Laconia*'s last known position. Harden circled U-156 for some time, both he and his crew observing the vessel and everything that was going on below them. The day was clear and fine, and he could not have failed to realise that such a mass of people on the deck of a U-boat and in the lifeboats being towed astern could only be survivors from a shipwreck, and the *Laconia* was the only vessel to have been sunk in that area during the last four days. Nor could he have failed to see the Red Cross flag draped over the U-boat's guns and bridge. (A statement by one of the survivors read that it was the guns only which had been covered with the flag. He made no mention of any flag draped over the bridge.)

Having circled U-156 for some time, Harden flew off in a south-westerly direction and reported by radio to Wide-awake Field, requesting orders. The American version of events was that Harden reported having challenged the U-boat to display its national flag, but without success, although Hartenstein made no mention of this in his log. Harden did say, however, that the U-boat responded with a Morse signal which he claimed he could not read properly, but which he thought was 'German, sir.' Although he mentioned the lifeboats being towed and the mass of people on the U-boat's decks, he did not say anything about the Red Cross flag which he could not have failed to see.

The Americans at Wide-awake Field were aware that there were no friendly submarines in that part of the South Atlantic at that time. It must also be borne in mind that British shipping in the Freetown area was dependent on the Americans on Ascension Island for protection. Captain Richardson had two options: to order the B-24 back to base or to attack. Another problem for the Americans was that Ascension Island did not monitor sea frequencies and could not communicate with shipping because their people could not read Morse signal lamps, which was rather strange, as most signals to and from ships or aircraft at sea were sent by Aldis lamp. Captain Richardson then conferred with Colonel Ronin, and they came to the conclusion that Harden might jeopardise the safety of the ships they were supposed to be protecting and abandon a legitimate and highly important target if he allowed them to proceed unmolested. They were also aware, however, that if he took action he would undoubtedly place the survivors at severe risk. Richardson ordered Harden, 'Sink sub.'

Harden turned back northwards and found the U-boat as he had left it, travelling on the surface and still towing the four lifeboats. Flying low, at a height of some 250 feet (75 m) he flew in, eager for a kill on his very first sortie. During the thirty minutes which had elapsed since the B-24 had flown off, everyone in the boats and on the decks of the U-boat had been searching the sea and sky, fully expecting to see a rescue ship heading towards them. Their elation quickly turned to horror as they saw the bombs falling from the underbelly of the aircraft.

Another extract from the log of U-156 reads:

> Aircraft of similar type approached. Flew over, slightly ahead of submarine at altitude of 80 metres. Dropped two bombs about three seconds apart. Aircraft of similar type approached ahead while four lifeboats were being cast off, the aircraft dropped one bomb in their midst. One boat capsized. Aircraft cruised around for short time then dropped a fourth bomb 2/3,000 metres away. Realised that his bomb-racks were empty. Another run. Two bombs. One exploded with delayed action directly under the control room. Conning tower vanished in a tower of black water. All hands ordered to don lifejackets. Ordered all British off boat. Batteries began giving off gas. Italians also ordered off. Had no escape gear to give them.

One of the bombs completely destroyed one of the lifeboats, which contained mostly Italians, killing most of them and maiming the rest in varying degrees. Another lifeboat was capsized by the blast. A survivor by the name of Tony Large, an able seaman RNVR, swam across to the capsized boat in order to organise efforts to right it, and discovered the bodies of four British dead who had been trapped inside.

Such was the discipline of Hartenstein that he did not instruct his crew to man his deck gun. Had he done so, and bearing in mind the low-level flight of Harden's

B-24 and his very limited experience of combat, there is little doubt that the gun's crew would have blown him out of the sky. That restraint showed should have been indication enough of his peaceful intentions. Not so the Americans, who appeared to be hell-bent on destroying not just the submarine but also the wretched survivors.

Ominous hissing sounds from below deck, coupled with the pungent smells of burning wiring confirmed Hartenstein's decision that it was then too dangerous to remain on the surface. The tremendous blast of explosions underwater are magnified many times, and the energy exerted by those American bombs had hammered against the hull of U-156 with such force as to cause her to shudder violently and leap about in the water like a mortally wounded beast. Lights went out, water poured from fractured pipes and people were thrown about with tremendous force. On deck, some of the survivors and members of the U-boat's crew had been blown into the sea, where many of them were drowned or taken by circling sharks.

The official report from Harden reads:

> One pass dropping three depth-charges was made, one hit 10 feet [3 m] astern, and two were about 100 or 200 yards [90–180 m] apart. Made two more runs and bombs failed to fall. This was fixed and a final run was made at 400 feet [360 m]. Two bombs were dropped one on either side, not more than 15 feet [4.5 m] away. The sub' rolled over and was last seen bottom-up. Crew had abandoned sub' and taken to surrounding lifeboats.

This last piece was nonsense from an inexperienced pilot.

Highly dangerous oceanic whitetip and blue sharks roam in abundance between the Tropics of Cancer and Capricorn and, as a result of inhumanity and criminal arrogance, the survivors of the *Laconia* once again found themselves swimming for their lives towards whatever lifeboats were left. Some were killed by those ferocious predators whilst others suffered severe bites. Most of the people who were inside the submarine when the attack began failed to reach the boats and were either drowned after being sucked under the sea when the U-boat dived, or succumbed to the ever-present sharks, ending their lives there in the South Atlantic even as imminent rescue was at hand in the form of neutral warships and enemy submarines.

After having completed the restoration of his boat into an effective fighting machine, Hartenstein submerged at 13.45 hours and proceeded on a course of 270 degrees. At 16.00 hours, he recorded in his log:

> All damage repaired as far as possible. Damage sustained: Air search periscope jammed. Fixed-eye periscope refuses to turn. Seven battery cells empty; others doubtful. Diesel cooling flange torn, DF set not working. Sounding gear and hydrophones not working. First-class repair job by technical personnel.

So much for Harden's capsized U-boat.

The lights burned late at U-boat headquarters in Paris that night, where an urgent meeting had been convened to discuss the situation in the South Atlantic. After reading out Hartenstein's signal to the hushed gathering of senior naval officers, Doenitz was put under some considerable pressure to abandon the operation at once.

Not being the kind of man to leave any job half done, however, he was determined to see it through whatever the outcome. He finally brought the meeting to an end by making it quite clear that he had no intention of deviating from his original plan for the rescue of shipwrecked mariners at sea. At midnight, he signalled U-506 and 507:

> You are in no circumstances to risk the safety of your boat. All measures to ensure the safety of your boat, including the abandonment of rescue operations to be ruthlessly taken. Do not rely on enemy showing slightest consideration. Boats will be kept in instant readiness to dive, and must retain at all times full powers of underwater action. You will transfer to the lifeboats any survivors you have on board your boats. Only Italians to be retained aboard your boats. Proceed to meeting point and hand them over to French. Beware enemy counter-measures both from air and by submarines.

(That signal was later used against Doenitz at his trial in Nuremburg, and it has since been used by certain historians to blacken him.

By the morning of the 17th, *Kapitän-Leutnant* Ekkehard Schacht, in U-507, had picked up as many survivors as he could take, and had taken no less than seven lifeboats in tow, in which there were 320 British and Polish survivors. Amongst them was the *Laconia*'s third mate, Thomas Buckingham. Inside the submarine were twenty-five very distressed women and children, and 163 Italians. All of those people crammed together in such a small space, along with the crew of fifty-two, would have made the situation below decks very uncomfortable. Moreover, with so many people in such a confined space, there was no possibility of the vessel launching any attacks on shipping or of being able to properly defend herself.

Schacht had already been informed by U-boat Headquarters of the bombing of U-156 the previous day but, even with that knowledge, he did not deviate from his task of rescuing those survivors. As a precaution, however, and with hindsight wisely, he placed one of his men on the stern of his vessel armed with a fire axe, with orders to cut the towline should an aircraft be sighted.

At 07.20 hours that same morning, Lieutenant Harden and his crew once more took to the skies in their B-24. Reaching the search area at 09.05 hours, he flew a grid pattern in his own search for survivors. At 10.30 hours, he spotted U-506, commanded by *Kapitän-Leutnant* Wurdemann, about 2 miles (3.7 km) away on his port bow. As with U-156, he could not have mistaken the significance of the fact that the U-boat's deck was crammed with people or that four lifeboats being towed astern. With a total disregard for the safety and well-being of those already deeply traumatised people, he increased his speed and roared into the attack. It was fortunate, however, that Wurdemann had also taken the precaution of placing a seaman aft with a fire axe.

Immediately the Liberator was sighted, the seaman at the stern cut through the towline with one blow of his axe, leaving the boats to drift away once more into the wild Atlantic wastes, just as Wurdemann gave the order to crash-dive. The conning tower of U-506 was already awash when the Liberator roared overhead at very low altitude. The bombs failed to release, however, saving U-506 and her pathetic passengers from almost certain destruction. Less than a minute later, Harden made a second pass, dropping two 500-pound (227 kg) bombs and two 350-pound (159 kg) depth-charges. The two 500-pounders fell harmlessly into the sea astern of the submarine, tossing the lifeboats about violently as they exploded, whilst the two depth-charges hit the sea directly above the submerging vessel, causing the U-boat to roll violently from side to side as they detonated, and causing varying degrees of injury to the people in the cramped space below. Her bows dipped sharply, her electric motors and violent concussion of the exploding depth-charges driving her into the depths. She was not damaged, however, and still with the survivors aboard Wurdemann levelled his U-boat and played a waiting game.

For the following forty-five minutes, Harden circled above the spot where the U-boat had disappeared, but Wurdemann had kept his nerve and, using one of the oldest tricks in the book, he sent up an oil-slick, which might induce an attacker to believe he had made a kill. More experienced pilots might have recognised that slick for what it actually was but Harden, inexperienced and eager to report another 'kill', broke off the engagement and returned to Wide-awake Field full of his own importance in sinking two U-boats in two days. He was later decorated for his achievements despite the fact that neither vessel was actually destroyed, and that he was responsible for the deaths of countless shipwrecked people.

The American garrison at Wide-awake Field was uneasy after the *Laconia* Incident. In nine missions by the First Composite Squadron on the 17th, only one significant report of survivors was forthcoming. Lieutenant Atkins reported that he had seen eight people adrift on a raft. When he returned to the area on the following morning, he reported finding four seaworthy but empty lifeboats. Another American pilot, Lieutenant McClellan, signalled that at 3°45'S, 13°15'W, he had seen a small vessel on a zigzag northerly course. That report was followed by another from Lieutenant Phillip Main, of two ships heading due north-west at 27°56'S, 13°35'W. He was instructed to shadow and try to identify those ships. In the meantime, Captain Richardson sent a query to the British authorities in Freetown. They replied two hours later with instructions for the Americans to shadow the vessels but not to interfere with their progress. They added: 'It would appear that they are searching for Italian survivors of the *Laconia*.'

Despite the evidence of the people crowding the decks of the U-boats and in the lifeboats being towed astern of them and the exchange of messages between those U-boats, Doenitz and the International Red Cross, which could not have failed to be monitored, the Americans claimed that this was the first inkling they had, six days after the sinking of the *Laconia*, that any rescue operation was underway. The two ships which were spotted by McClellan were the Vichy French cruiser *Gloire* and the sloop, *Annamite*, which had arrived on the scene the previous day and were then headed back to their base at Dakar with 1,041 people on board, who had been taken off the U-boats U-506 and 507. Another Vichy French sloop, the *Dumont d'Urville*, had picked up a further 42 survivors from the Italian submarine *Cappellini*.

The British claimed that, from the very beginning, they had assumed that Hartenstein was interested in rescuing only the Italian prisoners – an understandable assumption in the circumstances. Before the end of the year, however, the full gravity of the incident was known to all. It was also known that, in spite of Hitler's and Goebbels's commitment to psychological warfare, Germany did not use that incident for propaganda purposes.

On 27 September, the British prime minister, Winston Churchill, sent the following memo to the First Sea Lord:

> The report of 650 survivors being brought in from the *Laconia* and another ship shows that a very serious tragedy has taken place. Is it known what proportion are British personnel? There were nearly 3,000 people to be accounted for, so over 2,000 must have lost their lives.

The other ship referred to was the British freighter *Trevilley*, which was torpedoed and sunk on 14 September, and whose survivors had been taken aboard the French sloop *Dumont d'Urville*.

On 14 November 1942, the Admiralty received a secret message from Freetown which read:

> (1) NOIC [Naval Operational Intelligence Centre] Ascension confirms that only one attack was made by Ascension-based aircraft on 16 September. This was at 09.30 hours in position 5 degrees south and 11 degrees 40 minutes west. This was claimed as a definite sinking, but there is now strong evidence that this U-boat was undamaged. (2) COMMENT: Aircraft mistook British disembarked from U-boat to *Laconia* lifeboats for crew of U-boat abandoning ship.

That was a very different version of events to the one in the American report. The Americans, by their own admission, knew when they attacked Hartenstein's U-boat that the *Laconia* was carrying over 1,000 passengers, but were oblivious of the fact that she was also carrying nearly 2,000 Italian prisoners. Captain Richardson ordered the attack because he believed the German U-boat represented a threat to British shipping, which it was his responsibility to protect while they searched for the *Laconia*'s lifeboats.

It beggars belief that the Americans did not realise that the people crowding the decks of U-156 and the lifeboats that she was towing were not from the *Laconia*. Even if Hartenstein's Red Cross flag was not recognised in international law or was suspected as being a bluff, such high-ranking commanders must have been aware that lifeboats were not, indeed could not, be carried by submarines, no matter which side they were on. As for the American claim that their aircraft mistook the survivors for the U-boat crew abandoning ship, even such an inexperienced pilot as Harden would surely have known that there were enough people there to have manned a dozen U-boats.

The Americans claimed that the British never told them that U-156 was engaged in a rescue operation even though the naval authorities in Freetown knew of the situation because they were monitoring naval frequencies. They have also claimed that the British knew that the Germans had approached the Red Cross in Geneva but were never told of the German free passage statement. Bearing in mind Winston Churchill's penchant for sacrificing lives 'for the greater good', as he would say when explaining away any bungled operation, one needs to ask whether it was a deliberate ploy by the British to remain silent about the rescue operation because they were more concerned about their shipping in the area than about survivors in the water. Or was it a cover-up by the Americans, blaming the British when they knew that they had bombed shipwrecked survivors in order to make a kill? Or was it just a simple breakdown in communications between all concerned? Perhaps, after all these years, the full truth may never be known. One thing is certain, however: out of 692 military personnel and 2,562 passengers, including 1,793 Italian prisoners, only 975 survivors were eventually rescued.

# 6 Where Angels Fear to Tread

Since the days of Nelson, Malta stood as a bastion of British resolve in the Mediterranean, guarding the narrow and vitally important corridor through the central Mediterranean between Sicily and Tunisia. Its strategic importance was never more manifest than during the Second World War, especially the darkest days between January 1941 and April 1943. The vast quantities of arms, ammunition, aviation spirit, fuel oil and foodstuffs of every description which were needed, not just for the island itself but also for the British Army of the Nile in Egypt, made the free and uninterrupted passage of merchant ships through the Mediterranean and the blocking of enemy reinforcements to Tripoli of paramount importance. At the same time, Axis air power was striking deadly blows against Malta and the effective assertion of British sea power in that narrow waterway.

Up until June, 1940, the free passage of merchant shipping to and from Malta was uninterrupted, and merchant convoys passed through the Mediterranean unmolested. On 10 June, however, Benito Mussolini, who had formed his own Fascist Party as early as 1919, became envious of Nazi Germany taking all the spoils of war and, fearful of being left behind in the race for territory, he declared war on Britain and France. Having already taken Abyssinia and Libya, like some latter-day

Caesar he longed to extend his African empire, and cast his covetous eyes towards Egypt, with its fruitful Nile Delta and highly profitable Suez Canal.

The Western Desert became his chosen battleground, and it was in that harsh, unforgiving land of broiling daytime heat and freezing ice-cold nights that the battle for Egypt was fought and eventually won, under the most horrendous circumstances imaginable. But the battle was not just for Egypt, it was for the whole of the Mediterranean and the Middle East. Provided that Malta stood firm.

The morning after Mussolini's declaration of war, at 06.55 hours on 11 June, the sirens on Malta heralded the island's first air raid. A force of ten Italian bombers with a heavy fighter escort approached and branched into two attacking formations. Whilst one group attacked Marsamxett and the Grand Harbour, the other raided Hal Far and the Delimara area. Malta, totally unprepared for such a strike so soon after Italy had declared war, witnessed scenes of utter devastation as buildings collapsed into vast mounds of dust and rubble. As terrified mothers shielded their even more terrified children in cellars or any other makeshift shelter they could find, the anti-aircraft batteries were joined by the heavy guns of HMS *Terror* and HMS *Aphis*, both berthed in Marsamxett Harbour.

So began the long, heartbreaking years of siege, constant air attacks, starvation, death and destruction which Malta and its people were to suffer. With hostile forces on both sides, the European and the African mainlands, it was almost impossible for merchant navy convoys to get through.

By December 1941, the strain had been eased slightly with the recapture of Benghazi on the North African coast. As a consequence, and aided by bad weather and low visibility, one convoy of just three merchant ships did get through, losing just one vessel on the way, the ammunition ship *Thermopylae*. That good fortune, however, did not last. It was not very long before the situation deteriorated once again when General Rommel, who had previously been forced back to El Agheila, mainly because of lack of supplies, attacked once more on 21 January, sweeping the 8th Army eastwards once again. Benghazi was evacuated on 28 January – an ominous event for Malta, its garrison and citizens. The airfield of Cyrenaica, which until then had been providing fighter protection for ships taking supplies to Malta, were filled with German bombers which were then in a position to attack both the island and its best supply route from the west. They were, however, not capable of very much because of a lack of supplies, and were then held on a line running south from Gazala in early February.

Because of the devastating attacks on Axis shipping by British forces operating out of Malta, Hitler ordered the island's destruction.

Malta was exposed to invasion from the Italian ports and that, coupled with constant air attacks against the island, made it impossible to keep it as the main base for the Mediterranean Fleet, which was therefore transferred to Alexandria. Mussolini and several other Axis leaders favoured the early part of 1942 for the invasion of Malta, but Hitler had other ideas. He believed that sustained attacks by the *Luftwaffe* alone would force the island to surrender or, at very least, subdue its offensive operations against Axis convoys ferrying vital and badly needed supplies and reinforcements to General Rommel's Afrika Korps.

The intensified bombing raids by the *Luftwaffe* and Italian *Regia Aeronautica* had caused extensive damage and left many victims. Many areas had been totally wiped out. Valletta itself had lost many of its historic buildings, but the island was certainly not defeated. Between 1 January 1941 and 1 May 1942, for example, British submarines operating out of Malta had dispatched seventy-five Axis merchant ships, amounting to some 400,000 tons.

Axis air superiority, however, had made the risk of free passage for Allied convoys prohibitive, so merchant ships were forced to take the long, treacherous haul around the Cape of Good Hope. The Axis's net was tightening, with powerful enemy forces surrounding Malta from North Africa, Italy and Greece. Evidence of that new danger came very swiftly with the destruction of the next Malta-bound convoy.

On 12 February a small convoy, Operation MF 5, consisting of three merchantmen, the *Clan Chattan*, the *Clan Campbell* and the *Rowallan Castle*, sailed from Alexandria escorted by two cruisers, the anti-aircraft cruiser *Carlisle* and sixteen destroyers under the command of Admiral Vian. On the 13th, the *Clan Campbell* was narrowly missed by a stick of bombs and severely damaged, forcing her to limp as best she could into Tobruk. On the 14th, a direct hit was scored by German bombers on the *Clan Chattan*, causing severe fires throughout the vessel. That same afternoon, the *Rowallan Castle* was also hit and disabled. Both of those ships were subsequently destroyed by units of the Royal Navy, and no supplies reached Malta.

These events immediately precipitated a crisis in Malta, already desperately short of foodstuffs, medical supplies, ammunition and various oils (Admiral Cunningham reported on 7 February that Malta had sufficient petrol to last until 1 August, and that fuel oil and other essentials might last until the end of May). It was the severe shortage of wheat and flour which caused the greatest worry, however. The ability of Malta's defenders and civilian population to continue their resistance depended on their health, so in addition to petrol and fuel oil, bread was at the top of the list of priorities.

It had then become obvious to the Axis powers that if anything more was to be achieved in North Africa, Malta needed to be eliminated as a base for British forces. With the Russian campaign bogged down in the savage grip of winter, more German aircraft had become available for the Mediterranean Theatre. With the arrival of those aircraft, the siege was tightened and the real pounding of Malta began. Over the course of the following few months, all the buildings around the Grand Harbour were pulverised and many people were killed or maimed.

It was decided that another convoy should fight its way through at the earliest possible date. That convoy, MW 10, consisted of the naval auxiliary vessel *Breconshire* and the merchant ships *Clan Campbell*, which by then had undergone repairs and put back to sea, *Pampas* and *Talabot*. They set sail from Alexandria on 20 March. As luck would have it, their sailing coincided with the launch of the all-out bombing offensive against Malta by German forces based in Sicily and Sardinia.

Admiral Vian's escort group was one of the most powerful so far committed, with the three cruisers *Cleopatra*, *Euralus* and *Dido*, the anti-aircraft cruiser *Carlisle* and sixteen destroyers, plus another cruiser and a flotilla leader which had sailed from Malta to rendezvous with them.

In the early hours of 21 March the British submarine P.36 signalled that heavy units of the Italian fleet were leaving Taranto, whilst enemy air reconnaissance very soon reported that the convoy was at sea. Within twelve hours, Admiral Vian was aware that a major battle was then imminent.

The Italian fleet consisted of the battleship *Littorio*, mounting nine 15-inch guns, the cruisers *Gorizia* and *Trento* with 8-inch guns, and the 6-inch-gun cruiser *Giovanni Delle Bande Nere*, together with a ten-destroyer escort. With just one of his cruisers mounting 6-inch guns, Admiral Vian was seriously outgunned. Despite such tremendous odds, however, he had no doubts whatsoever about engaging the Italians. Whilst the convoy scattered and steamed on for Malta, the cruisers departed to engage the enemy fleet.

The ensuing battle, soon to become known as the Second Battle of Sirte, was one of the finest examples of cruiser protective action ever undertaken by the Royal Navy. The cruisers took full advantage of smokescreens, dodging in and out and manoeuvring their ships as though they were destroyers, and they were eventually able to turn a vastly superior enemy force away from the convoy. Fourteen British destroyers were damaged, but the Italian fleet finally retired without destroying the merchantmen. The British fleet returned to Alexandria.

Whilst all that was going on, the merchantmen, which had been delayed by the battle, were forced to continue their voyage with a final dash for Malta, dispersed and in daylight, and with minimal escorts. With just 20 miles (37 km) to go, the *Clan Campbell* was sighted by German bombers, which attacked immediately, sinking her with several direct hits. The *Breconshire*, with a vitally needed cargo of oil, got to within 8 miles (15 km) of the island before she was also hit and severely disabled. The high winds and heavy seas which had developed made it impossible for the cruiser *Penelope* to tow her into the Grand Harbour, so she was beached at Marsaxlokk. She was destroyed there two days later by German bombers. With the population of Malta lining the ancient battlements to cheer them in, the *Pampas* and the *Talabot* sailed into Valletta. They were both sunk at their moorings, by German bombers, however, with just 16,000 tons of the combined 26,000 tons of precious cargo unloaded. Despite winning a great naval battle, little had been achieved. Apart from the totally inadequate supplies which had been taken in by submarines and the supply vessels *Welshman* and *Manxman*, and the tiny amount salvaged from the March convoy, Malta had received no supplies since January.

The island, it seemed, was doomed. The German onslaught from the air was at its height, and it appeared that it was no longer a viable proposition as a base for attacking Axis supply lines to North Africa. By mid-June, starvation and surrender were only a matter of days away. The only wonder is that the Maltese people had not surrendered weeks previously, for the island was fast being reduced to a vast rubble heap by German and Italian bombers. By the end of May 1942, it had suffered 2,400 air raids. Those who remember the darkest days of the Blitz on London and other British towns and cities in the 1940s, and the interminable succession of days when the air-raid sirens wailed eerily in the misty twilight of morning or evening, will surely understand just what that meant. However, the longest number of consecutive days on which London was bombed amounted to fifty-seven, whilst Malta had endured no less than 155 days of continual day and night bombing.

In April, Malta's defences were reinforced by forty-seven Spitfires flown in from the British carrier *Eagle* and the American carrier *Wasp*, which promised some small relief; but so powerful was the Axis reaction that, within the space of three days, almost all of them had been destroyed on the ground. As well as food and fuel, ammunition for the anti-aircraft guns had to be strictly rationed, so the island's air defences were minimal. So intense was the bombing and the laying of mines offshore by both aircraft and E-boats that not even submarines could operate in and around Malta, and by the end of April these too had been withdrawn to Alexandria.

On 27 April, the Defence Committee met in London, and Churchill made it abundantly clear that he was prepared to run extreme military risks in order to save Malta from falling to the enemy. The Admiralty supported him, but the Army was unwilling to indulge in what General Auchinleck described as 'paying forfeits' in India and the desert just to succour Malta. Churchill had to order General Auchinleck to mount an offensive in the Western Desert to divert attention from Malta, and it was agreed that convoys should be fought through to Malta at the earliest possible date, and that a great deal of risk to the naval escorts should be accepted.

Rommel, meanwhile, had built up sufficient forces and supplies to make another attack, and by June the 8th Army was in full retreat.

So encouraging did the prospect in North Africa seem to the Axis forces that Hitler postponed the projected invasion of Malta. With Rommel's supplies coming in through Tobruk, the island was not as great a menace to his communications as it had been. But although the island was to be spared invasion, many more supplies were needed very quickly if the island population was not to starve. With Rommel's forces already at El Alamein, relief from the east via the Cape of Good Hope had become manifestly impossible, and the warships remaining in those waters were obliged to operate from the Levant ports and the Suez Canal. Everything therefore had to be staked on a convoy from the west.

There was one serious difficulty. The minimum speed at which a Mediterranean convoy could proceed without posing serious threat to the merchantmen was 16 knots (30 kph). There were many ships in the merchant fleet that were more than capable of this, but there was not one tanker which could work up more than 12 knots (22 kph). It was essential that a tanker be included in such a convoy as Malta was most in need of petrol and domestic fuel oil, and although high-octane aviation spirit could be carried in a general cargo vessel, only a large tanker would be capable of carrying the vast amounts of kerosene and domestic fuel oil needed to keep essential services running.

The tanker fleet of the Texas Oil Company of America were amongst the finest and fastest in the world at that time, but it seemed unlikely that the USA would be prepared to supply one after the losses sustained in the Caribbean, particularly for the highly dangerous waters of the Mediterranean. In the event, however, despite murmurs of disapproval in certain high places, American generosity prevailed, and America made available the brand new 14,000-ton *Kentucky* and, if another was needed, Texaco's other new vessel, the 14,000-ton *Ohio*.

The first convoy, which was conceived on a massive scale compared with previous Malta convoys, was to be run in two parts. The first, Operation Harpoon, was to depart from Gibraltar, and consisted of five large merchant freighters, the *Troilus*, the *Burdwan*, the *Chant*, the *Orari*, the *Tanimbar*, and the American tanker *Kentucky*, which carried between them approximately 44,000 tons of cargo. That convoy was to be escorted by Captain C.C. Hardy in the anti-aircraft cruiser *Cairo*, together with nine destroyers under the command of Commander B.G. Scurfield, and four minesweepers. Also included in the escort group were the ageing aircraft carriers *Eagle* and *Argus* with Admiral Curteis flying his flag in the battleship *Malaya*, and two cruisers and eight destroyers.

The second part of that convoy, code-named Operation Vigorous, sailed from Alexandria, and was made up of no less than eleven merchantmen – the *City of Calcutta*, the *Ajax*, the *Potaro*, the *Elizabeth Vakke*, the *Aagtekirk*, the *City of Edinburgh*, the *Bhutan*, the *City of Pretoria*, the *Rembrandt*, the *City of Lincoln* and the *Bulkoil* – carrying a combined cargo of some 70,000 tons. That fleet was to be escorted by Rear-Admiral Vian with seven cruisers, twenty-eight destroyers and a number of smaller craft (motor torpedo-boats, motor gun-boats, etc.), and several minesweepers. No capital ships or aircraft carriers had been included in that convoy, but the aged, remote-controlled target ship *Centurion* had been dressed up to resemble a battleship.

On the evening of 14 June, the Gibraltar convoy raised the Skerki Bank, suffering along the way the loss of just one merchant ship and the cruiser *Liverpool*, disabled by a torpedo dropped from a torpedo-bomber which struck in her engine-room. Those casualties were light considering the intense airborne attack which they had endured along the way.

Being unwilling, or indeed unable, to risk his Gibraltar-based capital ships in the narrows between Sicily and Tunisia, Admiral Curteis's supporting force consisting of the two battleships *Nelson* and *Rodney* withdrew that same evening, which left only Captain Hardy's anti-aircraft cruiser *Cairo*, the destroyer screen and the minesweepers as escorts.

The island of Pantelleria was raised at first light on the following morning when air reconnaissance reported to Hardy that a flotilla of two Italian cruisers with their escorting destroyers was no more than 15 miles (28 km) away to the north. Within minutes, the enemy was sighted as their shells began to rain down upon the lightly escorted merchantmen. Without a moment's hesitation, Commander Scurfield in the destroyer *Bedouin* led the destroyer screen in a furious attack, despite the superior odds which they were up against. In the meantime, HMS *Cairo* and the smaller escorts made smoke in order to cover the convoy.

Outgunned and outranged by the Italian cruisers, the British destroyers were forced to steam at high speed for several minutes before the enemy came within range of their 4.7-inch and 4-inch guns. Almost as soon as battle was joined, HMS *Bedouin* and HMS *Partridge* were disabled, and the Italian destroyer *Vivaldi* was also seriously damaged and out of the fight. When the escorts had laid sufficient smoke to screen the merchantmen from the enemy's view, HMS *Cairo* and four hunt class destroyers took a hand and the Italian admiral Da Zara, unsure of the size of the opposition, thought it prudent to withdraw. So devastatingly effective was the fury of the British attack that Da Zara believed 'with absolute certainty', to use his own words, that he was engaged with another Kenya class cruiser besides the *Cairo*.

The convoy, meanwhile, under the protection of the minesweepers, had suffered a heavy bombing attack in which the steamer *Chant* suffered a direct hit from three bombs, sinking within a few minutes of being hit, with only a dense column of black, oily smoke as her grave-marker. Later, the American tanker *Kentucky* suffered a near miss in which her main steam pipe was fractured. Taken in tow by the minesweeper *Hebe* she made only 6 knots (11 kph) and quickly fell astern of the convoy. Captain Hardy took the decision that the valuable ship and her cargo should not fall into enemy hands, and ordered that she was to be sunk. Once again, Malta was left without her life's blood, and a valuable ship had gone to the bottom despite the fact that repairs would have taken no more than about three hours. After another hour of the most ferocious air attacks, the steamer *Burdwan* came to a stop after a near miss by several bombs. She too was then scuttled.

The damaged *Bedouin* was later sunk by the Italian cruisers who were then circling the depleted convoy, reducing the original number of ships from six to two. At 14.30 hours, two Beauforts and four Albacores from Malta attacked the Italians, and although they did no damage, it somehow convinced Da Zara to withdraw at a rate of knots for less dangerous waters. The remaining merchantmen finally reached Malta safely with their precious cargoes intact.

It was well after nightfall before the vastly depleted convoy began to enter the partially swept channel of the Axis minefields. A minesweeper and three destroyers were damaged after hitting mines, and out of the six merchantmen which originally left Gibraltar, just two vessels, the *Troilus* and the *Orari*, eventually made port.

In the meantime, Operation Vigorous out of Alexandria had sailed only as far as 'Bomb Alley', the narrow waterway between Crete and Cyrenaica, when one of the merchant ships was damaged whilst another proved too slow to keep station with the rest of the convoy. On the 14th, another merchantmen which also proved too slow was forced to put into Tobruk. As late afternoon gave way to the twilight of early evening, a combined air, submarine and E-boat attack accounted for another merchantman sunk and one badly damaged, thus reducing the number of ships in the convoy from eleven to seven. Also in that evening action, the destroyer *Hasty* and the cruiser *Newcastle* were damaged by torpedoes. Whilst the *Newcastle* eventually reached safe harbour, the destroyer was too badly damaged to make way and was eventually sunk by other warships of the convoy.

Mere moments before the Mediterranean sun dipped below the western horizon, an RAF Maryland spotted two Italian battleships and four cruisers leaving Taranto and steering a course south to intercept the remaining ships. At 02.00 hours on the 15th, Admiral Vian received orders from Admiral Harwood, C-in-C Mediterranean, to steam back to Alexandria with the remaining ships of the convoy and the escort screen.

As dawn broke on the morning of the 15th, however, intelligence reports suggested that the Italian fleet, consisting of two of their most recent battleships, *Vittorio Veneto* and *Littorio*, escorted by two heavy cruisers, two light cruisers and twelve destroyers, was still approximately 200 miles (370 km) away to the north-west of the convoy's position. In the light of that information, Admiral Harwood then issued orders to resume course for Malta. However, when it became clear that the enemy fleet were still on a reciprocal course to intercept the convoy, ranging closer to them with every turn of their screws, that latest order was then rescinded and new orders issued to retire to Alexandria once again.

Whilst all of this was going on, Beaufort torpedo-bombers from Malta attacked the Italian fleet, disabling the cruiser *Trento*. Further attacks by other RAF planes and American Liberator bombers disabled both Italian battleships and Harwood changed his orders yet again: the convoy should resume its course for Malta. However, air reconnaissance reports soon indicated that the Malta aircraft had lost contact with the enemy, so he had to decide once again whether the convoy should proceed or return to Alexandria.

At that particular point, the Italian fleet was in retreat, but the enemy air attacks had been murderous, seriously damaging the cruiser *Birmingham* and the destroyer *Airedale*. Whilst the *Birmingham* was able to limp into safe harbour, the *Airedale* was far too seriously damaged to be salvaged and had to be sunk with gunfire. The Australian destroyer *Nestor* was also badly damaged and was later scuttled, and another merchantman was forced to turn back towards Alexandria. Admiral Vian reported that more than half his fleet's ammunition had been expended, and that what was left was fast disappearing. That report prompted the C-in-C to order all ships back to Alexandria. While returning, the cruiser *Hermione* was torpedoed and sunk, together with five destroyers and six merchantmen sunk and various others suffered varying degrees of damage.

The combined cargo of the two ships that did manage to escape the attacks and arrive in Malta consisted of little more than 15,000 tons, less than a month's rations for the beleaguered island. The food situation remained at a critical level, but with the loss of the *Kentucky*, the shortage of oil had become desperate. On 18 June, the C-in-C Mediterranean Fleet cabled Winston Churchill expressing his doubts as to the success of running another convoy to Malta after the failure of Harpoon-Vigorous. Churchill did not even consider giving up.

On 21 June, the second tanker which had been promised by the Americans, the *Ohio*, rolled in matronly fashion into the Firth of Clyde, loaded to her marks with petrol from the Texas oil refineries. In spite of the U-boat packs scouring the Atlantic sea lanes and the German long-range bombers, her voyage across the North Atlantic had been uneventful.

Immediately she discharged her cargo of 103,500 barrels of petrol at Bowling, she steamed out into the tidalway and came to anchor to await further orders. Although her ultimate destiny had been settled and agreed upon by both the British and American governments, no word of her destination could be allowed to leak out, much to the bemusement of her American crew and her owners, Texaco. Her skipper, Sverre Petersen, a one-time master mariner in sail from Oslo, Norway, was merely told that further orders would arrive soon. Two weeks later, after a great deal of confusion about the formalities, he received orders that his vessel was to be handed over to the British authorities. On 10 July, without any kind of formal ceremony and nothing in the way of goodwill, the American flag was run down from her jack. Thereafter the *Ohio* was to sail upon her short but magnificent voyage to fame and glory under the 'Red Duster'.

The British Eagle Oil and Shipping Company assumed nominal ownership of the big tanker on behalf of the Ministry of War Transport after being advised that she had been requisitioned for a special, top-secret convoy, and that the success or failure of her mission would depend largely on the quality and fortitude of her crew. After a countrywide search of the shipping offices for the best possible men available, a British crew was assembled and signed on. At the age of thirty-nine, Captain Dudley Mason, as well as being the youngest captain in Eagle Oil's fleet and a man of vast tanker experience, was also a man of integrity, vision and first-class leadership qualities.

Over the course of the next two days the other officers and crew began arriving and Mason, having sailed with most of them on previous occasions, was pleasantly pleased to see that they were all young, hand-picked men. Chief Engineer James Wyld was the first to arrive, greeting Captain Mason as an old friend whom he knew and trusted above all others. Immediately after him came the Chief Mate, Mr Gray, a tall, quiet young man of twenty-six from Leith, who had been a seaman for twelve of those twenty-six years. Second Mate McKilligan was a rather short, slightly overweight Scot from the western Highlands, aged twenty-eight, and Stephens, a happy-go-lucky 21-year-old went aboard as Third Mate. The engineers consisted of the Chief Engineer Wyld, Second Engineer Buddle from Cornwall and Third Engineer Grinstead, a burly South African and perhaps the oldest man aboard. In addition there were seventy-seven ratings, an unprecedented number for a tanker, including no fewer than twenty-four naval and military gunners. Amongst them was my late friend and companion, a chief bosun's mate and anti-aircraft gunner, Charlie Walker from Shrewsbury.

The ship was moved to the King George V Dock to be tied up under the shadow of the massive crane there. No sooner had she settled into her new berth than dockyard fitters, engineers and ordnance fitters began swarming all over her upper decks, supplementing her already impressive armaments in readiness for her forthcoming, highly dangerous voyage. She already carried a massive 5-inch gun aft and a 3-inch HA gun on her bows, both of which had been fitted in America. She was now fitted out with a 40-mm Bofors gun and six Oerlikons which were placed at strategic points on bridge wings, monkey island and boat decks. Without any doubt, it was the most powerful anti-aircraft weaponry her British crew had ever seen aboard a merchant vessel and, being veterans of the war at sea by then, they had a pretty good idea of what lay ahead. Captain Mason was later joined by a naval liaison officer, Lieutenant D. Barton.

The *Ohio* was also fitted with special engine bearings designed to reduce the shock of close explosions. With the fate of the *Kentucky* in mind, the steam pipes throughout the vessel were similarly strengthened and protected. Eventually, on 28 July, she was moved down the Clyde to Dunglass and loaded with 11,000 tons of fuel oil.

She then joined the rest of the convoy, which was already assembled and awaiting final briefing. Every ship had received similar reinforcements, armaments and complements, with naval liaison officers to assist with the complicated manoeuvring which was later to become necessary when negotiating the Mediterranean narrows and naval signallers and decoding operators. All was now ready for the last-ditch convoy to beleaguered Malta. The ships carried cargoes totalling some 85,000 tons, comprising flour, ammunition, shells, coal, bombs, medical supplies, military equipment, wines, spirits, cigarettes, chocolate, biscuits and highly volatile stocks of petrol, kerosene and aviation spirit, just in case the *Ohio* failed to get through – a very real danger considering the vast Axis forces that were operating in the Mediterranean Theatre.

Apart from the *Ohio*, thirteen large freighters had been assembled for Operation Pedestal at Gourock on Sunday, 2 August 1942. They were:

*Wairangi*, Captain H.R. Gordon, 12,400 tons, Shaw Saville & Albion
*Empire Hope*, Captain G. Williams, 12,688 tons, Shaw Saville & Albion
*Glenorchy*, Captain G. Leslie, 8,982 tons, Glen Line Limited
*Santa Elisa*, Captain T. Thomson, 8,379 tons, Grace Line
*Waimarama*, Captain R.S. Pearce, 12,843 tons, Shaw Saville & Albion
*Brisbane Star*, Captain F.W. Riley, 12,791 tons, Blue Star Line
*Melbourne Star*, Captain D.R. MacFarlane, 12,806 tons, Blue Star Line
*Dorset*, Captain J.C. Tucket, 10,624 tons, Federal Steam Navigation
*Deucalion*, Captain R. Brown, 7,516 tons, Blue Funnel Line
*Almeria Lykes*, Captain W. Henderson, 7,773 tons, Lykes Brothers Steamship Co.
*Rochester Castle*, Captain R. Wren, 7,796 tons, Union Castle Line
*Clan Ferguson*, Captain A.R. Cossar, 7,347 tons
*Port Chalmers*, Convoy Commodore A.G. Venables, (RN retired)

Nine of these vessels were to be sunk and the rest, including the *Ohio*, damaged.

In spite of it being late summer, dusk descended early in the evening of 2 August. The order to heave away came at 18.00 hours, aboard the assembled freighters, crews were becoming active as hooks were hove with a noise like a thousand iron gates being opened on rusty hinges, and engine valves were set to slow ahead. Silently and without fuss, like ghostly apparitions in the misty twilight, the fourteen big ships edged out of the Firth of Clyde. The Isle of Arran slid past on their starboard flank as a low hump of indistinct land. The ships were all blacked out as they slipped almost unseen into the darkening channel with their destroyer guardians, HMS *Bicester*, HMS *Ledbury* and HMS *Wilton*, frisking around them, nudging them into line like sheep-dogs herding a flock of recalcitrant sheep. Very few people witnessed their departure, and those who were could have no possible conception that on that handful of men and ships rested the fate of Malta, and possibly even the whole of the Middle East. The crews had been told that if they managed to get just one ship through and lost half the escorts the convoy would have been considered successful, and that the rewards of that convoy would be far greater than the sacrifice many of them would make. Little did they know then just how great that sacrifice was going to be.

Operation Pedestal, the greatest Mediterranean convoy of them all, was under way at a speed of 15 knots (28 kph).

The Axis forces in the Mediterranean were at the peak of their considerable strength, and were devoting their heaviest attacks to Malta-bound convoys as well as the island itself, although the attacks had eased somewhat after the fall of Tobruk.

News of Operation Pedestal had preceded the convoy, and even as they left the Clyde, German and Italian air and sea forces were being reinforced to meet them. The Royal Navy, however, had committed its greatest strength to the safety of the convoy, and were as determined to force it through to Malta as the enemy were to destroy it. Ships had been detached from units as far apart as Scapa Flow and Freetown, as well as units of the Mediterranean fleet and Force H from Gibraltar including the battleships, HMS *Nelson* and HMS *Rodney*. The convoy was forced to cross four lines of Axis defence, consisting of submarines, minefields, E-boats, and aircraft before encountering the Italian naval strike force of two cruiser squadrons comprising three 8-inch- and three 6-inch-gun vessels, together with their destroyer escorts.

The aircraft carrier HMS *Eagle*, commanded by Captain L.D. Mackintosh, DSC, was to be the first casualty. She had been stationed well over on the starboard quarter of the convoy, with HMS *Charybdis* keeping close station on her, and both steaming at 13 knots (24 kph), when four violent explosions occurred on her port side and she immediately developed a severe list to port. Black, oily smoke interlaced with orange and red flames curled away hundreds of feet into the still air, and superheated, high-pressure steam from her mangled 8-inch pipes could be seen pouring from her ruptured hull and decks, its noise deafening to the men on nearby ships. The tremendous force of those four explosions, and the secondary explosions within the huge hull, sent massive shock waves radiating out across the sea, causing the very air to shake under the force of the blast. The *Eagle* sank within six minutes of being hit approximately 75 miles (140 km) south of Cap de Ses Salines, the southernmost tip of the island of Majorca.

That skilfully executed attack had been carried out by the German submarine U-73, a 750-ton type VIIR U-boat operating out of Spezia and commanded by *Kapitän-Leutnant* Helmut Rosenbaum. Rosenbaum had detected the approach of the convoy through his hydrophones and had come up to periscope depth to make his stealthy approach. Fifteen minutes later, he had sighted the masts of a destroyer and, almost at the same instant, he had seen the aircraft carrier about 4 miles (7.5 km) away. He had crept cautiously nearer, determined to hit the carrier at any cost, achieving a magnificent coup for himself and his colleagues and a demoralising effect on the convoy. He did so with a full salvo of four torpedoes at a range of just 500 yards (450 m). Although the escorts went into immediate action, U-73 escaped unscathed.

Although the *Eagle* sank very quickly, sixty-seven officers and 862 ratings, including her captain, out of a total of 1,160 were rescued. Rosenbaum was later awarded the Knight's Cross for that brilliant action. It was, however, merely a dress rehearsal for the main event.

The loss of the *Eagle* was avenged to a certain extent on the night of the 11th/12th when HMS *Wolverine* obtained a radar contact at a range of 5,000 yards (4,500 m) on a bearing of 265 degrees. Depth-charges and guns were hurriedly prepared as she altered course and, working up to full revolutions, she made a tight turn to port, her wake boiling astern of her as she made, arrow-straight, for the unidentified object. At a range of 800 yards (730 m), the contact was identified as a submarine on the surface and, without a moment's hesitation, Lieutenant-Commander Gretton,

OBE, DSC, prepared his ship for ramming. Crash stations were sounded as *Wolverine*'s knife-edged bows squared up on her target as a speed of 26 knots (48 kph) and like a hot knife cutting through butter, she sliced through the submarine's pressure-hull squarely amidships, cutting it in half. The doomed vessel then simply rolled over and sank immediately. The submarine in question was the Italian *Dagabur* (*Tenente di Vascello* Renato Pecori commanding), a 700-ton boat operating out of Cagliari.

During the afternoon of 12 August, the merchant steamer SS *Deucalion*, under the command of Captain Ramsey Brown, brought down a Ju 88 during a heavy air attack with a few well-placed shells from the 4.7-inch gun mounted on her stern. In addition to carrying the usual cargo of war supplies, drums of fuel oil, petrol and kerosene, she was also carrying a large number of service personnel as passengers.

On the following day, at approximately 01.20 hours, the ship was straddled by three bombs. A fourth then scored a direct hit and penetrated her Number 3 hold and came out on her port side above the waterline before exploding. Seriously damaged, she slowed down rapidly. First her Number 2 hold began flooding then, as the after bulkhead of her Number 1 hold collapsed under the pressure of the inrushing sea, that hold also began flooding. In spite of the serious damage, however, Captain Brown was confident of getting his ship safely into Valletta, and after a twenty-minute delay, the engine-room reported that they could restart the engines. Having done so, her engineers were able to work the ship up to 8 knots (15 kph). Finding it impossible to keep up with the convoy, or even to catch up, Captain Brown ordered that they should attempt the inshore route through the Tunisian Narrows, escorted by the destroyer HMS *Bramham*. Listing very badly, the crippled freighter followed *Bramham* south, but later that afternoon the ever-vigilant *Luftwaffe* found them.

The southern part of the deep-water route through the Sicilian Channel is narrow, and winds tortuously between the sandbars of the Skerki Bank to form a funnel through which the deeply laden ships were forced to pass. The shoals and coastal hazards of the Tunisian coast formed a natural point of ambush for the E-boats, as the shallow water and constantly shifting sandbanks providing almost ideal conditions for the light enemy forces which had been deployed. The shallow draught of the E-boats allowed them a freedom of movement which the lumbering merchantmen lacked.

During the morning of the 12th, five Italian submarines had taken up position at the northern approaches to the channel. As night fell, they were reinforced by a second line consisting of motor torpedo boats of the 2nd, 15th, 18th and 20th Flotillas, nineteen boats in all, which the German Naval command planned to reinforce with boats of the 6th Flotilla out of Crete, six of which were even then speeding to the battle zone. Being almost undetectable against the black coastline, those very fast, very powerful little vessels posed a very great danger to the convoy.

The gently undulating sea was calm and serene, with hardly a ripple to mar the mirror-like surface as the reddening brilliance of the westering sun reflected like blood off the glassy-calm surface. The speed of the convoy was still 15 knots. At precisely 19.40 hours at 37°38'N, 10°25'E, the Italian submarine *Dessi*, launched four bow torpedoes at a range of 2,000 yards (1,820 m) at two steamers of

10,000 and 15,000 tons respectively, missing by more than 50 yards (45 m). The submarine *Axium* then attacked at 20.00 hours, causing chaos in the convoy lines. Rear Admiral Burrough's flagship, *Nigeria*, the anti-aircraft cruiser *Cairo* and the vital solitary tanker, *Ohio*, were all hit by that one salvo of four torpedoes, and all three broached to as they slewed out of line and came to a halt, throwing the convoy lines into complete confusion. The systematic extermination of Operation Pedestal had begun.

My friend Charlie Walker described the first strike on the *Ohio* thus:

I was stationed on one of the Oerlikons which had been mounted on the monkey island. We had been told to be on the lookout for enemy aircraft and E-boats, and that was what we were doing when that torpedo hit us. It was a beautiful evening as I recall, the sun was low down on the horizon, and the whole sky seemed to be coming alive with stars. The reflected glow resembled corrugated sheets of gold on the water. It was so peaceful and calm I could almost have forgotten that there was a full-scale war raging. I had my binoculars glued to my eyes at the time, searching the darkening sky to the north-east when someone shouted, 'Look out lads, torpedo coming.' The next thing I knew was that there was a tremendous explosion right under my feet and column of black smoke and flames shooting into the air on the port side. I was flung off the gun platform like a rag doll and sent flying through the air to land in a heap on the other side of the monkey-island deck against the bulwark. All the lads on the guns had been thrown about a bit, and we were all a bit stunned for a few seconds; but when we realised what had happened, we all just seemed to tense ourselves up for the exploding fuel and the ship disintegrating under us. As it turned out, she had been hit amidships just aft of the bridge and level with the pump room. As well as this whacking great hole in her side, the afterdeck had been ripped open on the port side and laid back to the centre line like a half-opened sardine can, the catwalk looked as though a gigantic hand had screwed it up like a wad of paper, and a column of flame shot up as high as the cross tree as the cargo ignited.

The stench of burning fuel oil and cordite was abominable. Columns of thick black smoke and blood-red flames curled high into the air, then, as the droplets began falling again, they showered the ship from stem to stern. The pump room was a complete shambles, and that too had been laid open to the sea. The main steering gear telemotor pipes had been mangled beyond recognition, and the lids of the kerosene tanks had been blown off and buckled into the most peculiar shapes imaginable. The fire then began spreading very rapidly, and the noise of it was enough to make our ears pop. It was just like a fast express train speeding through a tunnel. All of a sudden, all these men appeared on deck as if from nowhere, all carrying high-pressure foam extinguishers to fight the fires. The engines were stopped and all the engineers and greasers brought up from below as a precaution, but they were all okay.

Apart from the *Eagle*, I had never even seen a torpedoed ship before, let alone been aboard one, and as far as I was concerned, there was no way that ship was going to survive. She had been ripped almost in half. The force of that one torpedo had punched a hole in her side that must have measured about 25 feet by 30 feet [7.5 × 9 m] amidships, the main deck aft on the port side was a complete shambles with deck plates torn out and pointing in all directions, and when I looked over the side, that hole looked more like the entrance to the Mersey Tunnel, with the sea pouring in so fast – well, I thought we'd had it for sure. Ironically enough though, that incoming sea proved more effective in putting out the fires than the foam extinguishers that the crew were carrying, so that by just after eight o'clock, the fires had been brought under control.

Two gunners on the aft boat deck, Will Hands and Ernie Smith, a steward by the name of Ray Morton who had been manning a machine-gun on the boat deck and a young galley-boy, he could not have been more than fifteen or sixteen, were all lost when one of the lifeboats that had been lowered capsized. No one knew they had gone missing until the following day. The skipper hadn't given any orders to abandon ship, so they must have just taken it upon themselves to lower away.

I noticed the *Brisbane Star* had to reverse engines when we were hit so as to avoid a collision, and only just managed to avoid us. *Ohio*'s crew managed to shore up her keel later, but she could only manoeuvre sluggishly in circles for a while because her steering gear had been knocked out. Eventually, though, a hand-rigged steering position was set up aft and at half past eight she began moving ahead at about 7 knots [13 kph]. All the compasses and gyros had been badly damaged and were unserviceable, and we were all relieved to see the destroyer *Ashanti* closing the ship from astern. As she came alongside, Rear Admiral Burrough asked the old man if we required a tow. He said he did not, but asked for a guide ship to lead us through the Narrows. The destroyer *Ledbury* then rigged up a blue signal lamp on her stern post, and by following that dim light, we began to catch up to the convoy.

Within the narrow channel, yet another gauntlet had to be run: the mines which had been sown there. The minesweeping destroyers therefore forged ahead to lead the convoy through the Narrows, past the Cape Kelibia Light area.

At 20.30 hours, the final air attack of the day, which was carried out by more than a hundred German bombers out of Sicily and a squadron of Italian torpedo-bombers from a different direction scored several hits. The convoy's anti-aircraft barrage was in full voice, but *Ohio*'s crew were still frantically fighting her fires when the first of the bombers put in an appearance. She was narrowly missed on several occasions, but not seriously damaged.

In that attack, the destroyer, HMS *Foresight* was hit by one torpedo in her stern section and had to be disposed of by HMS *Tartar*. Almost immediately, the fleet carrier HMS *Indomitable*, was attacked by no less than forty Stuka dive-bombers. She was hit many times, disappearing under massive columns of smoke, flames and water as the bombs exploded on and around her. Even amidst all that devastation and confusion, her guns were still firing defiantly when she was hit by three bombs on her flight deck. Aviation spirit from her aeroplanes' ruptured fuel tanks ignited with a terrifying 'whoosh' and she turned downwind in an effort to fight the blaze, escorted by the cruiser *Charybdis* and several destroyers. It was the beginning of a hideous, heart-rending night of death and destruction in which nine German planes were destroyed. Admiral Syfret, the commander of Force H out of Gibraltar, had to turn back with the heavy escort of HMS *Nelson* and HMS *Rodney*.

The *Empire Hope* seemed to have been marked out for special attention as, during the following thirty minutes, no less than eighteen near misses were recorded around the vessel. Her skipper, Captain Gwilym Williams, who had commanded that vessel since her completion, steered her brilliantly through those attacks until she was finally hit amidships by just one bomb which disabled her engines and blew a 15-foot (4.5 m) hole in her side. Badly damaged, she broached to and stopped.

Drifting helplessly in the long, low swells, and dead in the water, she attracted still more bombers as the German pilots moved in for the *coup de grâce*. The attacks followed in such quick succession that they all seemed to be one. Many of her crew and gunners were killed or maimed by the bombs which were exploding on and around her. Some of them were blown overboard from decks and gun platforms under the tremendous force of the continuing blasts, whilst others were simply blown apart at their posts. Shrapnel from the bomb bursts reaped a terrible harvest in the smoke and murk of the half-light battle as frail human bodies were mown down like so much wheat at harvest time.

The *Empire Hope*'s luck finally ran out at 20.50 hours when the aft part of the vessel was struck by two direct hits. The Number 4 hold, which had been packed with high explosives, was pierced by one of the bombs, and the explosion and conflagration which inevitably followed spread rapidly to the boat deck where it ignited 45-gallon (205 l) drums of high-octane spirit which had been stowed there as deck cargo. Within the space of a few minutes, the whole after part of the ship had become a raging inferno, devouring everything in its path as ½-inch (1.3 cm) steel plates of decks and bulkheads began buckling and glowing evilly in the furnace-like heat. Companion ladders became twisted and misshapen as liquid fuel mixed with heavy paint, creating a fearful portrait of fire, death and destruction that not even the most hideous of horror stories could ever match.

Realising that his vessel was doomed, Captain Williams issued orders to abandon ship. A large number of the boats had been consumed by the flames and bombs, leaving very few for the surviving crew and passengers. The 45-gallon (205 l) drums containing aviation spirit which the ship had been carrying as deck cargo were split apart and high-octane spirit began to cascade over the side like a furiously burning lava flow, spreading rapidly across the surface of the surrounding sea in a terrifying curtain of flames. All around, dead fish of all sizes and descriptions floated and burned as men sought out any small space of sea which the fires had not yet reached. All those who had not been killed or seriously wounded in the attacks and resulting fires managed to get safely away, including Captain Williams.

Shortly after the *Empire Hope* went down, the *Brisbane Star*, commanded by Captain Frederick Neville Riley, was caught by an He 111 torpedo-bomber. A single torpedo ripped into her stem and, exploding on impact, tore a huge rent in her bows and blew in her forward bulkheads. Immediately, she began taking in huge amounts of water and, broaching to, she slid to a stop. Under the inspiring leadership of her skipper, however, her crew went to work and, within twenty minutes they had shored up her bulkheads and effected other vital repairs. The engine-room reported that they would be able to steam ahead at 8 knots (15 kph).

Commander Gibbs in HMS *Pathfinder* closed the *Brisbane Star* soon after she had been hit and decided that she would have no chance of keeping up with the rest of the convoy, and that Captain Riley's best course would be to head south to try and make his way past Kelibia, keeping the cover of Tunisian coastal waters.

Trusting to his fabled Irish luck that she would not be spotted, he put her helm over and she limped away in the darkness on her own.

At 21.00 hours, the 12,000-ton ammunition ship *Clan Ferguson* (Captain Arthur Robert Cossar commanding), was steaming at 15 knots (28 kph) approximately 7 miles (13 km) north of Zembra Island when a signalman on watch saw planes approaching from starboard, low over the water in classic attack formation, weaving from side to side like a plague of gigantic locusts. He shouted for the helm to be put over, but the ship did not respond quickly enough and was hit just aft of her midships superstructure by a single torpedo. Then in quick succession, she was struck along the full length of her after deck by a stick of four HE bombs. The colossal explosions which followed led all who witnessed the attack to believe that she had been blown to pieces with no survivors. Through the thick, rolling banks of smoke could be seen sheets of orange, yellow and blood-red flames tearing through the doomed vessel as she began settling rapidly at her stern. Vast tongues of fierce fire were shooting out of the engine-room skylights and the ship's side, lighting up the night like a monstrous beacon. Hatch covers were blown off the holds, and several landing craft which had been stowed on top of them were blown overboard. There then came a very violent explosion in her Number 5 hold, and the resulting sheets of flame set many of the lifeboats afire. No scene from Dante's *Inferno* could match the horror which was the burning of the *Clan Ferguson*, but despite the devastation sixty-four of her crew got safely away in the remaining boats and rafts, although it was recorded at the time that she had been lost with all hands. The ship sank some twenty minutes later.

This is how Charlie Walker described the moment when the *Clan Ferguson* was hit:

> I saw these three Junkers Ju 88s coming in low over the waves as they usually did, and watched them as they dived on the ship from her starboard quarter. The leading plane was hit by anti-aircraft shells from the ship's Bofors and Oerlikons, but not before it had dropped its bombs, scoring direct hits right along the length of her after deck. One minute, there was this fine vessel cutting through the sea at 15 knots [28 kph], and the next there was this massive detonation followed by a vast sheet of flame and she had gone. Or that was how it seemed at the time because she had just disappeared under a gigantic mushroom of smoke and flames. She just seemed to have disappeared in a flash. The other two Junkers were caught up in the blast and never reappeared. I did see some bits and pieces of debris falling into the sea, but it was a small price to pay for the *Clan Ferguson* and her crew. Huge chunks of the ship were splashing into the sea all around us, some of it landing on *Ohio*'s deck.

Burning ships littered the narrow seaway, making the sky as light as day as the erupting ships burned amidst the violent explosions. The nightmare, however, was only just beginning. Hour after horrendous hour the battle raged. The noise of exploding bombs and torpedoes, the ear-shattering *crump* of heavy and light anti-aircraft guns creating ribbons of white light arching like gigantic fireflies into the night sky, reverberated across the sea in a never-ending cacophony of tumultuous, ear-splitting pandemonium amidst the putrid stench of noxious cordite and burning corpses. It was a stark realisation of their darkest nightmares which those men lived and fought through on that hideous August night. Many of those sailors were little more than children of fourteen, fifteen and sixteen years old.

At 21.15 hours, the already damaged SS *Deucalion* had reached a position some 5 miles (9 km) from the Cani Rocks in the company of one destroyer when two Heinkel torpedo-bombers found them. Coasting in low over the water with engines throttled back, they caught both ships completely unawares. Neither ship's guns opened fire until it was far too late. The first plane launched its torpedoes from a height of approximately 50 feet (15 m) but missed. The second, gliding in even lower than the first, launched its torpedoes at the very close range of some 75 yards (70 m) and both missiles hit the steamer on her starboard quarter. Her Number 6 hold, which contained high-octane aviation spirit, exploded immediately, ripping the after section apart as though it were nothing more substantial than a cardboard cut-out. With his ship doomed, Captain Brown issued immediate orders to abandon. All surviving crew were taken on board the destroyer *Bramham*. By that time the *Deucalion*'s decks were awash, but she was still ablaze at 21.30 hours when *Bramham* turned away. There was one final, tremendous explosion and she sank within seconds.

Further to the east, the *Ohio* was finding it very difficult to hold her course astern of HMS *Ledbury* because the destroyer's stern light was not visible from the tanker's aft steering position, and all directions for course changes had to be passed via the one remaining intercom from the bridge amidships.

On the horizon could be seen a continuous semicircle of burning ships, lighting up the darkness in a fierce conflagration. Red, yellow and blue tongues of fire leapt grotesquely into the night sky, interlaced with the odious stench of thick, acrid-smelling smoke which hovered over the monstrous scene, burning cruelly into the sore nostrils of all who were close enough to ingest the noxious fumes.

By that time, the *Ohio* was making good progress despite her vast injuries, and, in spite of – or perhaps because of – the vast death machine which had been ranged against them, Captain Mason and his crew worked with pride, determination and courage to get their vessel through to Malta. A number of her compartments had been opened to the sea, trailing burning fuel as she approached the blazing hulk of the *Clan Ferguson*. The sea all around the foundering vessel was ablaze with burning fuel oil, but fortunately HMS *Ledbury*, realising the danger, steered a course well away from the rapidly spreading pool of fire.

In extended formation then, the convoy rounded Cape Bon at approximately 23.00 hours and sailed straight into the waiting guns and torpedoes of the deadly German and Italian E-boats. The merchant ships had all been equipped with PAC rockets and fast-action multiple (FAM) launchers, plus a vast array of defensive naval and anti-aircraft weapons, so each ship, with a service team of naval and military gunners, was able to give a very good account of herself.

The forward formation at that time consisted of the leading warships following astern of the minesweeping destroyers. Only three of the merchantmen had been able to keep up with that group, the *Glenorchy*, the *Almeria Lykes* and the *Wairangi*. All the others, including the *Melbourne Star*, the *Waimarama*, the *Santa Elisa*, the *Dorset* and the *Rochester Castle* were strung out astern with only the destroyer

*Pathfinder* as escort. Astern of them were the tanker *Ohio* and her escorting destroyer *Ledbury*. Still further astern were the SS *Port Chalmers* and the destroyer HMS *Penn*. The *Brisbane Star*, down at the head because of her badly damaged bows, was picking her own course close in to the Tunisian coast.

When the E-boats first made contact, it was with the main body of warships, which gave the merchantmen a brief respite. A fierce battle took place as all guns turned on the attackers of the Italian 18th Squadron with a devastating rate of fire. A running battle ensued past Kelibia Light as the sea was criss-crossed with the deadly tracks of numerous torpedoes whilst the darkened sky came alive with the arching lights of tracer shells and LA naval guns. The E-boats suddenly turned away in the face of such a fearsome barrage of firepower, and no ships were hit, nor were any E-boats. Finding their initial targets at the head of the strung-out convoy too well able to defend themselves, the E-boats slunk back along the line, where they soon found targets more to their liking in the form of isolated bodies of plodding merchant freighters.

A further serious danger to the convoy was provided by the coastal navigation lights off Cape Bon and Kelibia. Tunisia, being neutral, had kept their powerful beams working, shining with a pitiless glare on British and Axis shipping alike, making it visible at a range of 10 miles (18.5 km). In the event, Kelibia Light was to cost them dearly. Hearing the deep-throated roar of the powerful E-boat engines, all ships laid down a withering rate of fire in a barrage so intense that radar aboard the warships showed the E-boats wheeling away from the British ships as though every demon from the black pit of Hell was hot on their heels.

At precisely 01.10 hours, the cruiser *Manchester* was hit by two torpedoes on her starboard side, very near to her engine room. Her engineers thought at first that it would be possible for the ship to steam at 2 knots (3.7 kph) and that she would answer her helm at such a reduced speed. They hoped that they might make it back to Gibraltar but, despite all their very best efforts, the ship remained stubbornly dead in the water. The crew then took to Carley floats and whaleboats after scuttling charges had been set and fired. The cruiser, however, did not sink until 05.00 hours. Thirteen officers and 308 men were rescued, but the bulk of her crew were interned by the Vichy French when they made landfall on the Tunisian coast.

At 01.30 hours, the SS *Rochester Castle* spotted an E-boat quite close and immediately made an attempt to ram. But even before her helm could be put over, the E-boat had fired off a single torpedo which hit the *Rochester Castle* just above her bilge-keel in her Number 3 hold, blowing a massive hole measuring some twenty-five feet by twenty (7.5 × 6 m) in her bottom. The hold flooded at once and two lifeboats were wrecked by the tremendous force of the explosion. Despite the hit, coupled with earlier damage she had received, she was still able to steam at 13 knots (24 kph), although so well down at the head that her pressure wave at the bows swept over her foredeck like raging river rapids. It was a superb feat of seamanship by Captain Wren and his crew.

Throughout that hideous night, the slaughter continued unabated. At 01.50 hours, the leading group of warships was a little to the south of Kelibia when the E-boat Ms 31 found them. Just a little before 02.00 hours, the *Glenorchy* (Captain Leslie commanding), was illuminated in the fierce glare of a searchlight trained on the ship from the E-boat, which hit her with a fan of two torpedoes on her port side. The engine-room flooded at once, killing almost every man down there, whilst all the lifeboats on her port side were destroyed. The ship took on a heavy port list as two of the starboard lifeboats were swung outboard. She had been carrying aviation spirit which had ignited mere milliseconds after the torpedoes had struck, and the doomed vessel went up like a gigantic Roman candle.

There came a brief lull in the battle between 02.15 and 03.00 hours, but very soon the convoy was located by yet another wave of E-boats and the violent attacks began all over again. At 36°35'N, 11°22'E, *Wairangi*'s skipper, Captain Gordon, sighted an E-boat 500 yards (450 m) off the port bow, and also the track of the torpedo she had fired. There was no chance of avoiding the speeding missile, and the torpedo struck the ship between her Number 3 tank and the coffer dam on the fore part of the deep oil tank. At once there was a violent explosion, a massive flash which resembled a tremendous lightning bolt, and a huge column of water which mush-roomed upwards like an oversized rogue geyser. She took on a heavy port list whilst her engine-room and Number 3 hold began flooding rapidly, killing several men who had been working below. The Number 4 lifeboat had been wrecked in the initial explosion, and the pumps were unable to cope with the massive amounts of inrushing sea. Her gunners, however, continued to fight back with every available weapon as further enemy units engaged her.

The American steamer SS *Almeria Lykes* was also hit at that time. She had been steaming on a zigzag course at 13 knots (24 kph) at 36°40'N, 11°35'E when she came under attack from two German E-boats, one of which scored a direct hit on her port side. She was loaded with ammunition in all her holds, surrounded by 9,700 tons of general cargo and military equipment. Her Number 1 hold contained a consignment of bombs, but despite that very dangerous and highly volatile cargo, there was just one single explosion of the torpedo instead of the appalling chain reaction which had occurred aboard the *Clan Ferguson*. That one explosion, however, had split the ship's hull at the line of the forepeak bulkhead, although the resulting submergence of the bows prevented any estimate being made of the full extent of the damage. Her engines stopped about five minutes later, and after briefly abandoning ship, her crew were able to reboard her later.

At 05.50 hours, another American vessel, the *Santa Elisa*, was the next to go. Well armed with 20-mm Oerlikons which were being very rapidly and very expertly handled by the ship's armed guard party, she exchanged a vicious rate of fire with her first attacker, the Italian Ms 557, which raced past at high speed, spraying the exposed decks of the freighter with heavy machine-gun fire, killing four of her gunners at their posts. In response, she raked the E-boat fore and aft with heavy-calibre machine-gun fire and had the satisfaction of seeing her sheer off at high speed. Another E-boat then attacked, scoring a different torpedo hit at point-blank range in her Number 1 hold, starboard. As with most other ships in the convoy, her cargo included high-octane aviation spirit, which ignited at once in a roaring explosion, resulting in a conflagration which knocked several of her crew overboard. Although the ship was ablaze from stem to stern, the crew were able to launch three of her lifeboats, and all twenty-eight hands got clear away, although five had been very badly burned.

The convoy was bathed in a terrible glow of exploding ships burning like vast funeral pyres in the Mediterranean night, and all had become part of the same blood-letting machine. Against everything that the Axis forces could throw at them, there seemed very little that the remaining escort ships could do except to go down fighting. But, as a new dawn burst over the horizon in a fantastic blaze of celestial pyrotechnics of the most brilliant colours and hues, the E-boats melted away, that proved to be their last attack.

While that battle was being fought, an isolated British merchant captain was using all his considerable skill, patience and downright impudence to bring his ship safely through the many hazards of that deadly stretch of sea. After parting company from HMS *Pathfinder* earlier, Captain Riley had steered the *Brisbane Star* straight for the Tunisian coast and, once in the shallows, had followed the coastline south past Kelibia. Pushing on at his best speed of 8 knots (15 kph) he was crossing the Gulf of Hammamet by daylight.

After a couple of close encounters with the Vichy French and an Italian submarine which followed her for a little while but which, for some unknown reason, did not attack, she was finally stopped by a Vichy French gunboat and boarded.

Although the very essence of correctness and formality, the French officers insisted that Captain Riley should turn his ship around and follow them back to Tunis where he, his ship and crew would be interned for the duration of the war. Captain Riley, however, had other ideas. With his typical Irish wit and presence of mind, he proved himself more than a match for those French officers. Smiling a welcome, he made up a story about having to make some minor repairs in the engine-room and courteously invited them to his cabin suite for drinks and refreshment whilst the work was being carried out. Once there, he plied them with a potent concoction of French wines, whisky, gin and the very best French cognac, all liberally spiced with some kind of 'happy pills' plus a hefty helping of good old Irish charm. This mixture convinced the French officers of his innocent intentions, and they staggered out onto the open decks, fondly wishing Captain Riley and his crew *bon voyage*, as they returned to their own vessel, leaving the *Brisbane Star* to continue her voyage to Malta. Captain Riley was subsequently awarded the OBE for that little interlude, and by nightfall on the 13th the *Brisbane Star* finally nosed her crumpled bows into the relative safety of Valletta harbour.

The solitary tanker *Ohio* was also making good progress, but supreme efforts were needed to hold the battered ship together and on course. Her after deck had been split down the middle, right up to her midships section, and with every yaw of her helm, the torn and buckled metal groaned as it split a little more, threatening to tear the vessel in half at any moment. It had become necessary to keep a permanent 5 degrees of starboard helm in order to compensate for the pull caused by the great rent in her side. By 03.00 hours, however, her engineers had managed to reach the incredible speed of 13 knots (24 kph), so that by dawn she had almost caught up with the remainder of the convoy.

This meant that just half of the original convoy had survived that terrible August night, but those survivors were fully aware that daybreak would bring no relief, only the bombers and, for all they knew, the Italian cruiser and destroyer squadrons as well. Astern of them, they had left the Mediterranean sea lanes strewn with erupting ships, dead and dying seamen of both services, and a sea of flames. Aboard the depleted numbers of escorting warships, haggard and exhausted men stood ready to repel what would be the enemy's decisive attacks. Very few of those senior naval officers who were in a position to know gave themselves very much chance of getting through. Malta appeared destined to fall and Operation Pedestal seemed doomed.

The dawn, however, brought no sign of the expected Italian squadrons on the northern horizon. On the previous evening, the six heavy cruisers and eight destroyers of Admiral Da Zara's cruiser divisions had been concentrated about 100 miles (185 km) north of Ustica, and had changed course in order to bring the convoy to battle south of Pantelleria at first light. The position of the various Axis forces had been reported to Malta headquarters on the 12th, but it had been felt that there was no need for any undue alarm; the covering force of escort ships were still at full strength when Malta received the report, and the convoy was still intact. It was a great shock, therefore, when they received the news of the heavy casualties suffered by both convoy and escort that night.

It was a relief when, at 01.00 hours on the 13th, one of the aircraft which had been sent out from Malta to shadow the Italian ships reported that the enemy had turned to the north-east, away from the convoy. At 03.15 hours, another report was received to the effect that they were still maintaining a course of 060 degrees at a speed of 20 knots (37 kph) towards Palermo. A message was sent in plain language to the effect that the plane was to continue shadowing until a squadron of heavy bombers could arrive on the scene at dawn. There were no heavy bombers, but when he intercepted the signal, Admiral Da Zara demanded fighter cover. The Germans, however, did not think this was necessary and refused the request. The warships were therefore turned away on the personal orders of Benito Mussolini.

At 06.00 hours on the 13th, the *Santa Elisa* was hit by a stick of bombs from a Junkers Ju 88. The ship immediately caught fire and was subsequently rent asunder by several severe internal explosions. The main body of what was left of the convoy was brought under attack at 08.00 hours by a squadron of twelve Ju 88s some 30 miles (55 km) south-south-east of Pantelleria. The remnants were sailing in line ahead, with the *Rochester Castle* leading, followed by the *Waimarama*, the *Melbourne Star* and the *Ohio*. The *Port Chalmers* was several miles astern of those vessels when she was attacked by a flight of Ju 88s in a series of shallow dives from between 6,000 and 2,000 feet (1,800–600 m). The majority made straight for the *Ohio*, which was surrounded by bomb bursts and towering walls of spray. The escorts, however, forever watchful and alert, were successful in driving off her attackers, and she came through without further damage.

Three of the bombers then turned their attentions to the *Waimarama*. The first plane missed her entirely as a result of heavy flak from the vessel's guns exploding all around its nose. She was unable to avoid her next two attackers, however, which screamed down upon her at masthead height. The first released a five-bomb stick, and four of them scored direct hits, exploding very close together amidships. Her bridge superstructure disappeared in a flash of smoke and flame and the entire ship blew up with one enormous explosion. A massive ball of flame mushrooming skywards was followed by gigantic columns of black, evil-smelling smoke rolling and curling for many hundreds of feet, through which her masts and remaining superstructure could be seen collapsing inwards into the very heart of the fearful furnace which raged inside her melting hull.

Just before the bombs hit, the Chief Radio Operator, John Jackson, was in the chartroom talking to the naval liaison officer, Lieutenant Withers, who said to him, 'Jacko, I reckon we'll be in Malta in about four or five hours. We'll be all right, mate.' Then they heard the bombers screaming down onto their ship. Lieutenant Withers was the first to step over the coaming onto the bridge wing and, as he stepped forward, Jackson stepped involuntarily back. That saved his life because, as he did so, there was an enormous explosion and a solid wall of flame and the young lieutenant had gone, incinerated in a fraction of a second. Jackson, who was fortuitously wearing a kapok jacket, hated water and could not swim, but instantly leaped over the side, ending up very near to where a river of burning petrol was spewing through the rails and into the sea. There were a large number of screaming men around him in the water, some of them burning to death even as he watched, paddling away from those gruesome scenes and kept afloat only by his kapok jacket. He suddenly felt a strong hand take him by his collar and, looking around, saw that it was the 17-year-old Third Radio Operator who had pulled him clear of the suffocating heat and smoke. As Jackson looked around, taking stock of what he saw, he noticed a seaman by the name of Bo Dory standing on a heavy raft with his arms outstretched, as though in supplication to some divine entity. The raft was drifting inexorably back into the sea of flames and, realising that it was much too close to the fires for him to be of any help to the doomed man, Jackson turned sadly away, leaving Dory to his grisly fate. Even though there was nothing that young man could have done to aid his shipmate, that incident haunted him for the rest of his life.

There has traditionally been a gulf between the men of the merchant fleet and the Royal Navy, but nevertheless, there was a bond between them which the men of neither service could escape. That bond was never more manifest than on Operation Pedestal when they worked together with a will and determination that has known no equal in the annals of British seafaring life. The extreme courage of one captain and his crew stands out as proof positive of this bond. That man was Roger Hill, skipper of the destroyer, HMS *Ledbury*.

Before being detailed for Operation Pedestal, he had sailed with the Arctic convoy PQ 17, which lost twenty-nine ships from a total of thirty-nine because of an order for the escorts to turn away and the convoy to scatter. In a television interview some time ago, he spoke in almost subdued tones of the effect that the abandonment of that convoy by the Navy had had upon him and his entire crew, and of how the incident haunted him ever since. When speaking to his crew at the start of Operation Pedestal, therefore, he had said, 'As long as just one merchantman remains afloat we will go alongside and to hell with signals, no matter where they come from.' So badly had PQ 17 affected him that, when the *Waimarama* went up, he took his frail craft into the very heart of the fiercely burning sea and the crew of that small destroyer rescued forty-five merchant seamen from the most horrific death imaginable. If any men of the convoy ever deserved the highest naval award for bravery above and beyond the call of duty, those men were Roger Hill and his crew.

As well as a cargo of explosives and ammunition, the *Waimarama* had been carrying a deck cargo of petrol stowed in 45-gallon (205 l) drums all over her main and boat decks. They split apart and exploded at once when those four bombs burst amidships in a searing blast of furnace-like heat and flames which swept across her mutilated decks from stem to stern in a ball of fire which consumed everything in its deadly path, spreading in a roaring sheet of flame as the ship disintegrated. Within seconds she had listed heavily to starboard, righted herself momentarily, then went down very fast in a foul-smelling cloud of smoke and steam, leaving only a huge area of flaming sea and a dense, oily cloud of smoke as her grave marker.

Casualties were severe. All bridge officers had been killed, including her captain, R.S. Pearce. Eighty-seven men were killed. So intense were the flames that the *Ohio* and the *Melbourne Star*, following close astern, were both showered with debris as bits and pieces of the ship fell back into the sea. Charlie Walker described the event thus:

> I saw the bombs that destroyed the *Waimarama* hitting her squarely amidships. Four of them there was, all around her bridge. They never stood a cat in hell's chance. One minute she was there ahead of us, and the next she was gone. Huge chunks of steel was blown into the sky, some of it landing on our decks when it came down again. Huge steel plates, some of them about 6 feet [1.8 m] square, and other massive chunks of jagged metal rained down from the sky after the *Waimarama* went up, and with us being so close astern of her, all the lot seemed to come down on *Ohio*'s decks. There were shells, bullets, bits and pieces of guns, hull plates, deck plates, pieces of hatch covers, even a bloody winch came aboard – a huge great winch just blown out of her deck and thrown into the air like a football. I heard later that a 6-inch shell had crashed through the deckhead of the captain's cabin aboard the *Melbourne Star*. I'd never seen anything like it in all my life. In fact, we were in danger of our own cargo igniting from the heat as *Ohio* passed by. What was left of the *Waimarama* by then had just about gone, but even so, the fierce heat she was still generating threatened to ignite our cargo and blow us all to hell and gone. What was left of our paintwork just blistered and bubbled as though it were being treated with a blowtorch. Some of the lifeboats on our starboard side caught fire as Captain Mason swung the ship hard-a-port to try and avoid the worst of the flames. Eighty-seven members of *Waimarama*'s crew were killed in that one shattering explosion. In all my years at sea, that was about the most horrendous sight I have ever witnessed.
>
> We could do more than stand around and watch as we passed her by on our starboard side. Those of her crew who had survived the initial explosion we could see running across her twisted decks, most of them on fire as they tried to escape the blaze and just throwing themselves over the side and into the burning sea. That was just about the most horrible sight I have ever seen. As we passed, a great silence seemed to descend over our ship. We were all lining the rails, but no one spoke or uttered a sound. It was a silence broken only by the sounds of that burning ship and the bloodcurdling cries of burning men aboard her. Other than that, there was just this awful silence, the stench of burning oil and fuel and cordite.

As the long, wearisome day wore on, one assault seemed to merge with another, making it seem as though they were enduring one huge continuous attack. By 09.00

hours, the Stuka dive-bombers of 102 Gruppo once again found the unfortunate *Ohio* irresistible. HMS *Ashanti* had been equipped with many Oerlikon guns, which her skipper had ordered aboard before leaving Glasgow as being the best available to answer the Stukas. She nailed several aircraft as they attacked the *Ohio*, and once again the latter vessel came through those determined attacks without further damage, although a near miss by a 500-pound (227 kg) bomb which had exploded fine off her port bow flooded her forepeak tanks, twisting and buckling several of her bow plates. The huge tanker shuddered along her full length, shook herself free of the towering splash of the bomb burst, and just kept on going. But the battered hull and strained engines were unable to take very much more such severe punishment, as her crew were soon to find out.

One Stuka, hit in mid-dive by the combined fire of the *Ohio* herself and the *Ashanti*, was torn apart. Another was hit fair and square by 20 mm cannon shells from the *Ohio*, but they failed to stop it. At full throttle, it bounced off the sea and slammed into the *Ohio*'s side, crashing with a scream of tortured metal onto her poop deck. Once again, Charlie takes up the story:

> I was up on the poop deck when those two planes dived down on us, and together with the destroyer, *Ashanti*, I believe she was, we opened up on them with everything we had. I think it was one of the destroyer's guns that hit the first plane, and that just blew up in mid-air. But the second one, I had. I'm certain of that because I was following the line of tracer from my own gun and saw it rip into the plane. Anyway, it didn't stop her because she was too close. Everyone breathed a sigh of relief when we saw her hit the water just off our port quarter, then she bounced into the air again and all hell was let loose as she rose to deck level and smashed into the poop deck. Well, as you will know, the galley and all the crew accommodation is situated there, as well as the fiddley-top to the engine-room and stokehole, and as she slammed into the port bulkhead she just disintegrated in a flash. Flames and smoke engulfed the ship again, drifting over her like some monstrous funeral pyre, and that time, I thought we'd had it for sure. The single LA gun on the stern had been twisted out of alignment by the concussion and just hung there uselessly at an acute angle, and all the crew who had been manning that gun had either been killed or severely injured, but me and my crew were all right even though we were right above the spot where that plane hit us. The blast of hot air from the explosion though hit us like a furnace door being suddenly opened, but luckily we had all dived for cover when we saw what was going to happen, and as luck would have it, all the cooks were on deck helping to man the guns. We were short-handed because we'd had several casualties, and the cooks and stewards were helping out. But still the skipper and crew kept her under control, and still she came through it. The poop deck was like a charnelhouse though. There were bits and pieces of bodies and wreckage everywhere. It was just terrible. The pilot had been smashed to pieces, so there was no point in trying to find what was left of him. When the fires had been put out and everything had cooled down, we just threw what was left of the plane over the side.

In the same attack, at 09.45 hours, the *Dorset* was attacked by no less than six Stukas. Five bombs exploded close alongside, lifting her almost out of the water.

The fifth bomb, a heavy 500-pounder (227 kg), penetrated her Number 4 hold, collapsing the bulkhead between it and her engine-room, which flooded immediately. A large fire had erupted in the hold which was next to Number 3, in which was stowed high-octane fuel. All her electric pumps had failed owing to the lack of power as the engine-room filled with water, and there was no option but to abandon. It had been intended to use scuttling charges to finish her off, but they had been left in the flooded compartments when what was left of her engine-room crew came up on deck, and like so many ships before her, the *Dorset* was left a floating raging inferno. All her surviving crew were picked up by the HMS *Bramham*

At 10.00 hours, the *Rochester Castle* was rocked by three bombs which exploded under her bows, lifting her half out of the water and dislocating her engines. The resultant fires spread very quickly, necessitating the flooding of a magazine, which was in immediate danger of exploding. Her engines were restarted after a little while, but it took far longer to bring the blaze under control. It was then found that her steering mechanism had been damaged and, by the time the necessary repairs had been made, she had shipped over 4,000 tons of sea water, making course-keeping a nightmare.

The Axis forces had the aircraft with which to deliver the *coup de grâce* to what was left of the convoy, but RAF planes out of Malta, fully stretched and virtually blinded by lack of direction though they were, did some magnificent work in the afternoon. No. 248 Squadron provided sorties of four Beaufighters to escort the convoy from dawn to within 100 miles (185 km) of Malta, but failed to locate the ships. Short-range Spitfires were to take over fighter cover at a range of 70 miles (130 km) whilst long-range Spitfires, which were supposed to be operating at their extreme endurance range of 120 miles (220 km), were seen over the convoy at a range of 170 miles (315 km), so determined were they to get what was left of that vital convoy through.

Once again, the *Luftwaffe* came boring in with a further twenty Ju 88s attacking from dead ahead – yet another very dangerous assault with near misses churning up the sea around the freighters – and, once again, the already crippled *Ohio* suffered. A German bomber which had been heavily hit by AA fire skidded across the sea just 50 feet (15 m) from the tanker, slithering into her side in a shower of deadly flames. It had already dropped its bombs, but that additional shock, coupled with further explosions nearby, blew out the tanker's fires. All the engine-room lights went out and the ship went into emergency lighting as she stopped dead in the water whilst the rest of the convoy surged ahead. She was alone, crippled and drifting helplessly, completely at the mercy of the *Luftwaffe*.

At 23.00 hours, a force of twelve Italian SM 79s escorted by fourteen MC 202s was sighted dead ahead. While British Spitfires clashed with the Italian escorts in wild dogfights, the torpedo-bombers deployed for a low-level attack. At that point, the skipper of HMS *Pathfinder* took matters in hand and decided to make an attack of his own. Increasing speed to full revolutions, he turned her bows straight out to sea to meet the SM 79s head-on.

The torpedo-bombers were flying in at masthead height, and with great flair and dexterity, he steered straight for the centre of the formation. Her crew opened up with all guns as soon as she came within range, engaging on both sides with a withering rate of fire. The noise was tremendous as a continuous hail of tracer shells ripped into the planes in a devastating curtain of hot steel, with the nearest SM 79 almost within touching distance of the speeding vessel. The whole formation, surrounded by hundreds of shell bursts and tracer bullets, were seen diving, twisting and climbing in sheer panic at this unexpected counter-attack by one solitary vessel, and dropping torpedoes in all directions except that of the convoy. Several aircraft were on fire as the formation scattered in panic and hurriedly returned to Sicily. The attack broken up, the gallant *Pathfinder* turned under full power and rudder and returned to the convoy. Her vigorous and spirited action had thrown the Italian pilots into a state of complete confusion, and all of their torpedoes fell well clear of all ships.

Whilst the destroyer *Bramham* was engaged in picking up survivors from the steamer *Dorset*, the destroyers *Penn* and *Ledbury* were sent back to find the *Ohio*. The convoy was by that time, reduced to just three ships, but they had come under the aerial protection of the short-range Spitfires, and despite persistent attempts by enemy aircraft to destroy what was left of the merchantmen, those pathetically few pilots did some magnificent work in keeping the bombers at bay. By 14.00 hours, the Malta Escort Force had made contact with the remnants of the convoy, and was a very welcome reinforcement to the escort vessels. For the *Port Chalmers*, the *Rochester Castle* and the *Melbourne Star*, the worst of their ordeal was just about over, and by 16.00 hours, they had Malta in sight. At 18.25 hours, they steamed slowly through the minefield and into the still waters of Valletta harbour, there to be greeted by a rapturous crowd of cheering people and bands playing rousing tunes at the harbour entrance. Just three badly battered ships were there, from the total of fourteen, but without the cargo of that vital solitary tanker, the *Ohio*, even that achievement would be valueless.

She lay somewhere out to the west, and every effort was now concentrated on getting her, as well as the other two remaining ships, the *Dorset* and the *Brisbane Star*, into Valletta. For the *Dorset*, however, abandoned, listing, disabled and totally helpless under the grim shadow of enemy air bases, life was almost at an end. Throughout the day, the *Luftwaffe* had made several attempts to finish her off, but without success. Enemy aircraft had been active throughout the day, although the brunt of their attentions had been upon the *Ohio*. Finally, however, the *Dorset* was hit by a large bomb which burst on her foredeck, restarting the fires which had already ravaged her mangled hull. At 19.00 hours, she was hit for the last time by another 500-pound (227 kg) bomb which finally sent her to the bottom. She went down bows first with her 'Red Duster' still flying proudly from her jack.

The tanker *Ohio* had been left listing to an angle of 5 degrees and dead in the water, and *Ledbury* reversed her course to find her. Within thirty minutes of being disabled, after some desperate work in the engine-room, her engineers finally succeeded in getting her once more under way at the incredible speed of 16 knots (30 kph). She was brought under renewed air attacks, however, with a succession of near misses which shattered her electrical fuel pumps and tore the main switch from its bulkhead mounting. All her lights were extinguished as she slowed once again, and came wearily to a standstill.

Chief Engineer Wyld reported the full extent of the damage to Captain Mason, and it was severe. The captain asked for a full inspection of the ship and engines. After an hour of dangerous, painstaking work, this confirmed that the *Ohio*'s engines were finished. Nothing more could be done for the crippled vessel short of a tow, but no tug was available.

Lieutenant-Commander Swain, in the destroyer *Penn*, decided that, rather than lose the tanker altogether, he would attempt a tow with his own frail vessel. Captain Mason issued orders for Second Mate McKilligan to take a party of men to clear the forecastle head of litter and debris so that a messenger line from *Penn* could be passed across, carrying a 10-inch (25 cm) manila for the tow. Whilst they were engaged upon this strenuous task, the ship was bombed and strafed yet again by a lone Ju 88 which scored several near misses, only serving to aggravate that tanker's already severely weakened condition. Heavy-calibre cannon shells raked her devastated decks, whining in all directions as her crew cowered in any available corner they could find whilst her naval gunners, with a courage that had to be seen to be believed, poured a deadly hail of tracer shells into the plane's underbelly.

A messenger line was eventually passed from the *Penn* to the *Ohio* but, with no steam on deck to operate the winch, the work was slow and heavy as the manila, made heavy and unwieldy by its immersion in the sea, was laboriously hauled inboard by already exhausted men. The line was eventually secured, and as the little destroyer, a mere 1,500 tons, took the strain of the 30,000-ton tanker, her 40,000 shp engines seemed to groan aloud. The *Ohio* was drawing some 37 feet (11.3 m) of draught, and the massive rent in her hull began to counteract the tow, turning the ship inexorably to port. As the terrible strain on both ships and engines gradually increased, the tanker began pulling away from the destroyer until she was pulling at an angle of 90 degrees. The wind, blowing in from the south-west was also drifting the lifeless hulk astern.

Under the direction of her commander, the *Penn* tried to bring the ship's head round, but the only effect was to move her in slow, sluggish circles. Yet another attack followed and the *Penn*, in an attempt to manoeuvre to meet it, went hard ahead, snapping the towline with a sharp, rifle-like crack. Despite intense fire from both ships, one of the bombers placed his bombs close alongside the tanker where they exploded amidships under her keel. Already torn and stretched almost to breaking point, that explosion opened the rent even further. It became obvious that she was about to split apart.

As the attack died away, it became obvious that the only hope was to have two ships with towlines, one ahead and one astern, with the stern vessel acting as a rudder. This was not possible, however, because the *Penn* was the only escort then available.

In order to ensure the safety of her crew, there appeared no alternative but to abandon the *Ohio* for the time being. Consequently, at 14.15 hours, the tanker's weary sailors dragged their battle-fatigued bodies into the remaining lifeboats and were taken aboard the destroyer, where they fell into an exhausted sleep. Like their captain, as well as performing their normal duties of running a ship at sea, they had been at action stations for the previous three days and two nights, with no let-up from attack after attack, ranging from submarines to E-boats to aircraft.

Throughout the following hours, the *Penn* slowly circled the drifting vessel, waiting anxiously for reinforcements to arrive. No one aboard expected the *Ohio* to stay afloat long enough for another towing attempt to be made.

Axis aircraft continued to mount attack after attack upon the crippled ship, although their efforts were, to a large extent nullified by the extremely courageous efforts of the RAF fighter pilots. Between 16.00 and 19.00 hours, twenty-six Ju 88s and seven Heinkel 111s were sent out in groups, and at 15.00 hours, the Italians sent out five Stuka dive-bombers, powerfully escorted by no less than twenty-four MC 202 fighters in an attempt to bulldoze their way through the RAF fighter defence. The RAF, however, was maintaining a formidable barrier of sixteen Spitfires over the *Ohio* at all times, and in the ensuing dogfights, RAF pilots despatched three MC 202s and seven Ju 88s.

At 17.40 hours, the ocean minesweeper HMS *Rye* (Lieutenant J.A. Pearson, DSC, RNR, commanding), of the Malta Force, together with the motor launches ML 121 and ML 168, joined the *Penn* at 36°N, 12°59'E.

Barely refreshed by their very short respite, the *Ohio*'s crew volunteered to reboard her, together with a party of deck-hands from the destroyer, to assist in a renewed attempt to get her moving again. By then, the ship had settled lower into the sea, and was drawing 38 feet (11.5 m) of water with a slowly increasing list and her bows dipping even lower. Undaunted, merchant and naval crews toiled side by side in a nautical comradeship and devotion to duty that was as old as the sea itself.

At 17.45 hours, the tow was once more made fast and the *Penn* began moving slowly ahead. It was to no avail, merely a variation on a theme. The dead weight of the tanker turned the light destroyer to port and overran the tow. It became quite clear to everyone that no progress could be made with the rudder jammed, and so a party of volunteers were sent below to clear it. Within thirty minutes they had cast off the emergency gear and rigged a hand-steering gear by attaching cables to chains and reeving them through tackle-blocks. That enabled Captain Mason to report to Swain that they had fixed the rudder enough to give them about 5 degrees of star-board helm which, it was hoped, would counteract her port swing.

Once again the destroyer took up the strain and this time, with a quick shudder, the *Ohio* began to move. Carefully and with consummate skill, Swain increased speed until they were moving at 5 knots (9 kph). But the tanker stubbornly continued to yaw and edge, dragging the *Penn* back into her once again. After a short time, they were forced to stop. It was decided that, if 500 fathoms (900 m) of sweep wire were passed into the destroyer, *Rye* would act as stabiliser. That was done and at 18.30 hours both naval vessels went ahead together. Now their efforts met with success and, at 4 knots (7.5 kph), the tanker began to make slow but steady progress.

It was at this most critical and vulnerable time that German bombers put in yet another unwelcome appearance. Four Ju 88s appeared, dead ahead, having been missed by the fighter patrol. As they commenced their familiar dives, Captain Mason was aware that his ship's chances of avoiding being hit were very small and ordered all crew members who were working below decks topside. The four bombers then broke formation and, circling the ships, picked their easiest approach before making independent attacks from astern, where the amount of AA fire was at its lowest density.

Charlie Walker recalled with clarity the events of that day.

Moving as sluggishly as we then were, there was nothing we could do but sit and wait for it. It wasn't long in coming. One heavy bomb erupted astern of us and once again, the rudder became jammed. Another bomber then scored a direct hit. As far as I was concerned, that was it. I'd sailed on quite a few tankers before the war, and after the tremendous pounding that the *Ohio* had taken up until then, she should have been on the bottom. To this day, I'll never know what it was that kept that ship afloat; but if there really is such a thing as a God, then he was watching over us on that day.

We all watched, fascinated, as the bomb fell. It looked for all the world as though it was just a slow motion picture, but it was real enough. That bomb hit us dead square, bursting on our boiler tops after crashing through the fore end of the boat deck and starting a fire there. It blew a ventilator onto one of the Bofors guns, injuring some of its crew, but there was this one lad on the DEMS crew, a Gunner Brown it was, went and got himself trapped under the wreckage. He was all smashed up pretty bad, but we managed to pull him clear and transferred him to the *Penn*.

Although Gunner Brown was still alive when he was pulled from under the wreckage, he had received massive internal injuries and died later aboard the *Penn*.

Captain Mason's assessment of the damage revealed that the engine-room was completely wrecked, and the rudder useless. Moreover, in moving to meet the latest attack, the *Penn* had once again cast the tow. Miraculously, however, the ship was still holding together by her keel, although the severe strain was becoming intolerable, and under renewed attacks by the *Luftwaffe*, the motor launches went alongside *Ohio* to take off all hands.

Captain Mason and his crew were now completely exhausted, and fell into a deep sleep anywhere they happened to be. While they slept, the two naval commanders met again for a discussion on how best to get the *Ohio* moving and into Valletta. During the last air attack, the small group had been further reinforced by the destroyer HMS *Bramham*, which took up anti-submarine patrol duties around the small armada as a party of naval and merchant seamen, under the command of the *Penn*'s executive officer, Lieutenant G.G. Marten, boarded *Ohio* to make ready for yet another attempt to tow.

HMS *Rye* was now allocated as the towing vessel ahead, using chain cable instead of the more usual 10-inch (25 cm) manila, whilst the *Penn* ran in astern of the tanker and made fast. In that position, it was hoped that she could stop *Ohio* yawing, even without a rudder. It was 22.00 hours before the tow recommenced, but their efforts were successful, and good progress was made. All through that dark and dangerous Mediterranean night, the small flotilla moved forward at an agonisingly slow pace.

At midnight on the night of the 13th/14th, *Ohio* was still under tow, moving slowly at 4 knots (7.5 kph) and coming on very satisfactorily through the combined efforts of the *Penn* and the *Rye*. Although their progress was painstaking, there were high hopes that the end was almost within sight. The *Rye*, in the towing position ahead, then attempted a slight increase in speed. It was fatal. The tanker yawed badly to port and, with a crack like a cannon shot, the tow parted.

Lieutenant-Commander Swain decided to adopt a suggestion made by Lieutenant Baines of the *Ledbury*, that an alongside tow might work. Accordingly, the *Penn* went alongside the *Ohio* whilst the *Rye* made fast with a 10-inch (25 cm) manila to the tanker's bows, and towed from ahead. At 01.10 hours on the 14th, the flotilla went gingerly ahead. The tanker refused to move. Swain ran down for more power, but with little success. It became obvious that one destroyer did not have the power for such a gargantuan task and that any further attempts to tow in that fashion would only result in serious damage to the *Penn*. The attempt was abandoned.

Nothing more could be done for the *Ohio* until daylight, and for the next three hours, the *Penn* and the *Rye* circled the stricken vessel, which lay like a massive, badly wounded leviathan on the oil-coated sea, awkward and low in the water with her decks torn open, grotesquely twisted and broken, groaning hollowly with every movement of the sea. Her forward catwalk had almost completely disintegrated above the carnage of her once immaculate foredeck, whilst her aft catwalk had been twisted and buckled out of all recognition. Her poop deck had been smashed to such an extent that no access could be gained to her stern along her port side, both her fore and aft main decks were a shambles of torn and twisted shards of steel, and her midships superstructure had become a blackened, mangled parody of the handsome structure it had been mere hours before.

That brief respite gave the crews a few hours' much-needed rest, and by first light on the 14th they were fit enough to renew the battle to save the *Ohio*. Once again, the *Penn* went alongside and made fast, and at 04.00 hours they began moving, but the *Ohio* yawed badly and the tow parted. Next, the *Rye* made an attempt to take both ships in tow by using a 10-inch (25 cm) manila aboard the tanker and a sweep wire attached to the *Penn*'s cable. At 05.05 hours, that attempt also ended in failure as *Ohio* took control with her massive dead-weight swinging irresistibly away, parting both wires. It appeared to be an impossible task.

At 07.15 hours, they were joined by the *Ledbury*, returning from her fruitless search for the cruiser *Manchester*. The *Rye* then passed 3,000 yards (2,750 m) of sweep wire into the *Ohio* while the *Ledbury* made fast astern of the tanker to act as steering tug while the *Penn* remained clear. Once again they managed to get under way. As they did so, however, the *Ledbury* found it impossible to stop the stubborn tanker swinging away, and the hawsers parted once more. It had become a mind-numbing, nightmarish task, but by that time, the minesweeper *Speedy* and three motor launches from Malta had arrived. Commander Jerome of the *Speedy* was now the senior officer and took over the salvage attempt.

By now, the *Ohio* and the magnificent efforts to save her had become the talk of Malta and dockyard workers and civilians were already lining the ancient battlements and harbour walls, all wanting to be first to welcome her and her crew. Even a brass band was there, waiting and scanning the horizon to the west for the first sighting of their saviour. Her ordeal, however, was still far from over.

At 10.50 hours, the final air attack against the crippled tanker took place when five Ju 87s of the Italian 102 Gruppo, escorted by twenty MC 202s, made a last-ditch attempt to finish her off. Fortunately, the RAF had been maintaining their powerful umbrella over the ships. Besides the Beaufighters, there were always a minimum of sixteen Spitfires from 229 and 249 Squadrons overhead. They briskly engaged the Italian planes, but were unable to prevent one Stuka placing yet another bomb close by the tanker.

That bomb exploded hard in *Ohio*'s wake, flinging the ship forward as though she had been pushed by some gigantic hand, twisting her screws out of alignment and holing her stern. Already dangerously low in the water, a new inrush of sea into her engine room made her position critical. The RAF managed to destroy one Stuka and one MC 202 without loss to themselves, and thereafter parried the few half-hearted raids which followed. Although the final bomb-burst so close alongside appeared to have sounded the death-knell for the *Ohio*, but she still did not sink.

As the enemy bombers were being driven off by the RAF, the naval escorts sprang to life. *Bramham* was taken carefully alongside the tanker's port side and made fast. Volunteers, including survivors from the sunken *Waimarama* and *Santa Elisa*, as well as naval ratings from the warship, were placed aboard to man her remaining AA weapons and to assist in the new towing arrangements. All of those men knew that death aboard a tanker was neither quick nor clean, but they accepted the risk with stoic calm. Traditional rivalries were put aside as naval and merchant ratings and officers, with determination and courage, toiled together as one cohesive unit against impossible odds.

Lieutenant-Commander Swain edged the *Penn* up on the tanker's starboard side and made her fast there. Another party, armed with portable pumps from the destroyers to replace those which had been destroyed on the *Ohio*, went aboard to pump out the water from her engine-room and so increase her buoyancy. With a destroyer made fast to either side to keep her afloat and the *Ledbury* astern as a rudder, the *Rye* then positioned herself ahead as towing vessel. Around the group the minesweepers, *Speedy*, *Hebe* and *Hythe* formed a protective ring as they made ready for yet another bid.

Soon after the tow had commenced, however, it became apparent that the *Ohio* was not responding as she should have done; she was pulling the *Ledbury* slowly but surely around with her. Finally, the destroyer ended up alongside the *Penn*, and in attempting to rectify the drift the *Rye* lost the towing wire altogether. The group came to yet another agonising halt.

Commander Jerome organised a further effort, with both destroyers going slow ahead on either side of the tanker, and she finally began to move on a straight course. They had worked up to 5 knots (9 kph) when Captain Mason warned Commander Jerome that his ship would not hold together with any further increase in speed. At a snail's pace, then, they continued their journey to Malta, but with every tortuous mile gained, the level of water in the flooded engine-room increased, albeit more slowly than before because of the portable pumps. At noon, they suffered yet another setback when one of the *Bramham*'s wires parted under the ever-increasing strain. Under the direction of the *Bramham*'s first lieutenant, the Marquess of Milford Haven, OBE, the tow was cast off, a new wire secured, and the wearisome journey continued.

Under the scorching Mediterranean sun, the British flotilla pressed on and, late in the afternoon, the hazy coastline of Malta rose slowly over the distant horizon. The southern shores of the low-lying island gradually became clearer as the afternoon gave way to evening and they crawled laboriously towards their goal. There was still no certainty that the *Ohio* would make safe harbour, however. The waters around the island, and especially in the long approach to the main harbour, was thick with mines, and the only channel which was kept clear was very long, involving several abrupt course changes. In her present condition it appeared very unlikely that the tanker could be manoeuvred safely through it. Nevertheless no one involved considered the possibility of defeat.

As they approached the entrance to the channel off Delimara Point, the destroyers began the complicated and dangerous task of turning the 30,000-ton vessel and her deadly cargo into the gap in the minefields. As they turned with infinite care and precision to port, the towing wires, unable to withstand the extra strain, once again parted. Close to the mine-peppered waters, the whole complicated process of securing the tow began all over again.

By now, they had been joined by the ancient tug *Robust* and the salvage tug *Supply*. The King's Harbour Master was aboard the tug and he took command of the salvage operation. The *Robust* was secured to the tanker and, belching choking black smoke and thick flakes of soot from her ludicrously long funnel, she tried to move her. The tanker, however, contemptuously resisted the efforts of the old veteran and began pulling the tug into the side of the *Penn*. Furious attempts to unship the towing wire failed and she crashed hard into the destroyer, holing her above the waterline. With yet another round lost, the *Robust* was sent back into Malta while the destroyers resumed their arduous task.

As the evening wore wearily on, more ships put out from Valletta to render whatever aid they could, including the three tugs, *Carbine*, *Coronation* and the ancient 'rust-bucket', *Robust* again. Help was still very much needed, for as the towing formation reached Zonker Point, it became necessary for the tanker to execute another, different turn. Cautiously, the *Penn* and the *Bramham*, still both alongside holding the *Ohio* afloat, nursed her around. With the turn only half completed, however, the *Ohio* again began to make her incurable drift, edging herself and the two helpless destroyers into the minefield.

The *Ledbury* then went alongside and passed her 6-inch (15 cm) manila into *Ohio* in an effort to pull the three ships around again, whilst two of the motor launches pushed hard against the destroyer's bows. It was an agonising, heartbreaking battle, with little movement either way. For some time it was touch and go whether or not the whole flotilla would end up in the minefield so close to their goal.

At 18.00 hours, the situation was remedied by the arrival of the Malta tugs, one of which placed herself astern and the other ahead. With the two destroyers lashed one on either side, the *Ohio* was once again coaxed, cajoled, bullied and pushed up-channel towards the main harbour.

For fourteen hours, men and ships toiled in determined, backbreaking labour as they nudged the tanker into every dangerous turn. Finally, at 08.00 hours, their efforts were rewarded as they passed through the minefield and into Valletta harbour to a rapturous welcome. Wildly cheering throngs of people, yelling, crying, laughing and pointing, choked the harbour and battlements as a band played patriotic tunes. Nevertheless, the final mile from entrance to berth was a nerve-wracking experience for all concerned. With her decks awash and her torn and mangled hull still protesting at every movement, there was still a grave fear that, even at that eleventh hour, the *Ohio* might sink and block the channel.

The *Penn* had been cast off as they neared the *Ohio*'s berth, leaving the *Bramham* to try and hold the vessel together for the final few hundred yards. Slowly and with infinite care, the gallant tanker crawled past the wreck of another tanker, the *Plumleaf*, which lay at its original berth with its upper works barely above the surface. The *Bramham* was cast off and the naval auxiliary *Boxol* took over. At long last, the *Ohio* slid gently and obediently into her allotted berth. While she was still being tied up, gangs of dockyard workers swarmed all over her with pumps and pipes to unload her precious cargo before, like the *Plumleaf*, she settled to the bottom of the harbour. The *Boxol* also made her contribution by taking some of the *Ohio*'s cargo into her own tanks. Another race against time and gravity had begun, because as the tanker's fuel was being pumped out of her fore tanks, so her bows rose whilst her aft section continued to sink, threatening to break her in half at any moment. As though that was not enough, it was now full daylight, and a sneak bombing attack could not be ruled out.

Strangely enough, however, as though finally accepting defeat, the *Regia Aeronautica* and the *Luftwaffe* made no attempt to disrupt the discharging of any of the surviving ships once they had reached harbour. Already, the *Rochester Castle*, the *Melbourne Star* and the *Port Chalmers* had completed their own discharging, and the gallant *Brisbane Star*, which had reached safety on the previous day under an umbrella of Spitfires, was similarly also empty.

Hundreds of rescued men of both services were aboard the tiny destroyers and the *Ohio*, being an American vessel, had been well stocked with food of every description as well as many luxury items and Christmas fare. Before they docked in Valletta, Captain Mason had given permission for her crew to open up the food lazarettes, freezers, bond store and fridges and help themselves to whatever they desired. Cigarettes, chocolate, alcohol and Christmas stores of all descriptions were handed round and ravenously devoured by all the men aboard all the ships involved in the battle to save *Ohio*. The most amazing thing of all, however, was to see naval and DEMS gunners manning their weapons wearing all kinds of bizarre clothing and ridiculous paper hats. Perhaps the German and Italian pilots, witnessing such idiocy in men who had been bombed, machine-gunned and torpedoed almost out of existence, merely gave up and went home.

The crowd of wildly cheering people lining the bomb-battered quays and walls of Valletta harbour erupted as the *Ohio* entered her berth. The bands played different tunes all at once, people screamed, cheered, laughed and cried as though the *Ohio* had won the entire war all on her own. Charlie Walker described it as 'a most amazing, wonderful sight', as the bedraggled crew of the tanker and the pitiful survivors of the ships which had been sunk were shepherded ashore.

The crew of the *Ohio* were later paraded through the streets of Valletta through yet more throngs of wildly cheering people lining the rubble-strewn streets. As they proudly passed by, one tiny old lady holding black garments around her frail body suddenly stepped out of the crowd and gave to the man nearest her, a DEMS gunner by the name of Bill Hendy, a little wooden crucifix and said to him, 'Thank you my son, and may God bless you.' After all the death and destruction suffered by the courageous Maltese people through the years of intense bombardment, it filled those men's eyes with tears that such a gesture of compassion and goodwill could still be made to those who, in Charlie's words, 'had suffered only five days of such hell'.

Overlooking the entrance to the Grand Harbour, the Siege Bell extends over a long site on the bastion adjacent to the Lower Barrakka Gardens. It is a memorial consisting of a neo-classical cupola with a bell inside it and a recumbent figure on a catafalque lying before it. That bronze sculpture represents all of Malta's war dead, and can be interpreted as a sailor, soldier, airman or civilian. Beneath that bell, there is a plaque which reads, 'This bell tolls in memory of those who gave their lives during the siege of Malta – 1940–1943.' It is a tribute to the 7,000 servicemen, merchant seamen and civilians who made the ultimate sacrifice in defence of the island. The book of remembrance of civilians and servicemen killed between 1940 and 1943 is in the National War Museum of Fort St Elmo, Valletta, along with the George Cross awarded to Malta by King George VI on 15 April 1942. Because of persistent enemy action, however, the ceremony for the handover of the medal could not be held until 13 September, when Lord Gort, VC, presented it, together with the King's citation, to Chief Justice Sir George Borg, who received it on behalf of the Maltese people.

The successful arrival of the remnants of Operation Pedestal was linked by the Maltese to the Feast of Santa Maria. As the last gallons of precious, life-preserving fuel were being pumped clear of the *Ohio*, her final task painfully accomplished, she settled, almost gratefully, to the bottom of Valletta harbour. Operation Pedestal had come to an end, and there was renewed hope of ultimate salvation for Malta, its gallant citizens and military defenders. The extreme courage of the men of both the Royal Navy and the merchant fleet had once again turned defeat to victory against seemingly insurmountable odds. The amount of vital cargo which had been discharged at such a harrowing cost in men and ships was far less than had been hoped for, but it still meant that Malta had been given a breathing space for a further two months.

Vital as the stores, provisions and ammunition were, the *Ohio*'s cargo of precious fuel oil, without which all the defensive and offensive capability of the island would have come to a standstill, was of paramount importance. The master of the tanker, the gallant Captain Mason who just would not accept defeat, was deservedly awarded the George Cross for his superb contribution in taking his ship into Malta despite her impossible condition. Her crew, however, without whom Captain Mason would have been totally impotent, received nothing but their pathetic remuneration. Other masters of the convoy also received just their awards for their determination and courage. The bravery of those 'non-combatants' in the face of the heaviest air and sea attacks ever mounted against a merchant convoy was remarkable, but the equally remarkable merchant seamen received only a pittance for wages.

The *Ohio* was destined never to sail the seas again. Some time after the completion of her discharge, her badly battered hull was pumped dry and she was towed away to a remote part of Valletta harbour, where she finally broke in half. She was then converted and continued in use as a stores and barracks for the remainder of the war. She was finally towed out of Valletta in September 1946 and sunk by gunfire. During the five short days of Operation Pedestal, however, her name became an enduring legend in the annals of seafaring.

The other surviving merchant ships did not reach their home ports again until spring 1943, by which time, the stranglehold of the German submarine offensive in the Western Ocean was about to be broken.

Operation Pedestal was by far the most costly of all the Mediterranean convoys, and that at a time when every Allied ship was worth its weight in gold. The losses of HMS *Eagle*, HMS *Manchester*, HMS *Cairo* and HMS *Foresight* were all grievous blows, but in addition the Navy had the *Indomitable*, the *Nigeria*, the *Kenya*, the *Ithuriel*, the *Wolverine* and the *Penn* all put out of action for a considerable period of time; and those were only the losses incurred in ships and *materiel*. The casualties amongst the merchant seamen and Royal Naval personnel were equally severe – 350 officers and men, more, even than the disastrous PQ 17 Arctic convoy which had been slaughtered the previous month.

Considering the heroic efforts needed and the severe losses in men and ships of both services in keeping Malta supplied, one must ask whether they were necessary on such a scale. The answer is that in the circumstances of the time, not only were they necessary, but their eventual success also proved to be a vital factor in the future course of the war in the Mediterranean and North Africa and probably in Europe as well. The situation in Malta at the time is an outstanding example of the price that must be paid for parsimony in times of peace. It must have been obvious that, in a war with Italy, Malta would be isolated for long periods and would, most certainly, be attacked from the air. Had steps been taken before the war – which could have been foreseen as early as 1935 – to accumulate provisions and supplies and to provide an effective air defence together with oil, ammunition and armaments, many lives, ships and planes might have been saved, and the Maltese people themselves might not have had to endure the severe hardships that they did.

The building of rock shelters on Malta had been proposed on numerous occasions from 1935 onwards by the three successive commanders of the Mediterranean Submarine Flotilla at an estimated cost of just £300,000, using mainly local labour. Those proposals were never accepted, however. Such shelters for submarines and minesweepers would not have been difficult to build, and would have proved a valuable asset to the defensive and offensive capability of the island. Although it is true that in the belated and half-hearted attempts at rearmament of the pre-war years, such things were all too easily swamped by more urgent matters closer to home, the highly strategic island had been left badly defended and totally unprepared for the terrible ordeals it ultimately suffered.

# 7 PQ 18: A Convoy to Hell

Some years before his death in 1980 my father told me about some of the wartime convoys in which he had sailed. Some of them have stayed with me through the years as being of particular poignancy and historical interest, encapsulating all the terror that lurking U-boats and diving torpedo-bombers can evoke.

One convoy in particular stands out in my memory, not only because of the horrendous circumstances surrounding it, but also because of the sea area in which it was fought. That convoy was code-numbered PQ 18, and sailed from Loch Ewe in September 1942. My father told me about it from his own perspective, but he was not in a position to tell me about the background. I have therefore researched the convoy more fully, mostly in memory of my father but also to bring home the contribution that was made to the war by Britain's merchant seamen who, having survived bombing, torpedoing, shelling and mining, simply went home for a few days' rest, before nonchalantly signing on again and going back to sea.

Between the east coast of Greenland and the north-west coast of Norway, a distance of almost 1,000 miles (1,850 km), are to be found some of the most violent maelstroms on earth. It is one of the most turbulent stretches of ocean in the world.

Across its intensely cold, leaden grey waste rages a never-ending succession of severe storms which drive before them stinging rain, hail, sleet and snow. As they hurtle north-eastwards, they raise the seas to incredible heights before eventually smashing themselves against the rugged north coast of Norway. From there, they race with a savage fury around the North Cape before entering the Barents Sea where, their business complete, the high barometric pressure over the polar icecap forces them into the upper atmosphere.

The warm, meandering waters of the Gulf Stream flow northwards along a boundary which separates the warm, saline water of the Sargasso Sea, from the colder, slightly fresher, Continental Slope Water to the north and west. Originating in the warm, subtropical waters of the Gulf of Mexico, it flows along the rim of the warm North Atlantic Water northwards from the Florida Straits along the continental slope of North America to Cape Hatteras. There it turns north-eastwards towards the Grand Banks off Newfoundland where it breaks up into swirling currents. At that point, a part of the current loops back on itself to flow south and east towards Spain and Portugal. Another part flows eastwards towards the west coast of Britain, while the remaining water flows north-east-wards as the North Atlantic Drift into the northernmost regions of the North Atlantic.

This pelagic current flows on past Iceland, the Shetlands and the Faeroes, reducing in both temperature and energy the further north and east it flows, but still incorporating a residual warmth as it flows past the Norwegian coast and around the North Cape. There, it encounters the high-pressure air mass and icecap of the high Arctic, where its less dense waters resist the incursion of the eutrophic polar seas.The colder waters of these polar seas slip unobtrusively beneath the warmer waters of the current, forming layers of differing densities. The current is cooled and its navigable width narrowed in winter to approximately 80 miles (150 km) between the North Cape and the southernmost edge of the pack-ice, before finally exhausting itself off the entrance to the Kola Inlet.

A similar very slow but perceptible encounter also takes place in the air above, where the less dense residue of tropical air succumbs to the cold, high-pressure winds which flow southwards from the North Pole. Churned up by the influence of the spinning earth, this collision of winds causes intense, very deep depressions, resulting in the storms of exceptional violence I have mentioned. Although the massive seas which these winds generate are not freezing when they break over the bows of ships at sea, they are turned very rapidly to ice as they are dashed into spray in the frigid air and come into contact with the vessels. Ships caught up in these storms are consequently prone to a build-up of ice on their upper works, until there is a heavy encrustation of obstinate ice which, in such freezing conditions, is almost like hardened steel. Under these conditions, when masts, cross-trees, stays, rigging, halyards, guard rails and companionway steps expand to three or four times their original size, and when weapons and deck machinery seizes up, watch-keeping becomes a savage, nightmarish ordeal of unimaginable misery. The weight caused by this rapid build-up of ice adds enormously to the seaman's ultimate horror – the very real risk of his ship capsizing in a sea so cold that it can kill within a very few minutes of immersion. That would be the kindest way to go, but if anyone who is able to get into a lifeboat is not rescued very quickly, their end would be a slow, painfully freezing ordeal.

According to my father it is this penetrating, omnipresent cold and the awful dead smell of the Arctic wastes that the men who ran the Russian convoys remember most – the misery of damp bulkheads and steel decks running with condensation, the chill, reeking odour intruding into every nook and cranny, the biting cold which froze the condensation solid and turned exhaled breath into rime and sea spray to ice, the intricate patterns that the ice formed on bridge screens and portholes. Everywhere, even when out of sight, the ice is omnipresent, forever beautiful, forever deadly.

Paradoxically, however, the high Arctic is not always a nightmare of penetrating cold and violent storms. Like the South Polar regions, the Arctic also has its more serene and tranquil countenance, a cold but calm, clear beauty during which the temperature inversions can increase visibility by up to 30 miles (55 km) or more. The air stream which predominates from the south-west, and which manifests itself in the violent gales is in stark contrast to the high pressure of the polar regions, and the barometric pressure can shift quite suddenly and dramatically. The mirror-calm sea on a perfect summer day can be marred by sudden fogs, during which only the topmasts of ships at sea can be seen from the air, but the Arctic can also produce many wonders, as in a ship surging through sea ice, rising and falling in a gentle swell, resembling the tinkle of breaking glass, the sudden loud crack of an ice floe breaking up, or the unforgettable vision of the aurora borealis undulating sinuously across the sky in a vast kaleidoscope of fantastic colours. The high Arctic in summer resonates with lonely sounds: the forlorn cry of a solitary seabird, or the echoing blow of a surfacing whale. But again like the South Polar regions, it can also echo with inactivity and virtual, unnerving silence, placing the nerves of already over-stretched, desperately tired men on a knife-edge of uncertainty.

This, then, was what the Russian convoys were all about. Add to that the misery of winter's constant darkness or the danger of twenty-four hours of summer daylight, the ever-present *Luftwaffe* operating from their bases in northern Norway, the lurking U-boat packs and the very real threat of the *Kriegsmarine*'s heavy units, their 'fleet in waiting', riding at anchor in the Norwegian fiords, and one has the kind of nightmare voyage which cannot even be imagined by anyone who was not involved. And it was into that deadly mix of weather, cold, enemy guns, bombs and torpedoes that PQ 18 sailed on that fateful September day.

Approximately 100 miles (160 km) east of Warsaw, the River Bug flows south to disgorge its waters into the Black Sea at Odessa. Along the eastern bank, on a 500 mile (800 km) front, Hitler placed more than 7,000 pieces of artillery and a large part of his *Wehrmacht* troops. In the early hours of the morning of 22 June 1941, the fierce bright light of those guns rent the night asunder, marking the opening shots of Operation Barbarossa. The German invasion of the Soviet Union had begun, an invasion which would eventually cost the lives of more than 20 million Russians – more Russians died during the siege of Stalingrad alone than in Britain and America combined, with an average loss of 4,000 people per day.

At that stage of the war, the Royal Air Force had already defeated the *Luftwaffe* in the skies over south-eastern England and, as a result, Hitler had postponed Operation Sea Lion, his proposed invasion of Britain, indefinitely. Britain, however, still stood alone against the might of Germany and, in spite of her victory, day and night bombing raids over Britain continued unabated. France, the Low Countries, Norway and the Balkan states had all been overrun, giving easy access to the Western Ocean for German U-boats and surface vessels and paving the way for Arctic submarine and air offences against Allied shipping from northern Norway. Operation Barbarossa was therefore fortuitous for Britain's hard-pressed military and political leaders insofar as it kept pressure off the western theatre of operations.

The Soviet Union crumbled before the German onslaught. It was in no position to put up much of a fight, partly because of Stalin's earlier purges of senior military officers, but mostly because it had not geared itself up for war, and its forces were poorly equipped. The Germans therefore advanced a staggering 600 miles (960 km) in just three months. Stalin, however, had made contingency plans for a mass evacuation to the icy wastes of Siberia, not just of people, but of whole factories. One thousand five hundred war factories were dismantled right under the noses of the Germans and put aboard 1,800 trains to be reassembled in a place where the Germans could not reach them. Whilst this was going on, however, the Soviet Union was in need of Western aid, and so early in 1942 Churchill went against the advice of the Admiralty and promised Stalin three convoys of war aid every two months, some of it from Britain but most from America.

The destination of these Arctic convoys was either Archangel or Murmansk, the former being seasonally and the other permanently ice-free. Murmansk's more temperate climate was offset by the fact that, in 1942, it was just 30 miles (48 km) from the front line. The Russians therefore preferred to use Archangel, undertaking to keep that port free of ice with ten ice-breakers. In the event, only two of them ever materialised, and after one of those was hit by a bomb in January, 1942, five vitally needed British merchant ships were frozen into the ice for the remainder of that winter.

As with the Western Ocean convoys during the early years of the war, the principal problem with the Arctic convoys was a shortage of escort vessels. Added to the natural hazards of the voyage, the inadequacy of the ice-breaking and discharging facilities, the lack of adequate medical care when they finally reached Russia and the failure of the Russians to provide coal, ballast, stores and fresh water for the return voyage, the U-boats, the planes and the ever-present threat of German heavy units, this made for a nightmare voyage of monstrous proportions.

The ships which were employed on the Russian convoys were some of the most modern of the British merchant fleet. They had to be specially fitted out in order to withstand the awful Arctic climate and mountainous seas, and once so equipped, they were virtually restricted to the Arctic run. Having all those merchant ships tied up every month became a severe drain on the hard-pressed merchant fleet.

German opposition did not have any impact upon the first twelve convoys, all of which reached their destination intact. PQ 12, however, was the last to do so. PQ 13 lost some 30,000 tons of merchant shipping and, from that point on, the losses increased. In June of that year, convoy PQ 17, consisting of thirty-eight merchant freighters and one tanker, set sail for Archangel. After the escort was ordered to withdraw and the convoy to scatter, it was decimated by German bombers and U-boats, losing a total of twenty-nine ships.

For the men of the Royal Navy that débâcle was a source of shame and extreme embarrassment. Upon their return to Scapa Flow, Rear-Admiral Burnett made himself even more unpopular when he tried to explain the reason for that order, but only succeeded in confirming his nickname of 'Bullshit Bob'.

Winston Churchill had much to think about after PQ 17, not least how to bolster the shattered morale of Allied merchant seamen and remove the shame felt by the men of the Royal Navy. The Admiralty had placed a complete embargo on further Russian convoys during the continuous hours of daylight of the northern summer, but Churchill instructed Admiral Pounds to fight yet another convoy through the Barents Sea with integral and heavy naval support. In his own words, 'If a naval battle should ensue, so much the better.'

To say that Admiral Pounds was not keen would be something of an understatement. There were several difficulties involved in such an undertaking, not least of which was the lack of facilities in Murmansk and Archangel should any of the naval vessels become damaged through enemy action. Moreover, the fleet aircraft carriers which Churchill had suggested were simply not available.

Churchill, however, chose to disregard Pounds's advice. Four photo-reconnaissance Spitfires, No. 210 Catalina Squadron and No. 144 and 255 (RAAF) Squadrons of Hampden bombers were sent to northern Russia to provide air cover over the Barents Sea. Several of the Hampdens were shot down by first the Germans then the Russians in what turned out to be a complete débâcle.

One of these, which was shot down over Norway, was carrying secret papers regarding the defensive plans for PQ 18 and QP 14 (the returning ships of PQ 17), which subsequently fell into German hands. Why such sensitive documents should have been put aboard an aircraft performing frontline duties is something of a mystery. Forewarned, the German High Command made preparations for attacks against PQ 18 with the *Luftwaffe* and *U-bootwaffe*, whilst QP 14 was to be attacked by the *Panzerschiff Scheer*, together with the cruisers *Hipper* and *Köln* which, covered by a destroyer screen, moved north to Altenfjord on 1 September.

Admiral Tovey, meanwhile, was preparing a strong destroyer escort screen which, whilst adhering to convoy defence, could be deployed independently if circumstances warranted. The battleship *King George V* was kept swinging at her anchorage in Scapa Flow, and units of the Home fleet were deployed under the command of Vice-Admiral Fraser (later to become Lord Fraser of the North Cape) in the battleship *Anson*.

Approximately 7 miles (11 km) to the north of Gairloch on Scotland's north-west coast, and some 20 miles (32 km) east of the Isle of Lewis, lies the deep-water inlet of Loch Ewe. It is about 20 miles (32 km) long from its sea outlet at Greenstone Point on the Minches to its eastern end, and about 5 miles (8 km) wide at its widest point. It was there that the thirty-four merchant ships destined to make up convoy PQ 18 were ordered to gather. The decision to assemble them there instead of the more usual anchorage at Hvalfjordur was taken as a precautionary measure designed to confuse an enemy which was already in possession of all the details about PQ 18. In any case, the convoy was obliged to sail first to Hvalfjordur in order to join up with several Russian merchantmen waiting there.

For the first time on the Russian convoys, PQ 18 was to sail in company with an escort carrier. Commanded by Commander A.P. Colthurst, the fleet aircraft carrier HMS *Avenger* was a light, unarmoured vessel of 8,200 tons. Designed on the hull of a merchant vessel, she had been built in the USA for the Royal Navy under the lend-lease arrangements. A stubby, ungraceful little ship, she had a maximum speed of just 17 knots (31 kph) and an overall length of 468 feet (142.6 m). She carried a maximum of fifteen aircraft, but had only a half hangar under the after end of her flight deck. She embarked twelve Sea Hurricane fighters and three Fairey Swordfish biplanes, the archaic torpedo-bombers which played such a major role in the destruction of the German battleship *Bismarck*, and which were being tried out for the first time as an anti-submarine aircraft. However, the young Fleet Air Arm pilots who were to fly those aircraft would have to work out their own tactics as they went along and learn the hard way. *Avenger* was to have her own close escort of two hunt class destroyers, HMS *Wheatland* and HMS *Wilton*.

The fighting destroyer escort (FDE) was under the command of Rear-Admiral Robert Burnett ('Bullshit Bob') in his flagship, HMS *Scylla*, a light anti-aircraft cruiser fitted with eight 4.5-inch high-angled guns. The destroyer screen was divided into Force A, comprising HMS *Onslow*, commanded by H.T. Armstrong, Senior Officer, Captain (D), HMS *Onslaught*, HMS *Opportune*, HMS *Offa*, HMS *Ashanti*, HMS *Eskimo*, HMS *Somali* and HMS *Tartar*. Force B was made up of HMS *Milne*, commanded by I.M.R. Campbell, Senior Officer, Captain (D), HMS *Marne*, HMS *Martin*, HMS *Meteor*, HMS *Faulkner*, HMS *Fury*, HMS *Impulsive* and HMS *Intrepid*.

Because Admiral Burnett's destroyer force would need frequent refuelling, a third force designated Force P, made up of the fleet oilers, *Blue Ranger* and *Oligarch*, along with the destroyers HMS *Cowdray*, HMS *Oakley*, HMS *Windsor* and HMS *Worcester*, were sent ahead to Stor Fjord, Spitzbergen, as an advanced refuelling force. The tankers *Grey Ranger* and *Black Ranger* were to form Force Q, which was to be a part of PQ 18.

Fuel rationing was of the essence. Because of the U-boat war in the Caribbean and the Gulf of Mexico between January and August 1942, the total reserve of fuel oil left in Britain in August of that year was just three weeks' supply, and although that situation was considerably eased when America finally had a convoy system working in the Caribbean, the continuing Battle of the Atlantic coupled with several heavy German U-cruisers operating around the Cape of Good Hope and the Mozambique Channel, kept Britain desperately short of fuel supplies for quite some time afterwards. The fact that the ships were operating at high speed, plus the fact that they were to be under way for a much longer period than was usual, meant that the rationing was critical for PQ 18. Moreover, since the seasonal retreat of the ice during early autumn permitted convoys to sail much further north, they did so for added safety, but that only added considerable distance to an already lengthy voyage.

Anticipating another PQ 17, a formidable array of the *Luftwaffe* made ready for their attack on PQ 18 from their bases around Norway's North Cape. Forty-two

Heinkel He 111H-6 torpedo-bombers of KG 26 were supported by thirty-five Junkers Ju 88A-17s of KG 26. They were the faster version of the Ju 88 which had been specially flown north from France for the specific purpose of destroying PQ 18. Supporting those attack aircraft were the long-range Condors and Blohm and Voss flying boats, further supported by Ju 88 bombers of KG 30.

The German plan was to use a tactic known as the 'golden lange', also known as the 'golden comb', a joint low-level torpedo attack led by the Heinkels and supported by diversionary, medium-level dive-bombing attacks. It was envisaged that such a tactic would disrupt the convoy's defences and enable the torpedo-bombers to duck under the radar screens to press home a devastating onslaught – a tactic in which the Heinkel torpedo-bomber pilots had become exceptionally skilled.

PQ 18's close escort group had been placed under the command of Commander A.B. Russell aboard the destroyer *Malcolm*. It included the ageing *Achates*, the anti-aircraft vessels *Ulster Queen* and *Alynbank*, the corvettes *Bergamot*, *Bluebell*, *Bryony* and *Camellia*, the minesweepers *Gleaner*, *Harrier* and *Sharpshooter*, and the submarines P 614 and P 615. In addition, there were four anti-submarine trawlers, the rescue ship *Copeland* and three motor minesweepers which were being transferred to the Russian Navy and operated in the convoy as rescue ships. The submarines *Tribune*, *Tigris* and P 34 were patrolling off Narvik, but were later transferred to the North Cape, there to be reinforced by the *Unique*, the *Unreal*, P 456, P 540 and the Free French minelayer *Rubis*.

With my father on board, the 6,327-ton *Empire Snow*, her cavernous holds packed with TNT, HE bombs and shells, Matilda tanks and trucks together with a deck cargo of crated Spitfires and Hurricanes, prepared to get under way from Loch Ewe on the cold, grey, blustery morning of 2 September 1942. Her position in the convoy was to be Number 31, a position which placed her in the first row of column 3 on the port flank.

Other merchant ships in the convoy were:

### British
    *Empire Baffin*, 6,800 tons
    *Empire Beaumont*, 7,044 tons
    *Empire Tristram*, 7,167 tons
    *Empire Morn*, 7,090 tons
    *Empire Stevenson*, 6,202 tons
    *Athel Templar*, 8,992 tons
    *Temple Arch* (commodore vessel), 5,138 tons
    *Ocean Faith*, 7,137 tons
    *Goolistan*, 5,851 tons
    *Dan-Y-Bryn*, 5,117 tons

### American
    *Kentucky*, 5,446 tons
    *Charles R. McCormick*, 6,027 tons
    *St Olaf*, 7,191 tons
    *Exford*, 4,969 tons

*Hollywood*, 5,498 tons
*Patrick Henry*, 7,190 tons
*Esek Hopkins*, 7,191 tons
*Meanticut*, 6,061 tons
*Sahale*, 5,028 tons
*Lafayette*, 5,887 tons
*Campfire*, 5,671 tons
*Schoharie*, 4,971 tons
*Nathaniel Greene*, 7,176 tons
*John Penn*, 7,177 tons
*Virginia Dare*, 7,177 tons
*William Moultrie*, 7,177 tons
*Wacosta*, 5,432 tons
*Mary Luckenbach*, 5,049 tons
*Oregonian*, 4,862 tons
*Oliver Elsworth*, 7,191 tons

**Panamanian**

*Afrikander*, 5,441 tons
*MacBeth*, 4,885, tons
*White Clover*, 5,497 tons

**Russian**

**(Joined convoy at Iceland)**

*Stalingrad*, 3,569 tons
*Sukhona*, 3,124 tons
*André Martin*, 2,352 tons
*Komiles*, 3,962 tons
*Petrovski*, 3,771 tons
*Tbisi*, 7,169 tons

The *Empire Morn* was a catapult aircraft merchantman (CAM) equipped with a Hurricane fighter.

A moderate gale of force 7–8 blew steadily across the leaden grey waters of the Minches, the seas rising ominously as the 34-ship convoy, under the command of Rear-Admiral E.K. Boddam-Whetham, DSO, RNR, prepared to form up in columns in readiness for the first leg of their voyage to Archangel via Iceland. There, at Hvalfjordur, they were scheduled to pick up the Russian freighters which were to join them before turning north through the Denmark Strait.

Operation EV finally began to move at 16.10 hours on the evening of 2nd September, and as early dusk began to settle over the water, they headed north for their rendezvous with the various other freighters and warships that would finally make up convoy PQ 18. The merchantmen were stationed in two columns for the night passage, and speed was at 8 knots (15 kph). They were bound for the White Sea port of Archangel and the unknown and, as an indication of the kind of weather they could expect, as they left the sea loch, the barometer began dropping like an elevator in free-fall.

By the time they had cleared the Minches and left Cape Wrath and the Butt of

Lewis astern, they were pounding through high winds and heavy seas of severe gale force 9 to storm force 10. The heaped up seas, rising to 60 feet (18 m) or more raced across the ocean with incredible power, battering the ships as they steered a course of 313 degrees, which would ultimately take them to the anchorage at Hvalfjordur, 700 miles (1,300 km) distant.

The severe weather conditions almost immediately scattered the formation, and the task of keeping thirty-four slow, cumbersome merchant ships within sight became a nightmare for Commodore Boddam-Whetham. The American and Panamanian ships in particular played havoc as they had no previous experience of convoy work, paid very little attention to signals, and knew virtually nothing about station-keeping. The only knowledge they had was based upon the rumours they had heard about PQ 17 which, unfairly, were more than a little scathing about the Royal Navy as a protective force. The American merchantmen, having entered the war just nine months earlier, did not have the battle-hardiness of their British counterparts, who already had four years' experience during the First World War and three years during the Second.

The merchant ships were very soon in trouble. The *Campfire* reported a south-westerly gale and very heavy seas, whilst a further two ships had been observed hoisting their 'out of command' signals. Aboard the American liberty ship *Patrick Henry*, the wind was reported as force 9–10 with a rough and very dangerous beam sea. The forecastle gun crew had been taken off duty because it had become too dangerous for them to maintain their exposed positions. By 20.00 hours that evening, her master had had more than enough of trying to hold his position in the line. He reduced speed and put the helm over to port, leaving the convoy. She rejoined the following morning, but she was not the only freighter to be left astern or to choose her own course.

The first leg of that voyage was a nightmare for the ships of the Royal Navy. Whilst for the big merchantmen the gale was no more than an uncomfortable experience, for the crews of the smaller naval ships there was quite a considerable degree of danger. Pitching like wild stallions over one sea and going straight through the following two, the destroyers were rolling their scuppers under all the way across the 'Rose Garden', the stretch of water between Iceland, the Orkneys and the Shetlands, which had been peppered with British mines, making life aboard them a dangerous misery of cold, hunger, fear and extreme endurance.

So great was the storm that it delayed the progress of the convoy and they were thirty-six hours late for their rendezvous with their ocean escorts. Despite the poor weather, the convoy could not conceal itself from the watchful eyes of the German U-boat crews, and even before it reached Iceland, it had been spotted and reported by Teichert, commanding U-456. Several submarine sightings kept them all on their toes on that first leg, but good counter-attacking by the escorts kept the U-boats at a safe distance.

The dark, grey morning of the 7th found PQ 18 rounding the south-west corner of Iceland at Reykjanes, and the various complicated arrangements were put into action for the rendezvous with the remainder of the convoy and its ocean escort group, which comprised the *Ulster Queen*, the *Alynbank*, two anti-aircraft vessels, three destroyers, four corvettes and four armed trawlers. The local escorts were then sent into Hvalfjordur and the close escort, together with the anti-aircraft ships and the Russian merchantmen, were finally rounded up. Then the whole armada set course northward through the Denmark Strait along the west coast of Iceland.

At 06.00 hours on the 8th, the two British submarines P 614 and P 615 had sailed from Seidisfjord, escorted by *Sharpshooter* and, at around midnight on the 8th/9th, they reinforced the convoy at 68°36'N 17°55'W. Then the *Bryony* took over and her two surfaced submarines occupied positions to port and starboard astern.

On the 9th, Rear-Admiral Burnett, in command of the FDE and flying his flag in the cruiser *Scylla*, joined the convoy, along with the escort carrier *Avenger* and ten of the eighteen destroyers which had been selected for the operation. The other eight had forged ahead to refuel from the tankers *Oligarch* and *Blue Ranger*, which were already stationed at Spitzbergen.

Even though PQ 18 was already covered by a powerful naval force, another five cruisers and five destroyers had been made available for its defence. The cruisers *Cumberland* and *Sheffield* with the destroyers *Amazon*, *Echo*, *Eclipse*, *Venomous* and *Bulldog* patrolled off Spitzbergen, whilst the other three cruisers, the *Norfolk*, the *Suffolk* and the *London* were in a supporting group off Bear Island.

More distant cover had been made available in the form of the battleships *Duke of York* and *Anson*, the cruiser *Jamaica* and the destroyers *Keppel*, *Montrose*, *Mackay* and *Bramham*, all under the command of Admiral Sir Bruce Fraser, flying his flag in *Anson*. That force was operating between Seidisfjord and Jan Mayen Island, but was not continously at sea because of the deployment of such a large number of destroyers to the FDE.

Ten hours after leaving Hvalfjordur, the convoy rounded the northern tip of Iceland at Straumnes, and there set a north-easterly course towards Jan Mayen Island and Spitzbergen. Eight hundred miles (1,482 km) later, in the Greenland Sea on the 10th, powerful winds raised a high, rolling sea with heavy and persistent rain which, in the late afternoon, gave way to a grey blanket of fog which fell over the ocean like an opaque shroud, but which at least hid them from enemy eyes. The ships lumbered and wallowed their cold, weary way north and east while the destroyers in the outer screen criss-crossed astern investigating Asdic contacts. The submarines *Tigris* and *Tribune* both made unsuccessful attempts to torpedo the three heavy German units *Köln*, *Hipper* and *Scheer*, which were at the time moving north in the direction of the Barents Sea.

The morning of the 11th dawned as grey, bleak and gloomy as the 10th. The heavy rain squalls had given way to equally heavy showers of snow. Station-keeping amongst the American and Panamanian ships remained poor and the Commodore, his broad pennant flying from the foremast of the *Temple Arch*, had to chastise his wayward charges on many occasions, warning them in the process that enemy action was virtually certain within the following forty-eight hours. 'Ships,' he signalled, 'must be kept closed up to two cables and be prepared to assist with mass fire.'

The M Class vessels of the 3rd Flotilla were by far the most potent of Admiral Burnett's destroyers because, although they did not possess a main armament of dual-purpose guns, their 4.7-inch weapons could elevate to an angle of 50 degrees, and on their decks, they carried a formidable array of torpedo tubes. With that in mind the Admiral left the convoy in the *Scylla* at 11.40 hours, taking with him the *Martin*, the *Meteor*, the *Milne*, the *Marne* and the *Intrepid* to refuel from the oilers *Oligarch* and *Blue Ranger*, both of which were then at anchor in Axelfjord, Spitzbergen, in an attempt to bunker before the convoy suffered its first airborne assault. They entered the Bell Sound on the following evening, and had bunkered and sailed by 14.00 hours on Sunday, the 13th. By that time, however, PQ 18 had suffered its first casualties.

Saturday 12 September dawned intensely cold under a low cover of overcast and intermittent snow showers, but with a moderate north-westerly breeze of force 5 and good visibility clear to the horizon. It was by an unfortunate coincidence that a Blohm and Voss BV 138 dropped out of the cloud cover and spotted the convoy. The *Avenger* immediately flew off a flight of four Sea Hurricanes but, much to their chagrin, they failed to destroy their shadower, which easily evaded their efforts in the overcast. One tiny morsel of good news was that aerial reconnaissance had revealed that the *Hipper*, the *Scheer* and the *Köln* were still snugly tucked away in Altenfjord.

Throughout that day, Huff-Duff (High-Frequency Direction Finding) bearings had betrayed the presence of the expected U-boats, causing frequent alarms and depth-charge attacks by the outer destroyer screen, which in turn created a tidal-wave of tension within the convoy ranks. At 21.00 hours, just as the *Faulkner* was crossing ahead of the convoy at high speed, her Asdic located the firm echo of a submarine at a range of just over 2,000 yards (1.8 km). Her skipper, Scott-Montcrieff, immediately went into attack mode and, dropping depth-charges a few minutes later, was actually in the act of turning in a tight circle to deliver a second pattern when his acoustics picked up the unmistakable sounds of a U-boat breaking up underwater. Moments later, the nauseating stench of oil hung in the air, as a grey slick spread itself across the swells in the evening twilight, the only grave marker of Bohmann's U-88 and its forty-man crew.

At 08.15 hours, one of the Swordfish spotted a U-boat on the surface some 20 miles (37 km) astern of the convoy, patiently following it and transmitting homing signals in the classic manner used by the U-boats to call up other boats in the area. Spotting the Swordfish from a distance of about 3 miles (5.5 km) the U-boat dived, leaving the aircraft with no accurate position to select for a successful depth-charge attack.

By that time at least two of the U-boat pack were submerged to periscope depth and in good attacking positions astern of the convoy. Both U-408's and U-589's captains chose almost the same moment to press their firing buttons at their selected targets which were freighters in column 10. At 08.55 hours, two of their torpedoes struck home. The 3,560-ton Russian steamer *Stalingrad*, which had been steaming in position 103, was hit by a single torpedo on her starboard side, sinking her within fifteen minutes in a maelstrom of swirling water and debris. A female mate was pregnant at the time and actually went into labour when the torpedo hit. Her child was stillborn but, in spite of the ship having gone down so quickly, it proved to be the only casualty. Rescue ships and escorts were quickly on the scene, picking up every member of the crew uninjured.

The second victim of that salvo was the American liberty freighter *Oliver*

*Elsworth*, a vessel of some 7,000 tons. Proceeding at a speed of 9 knots (17 kph) in position 105 at the rear of the starboard column, she was loaded to her marks with a full cargo of crated aircraft and ammunition. The torpedo struck on her starboard side between her Numbers 4 and 5 holds. The damage was almost entirely below the surface and therefore no assessment could be made. Her captain gave orders to abandon ship, and with the exception of one of the armed guard party, all got safely away in the lifeboats.

Throughout the remainder of that day, the persistence of the U-boats in attempting to penetrate the strong close-escort screen was matched only the skill, determination and alertness of the destroyer crews, and the two merchantmen were their only victims for that day.

After some high-speed refuelling in Bell Sound, Rear-Admiral Burnett sped back to rejoin PQ 18. At 11.30 hours, he received the news of the two torpedoed merchantmen and increased speed in order to make as early a rendezvous as possible with the convoy. With the frigid Arctic waters teeming with U-boats and the grey skies above full of enemy planes, PQ 18 was then very much at bay. By 14.00 hours, Burnett's flotilla had sighted the masts of PQ 18 off the port bow.

Elation very soon turned to concern, however, when *Avenger* was seen from *Scylla*'s bridge to draw out of the convoy and fly off five of her Sea Hurricanes. The *Luftwaffe* was about to take a hand in the proceedings. At 14.00 hours, a large group of enemy aircraft were reported heading towards the convoy at a range of 60 miles (110 km). Fifteen minutes later, another group of Sea Hurricanes were flown off to patrol in the direction of the contact and, at 15.00 hours, six separate groups of enemy aircraft were being reported by radar. At 15.30 hours, the Sea Hurricanes were reporting that they were in contact with five Ju 88s, which they chased off into cloud cover. In doing so, however, they had expended all of their ammunition and no more fighters were then available to reinforce them.

The first of the German bombers began an attack on PQ 18 at 16.00 hours, which continued intermittently for thirty minutes. Only about six of the Ju 88s managed to break through the defending fighters, however, while the rest played games of hide-and-seek in and out of the cloud cover. The six attacking planes made individual bombing runs out of the cloud cover but failed to score a hit because of the heavy concentration of intense AA fire from all the ships in the convoy. But worse was to come.

A German force was scheduled to strike at the convoy later that afternoon. It was to consist of twenty-eight He 111 torpedo-bombers from Bardufoss in two waves immediately after 111/KG30 had made its diversionary attack with twenty Ju 88 torpedo-bombers of 111/KG26 commanded by *Hauptmann* Klaus Nocken, all from Banak airfield near to Hammerfest, with seventeen Ju 88s of 1/KG30 from the same base. A very special effort had been called for to eliminate the aircraft carrier. When the torpedo-bombers were within half an hour's flying time of the target, they were to be met by one of the shadowing Ju 88s, which would then lead them straight to the convoy to help in the surprise attack.

It was late into the afternoon when the Heinkels took off from Bardufoss and flew down Malangerfjord and out over the lonely, windswept Lofoten Islands to form up before their rendezvous with Nocken's force. The attack was scheduled to hit

PQ 18 about 400 miles (740 km) from their bases, and the Heinkels and Junkers flew at economical speed to conserve fuel. At low level, they thundered north-west across the icy waves towards the distant convoy for two hours. The cloud base had been reported at 2,400 feet (730 m) with a cold, light rain and drizzle which soon reduced visibility to a mere 6 miles (11 km).

*Hauptmann* Klumper's force at first missed both the convoy and the guiding aircraft. But a few minutes later, and almost at the extreme endurance range for their outward leg, the formation turned east and soon sighted the solid phalanx of PQ 18 below them. They failed to find the *Avenger*, however, and in trying to locate her they simply wasted time and precious fuel. At the same time, the flak from the outer destroyer screen was becoming ever more intense. Klumper climbed to 150 feet (45 m) in an effort to avoid the worst of it and in a single line abreast, the 'golden comb' pressed in towards the starboard flank. The time was 16.27 hours.

The men of the convoy watched fascinated as the 44-plane formation rose up over the rim of the earth and deployed towards them like a flight of gigantic nightmare locusts, extending far out on either side of the convoy. Their stomachs turned somersaults as the planes lined up in a classic attack formation, rising and falling like the waves beneath them as they pressed on in perfect unison, seemingly oblivious to the withering fire from the escorts and merchant ships.

A massive flash of flame tore the heavens apart as the destroyers and merchantmen on the starboard outer screen opened up with every weapon which could be brought to bear, from 4.7-inch to 20-mm Oerlikons, 2-pounder pom-poms to light machine-guns and everything in between. Gunfire from the large screen was intense as the torpedo-bombers flew in at low enough altitude for even the destroyers' main armament of low-angled 4.7-inch guns, which could only elevate to 40 degrees in most of the vessels, to join in the barrage.

Since that cold, dismal afternoon there have been conflicting reports of the number of enemy aircraft shot down in that first attack. British naval historians claim that just five were destroyed. However, Captain Richard Hocken of the American liberty ship *William Moultrie* was awarded the Mercantile Marine Distinguished Service Medal for shooting down three torpedo-bombers and assisting in the destruction of six more. Another American ship, the *Nathaniel Greene*, claimed four destroyed, and the American *Virginia Dare*, on her maiden voyage with a 'green' crew credited themselves with the destruction of no less than seven. These were quite remarkable claims when one considers that, with more than eighteen warships and merchant vessels firing into the formation with a wide variety of weapons, it must have been nigh on impossible to be positive that it was one ship's shells out of all the thousands that scored the hits.

The contingency plan for a massed torpedo attack which had previously been made by Boddam-Whetham and his staff was simply a forty-five degree turn to port or starboard as the situation demanded, using the appropriate sound signals and a single flag hoist. The success or failure of those signals was entirely dependent on good watch-keeping, instant responses and a repetition of the signals down the line of ships. A vast pall of thick, black, acrid smoke hung over the convoy like a gyrating curtain on the starboard flank as Boddam-Whetham made his signal, and the convoy duly made a forty-five degree turn to port. Boddam-Whetham was horrified, however, to learn that the ninth and tenth columns had failed to respond and the outer starboard ships which had failed to execute the turn were about to bear the full fury of the attack.

Criss-crossed with continuous streams of crimson tracer and interspersed with puffballs of bursting shells, the sea had become an inferno of burning oil and exploding ammunition as swarms of torpedo-bombers thundered in to the attack, diving into separate groups as they flew past the *Scylla* at masthead height. Undeterred by the prodigious gunfire, each plane dropped two torpedoes as they came into position, then banked steeply as they swept off astern, some of them on fire as they roared off leaving a vast trail of smoke and flame in their wakes. Those that were still intact pressed home their attack with suicidal daring as they flew in amongst the ships, dropping torpedoes at very close range. One flew so close that its torpedo failed to drop into the water at all but instead, dropped through the hatch of the *Wacosta* and exploded inside her hull.

Ahead in the ninth column, the *Empire Stevenson* was suddenly enveloped in a gigantic plume of smoke and flame, which seemed to rise for thousands of feet into the air. When it cleared, it left only a thick, burning, evil-smelling oil-slick on the heaving surface of the sea. The ship had been pulverised and scattered like so much chaff in the wind by the tremendous power of the explosion, and there was no trace of her whatsoever. A massive column of smoke and dull red flame lit up the inverted bowl of sky for seconds only, then there was silence. Everyone who witnessed that spectacle became momentarily dumbstruck with awe and shock. Such was the awful price that the merchant seamen paid for carrying explosives to the Russian front. There were no survivors from the *Empire Stevenson*, but all the crew of the *Wacosta* were quickly rescued.

Loaded with tanks and war materials, the Panamanian freighter *MacBeth*, the second ship in the tenth column, succumbed to two torpedoes which came in with startling rapidity, ripping a massive hole in her starboard side. Then, just moments later the *Oregonian*, which had been plodding along just ahead of the *MacBeth*, quickly capsized after three torpedoes stove in the whole length of her starboard side. Just twenty-seven of her fifty-five man crew were subsequently rescued by the *St Kenan*, many of them in a fearful condition from wounds and from having been immersed in the freezing sea and ingesting fuel oil.

Torpedoes also hit the Panamanian ship *Afrikander*, which had been on charter to the US Maritime Commission. Both were quickly abandoned as they sank, their crews being picked up by the small vessels of the close escort. With the exception of the *Mary Luckenbach*, the two outer columns had been completely annihilated. The *Empire Beaumont* had been set on fire after a torpedo had struck the only hold not containing explosives. She was successfully abandoned and her crew rescued.

Less fortunate were the crew of the American liberty freighter *John Penn*. Three men who were on duty in the engine-room were killed instantly when two torpedoes exploded in their midst. With billowing smoke and high-pressure steam pouring out through the rent in her side, she heeled over as the ocean thundered through her hull, but although the torpedoes did not sink her, she was later sent to the bottom with gunfire from one of the warships, as there was no question of salvage.

Amidst the confusion of roaring aircraft, exploding bombs, blaring sirens, venting high-pressure steam, chattering machine-guns and booming heavier guns, the *Copeland*, with the trawlers and smaller vessels, picked up merchant sailors from rafts, boats and out of the freezing sea. Their minds full of nightmares and wild imaginings, some of the men claimed to have seen periscopes amongst the convoy. Whatever the truth, the stark fact was that eight ships had been lost within the space of fifteen minutes and, despite the claims of the American merchant captains and gunners, German losses amounted to just five aircraft.

The fact that the other seven victims of the attack did not suffer the same fate as the *Empire Stevenson* seemed to disappoint the Soviet Admiral Arseni Golovko, a spiteful man who sneeringly recorded: 'The only one of the first ten to sink at once was the *Stalingrad*. The remaining nine, flying Allied flags remained afloat and were finished off with gunfire from the escorts. Evidently, it causes them no great heartache to complete the destruction of vessels loaded with cargo for us.' He made no mention of the civilian merchant seamen whose lives had been sacrificed to carry that cargo.

As the surviving German bombers winged their way swiftly into the distant gloom, surrounded by the last few isolated pockmarks of long-range flak, they left behind them a stricken convoy, stunned by the speed and extent of their power. With the exception of the American liberty freighter *Mary Luckenbach*, which was later placed in column eight, astern of the *Dan-Y-Bryn* and ahead of the *Virginia Dare*, columns nine and ten had ceased to exist, and where minutes before had steamed eight proud ships, there remained only a sea of burning, foul-smelling oil and debris, little clusters of men in the water, some of them already dead from injuries or cold or both, and the acrid stench of charred and burned flesh. The time was 16.40 hours.

The next attack was, by comparison, a half-hearted affair carried out by Heinkel float planes of the *Kriegsmarine* which hovered just outside the range of the convoy's guns before going in in two groups, which were subsequently driven off without loss. One He 115 was attacked by four of the *Avenger*'s Sea Hurricanes of 802 Squadron, but managed to escape after shooting down 802's leader, Lieutenant E.V. Taylor. Shortly afterwards, the *Faulkner* reported enemy aircraft dropping mines ahead of the convoy. This caused a bold alteration of course to be made to port until 20.15 hours when the original course was resumed.

By 20.30 hours the skies had darkened substantially as a dozen He 115s from Billefjord approached from the south-west. Once again, the ships put up a fierce barrage, which drove the attackers off. One of the planes plummeted into the sea alongside *Opportune* and another was shot down in flames. While a British destroyer rescued the crew of the first plane to go down, the crew of the second were picked up by U-504, which was trailing the convoy at the time.

The morning of the 14th dawned as grey, black and hopeless as the 13th, and started with another blow to the already devastated convoy. Returning to her station from investigating an Asdic contact she had been pursuing, HMS *Impulsive* obtained a second echo and had already begun a depth-charge run when, at 03.30 hours, the U-boat she had been trying to destroy fired at the target she had been stalking, the tanker *Athel Templar*. The *Impulsive* then lost the contact as

*Korvettenkapitän* Brandenburg dived U-475 under the convoy, hiding the sounds of her screws amidst those of the surface ships.

Hit in the engine-room, it was indeed fortunate that the tanker's volatile cargo did not explode on contact, but the fires which then roared out of control as her cargo ignited soon made it impossible for her crew to do more than abandon ship. They were picked up some little time later by the *Copeland* and the *Offa*. The close proximity of other U-boats which were in contact with the convoy discounted any attempt to salvage the burning vessel, and the minesweeper *Harrier* was ordered to sink the 9,000-ton ship and her cargo of fuel oil. Blazing furiously from stem to stern by that time, the tanker was left astern, burning for several hours like a monstrous funeral pyre in the early Arctic dawn as her decks, superstructure and steel companion ladders twisted and buckled into grotesque shapes before she finally sank. Only then was the conflagration extinguished by the cold, grey waters of the Barents Sea.

At approximately 09.45 hours that same morning, the duty Swordfish from the *Avenger* reported a surfaced submarine 6 miles (11 km) away on the starboard bow of the convoy and marked the spot with a smoke float. HMS *Onslow* was despatched to locate the float and sighted the U-boat, which immediately crash-dived. At about 10.50 hours, the *Onslow* picked up a firm echo on her Asdic at a range of 1,900 yards (1,740 m). Captain Armstrong immediately gave chase, closing the gap very rapidly and, after dropping a pattern of shallow-set depth-charges, proceeded to saturate the area. At first just oil and air bubbled to the surface but, aware of the tricks employed by U-boat skippers in their efforts to escape, Armstrong was not satisfied and persisted with his attack. His persistence finally paid off when a tremendous explosion heaved the ocean upwards as though an underwater earthquake had taken place and great geysers of escaping air added to the turbulence. Fuel oil, wooden crates, food, vegetables and a variety of other debris appeared on the surface, confirming the destruction of one more wolf of the sea.

After intermittent air attacks throughout that morning, twenty-two He 111s and eighteen Ju 88 torpedo-bombers under the command of Klumper and Bloedorn flew in from Bardufoss at 14.00 hours. Making a wide sweep around the convoy, they attacked from ahead in the mistaken belief that the carrier was in that position. Instead, they found the *Scylla*'s high-angle anti-aircraft guns waiting for them, and four Hurricanes hot on their tails. Impervious to the fact that they were then diving into their own flak, the Hurricanes followed the German planes down, pouring their own lightweight fire into their fuselages.

Thwarted by the ferocity of the unexpected defensive barrage, very few of the German bombers were able to manoeuvre into a position where their torpedoes could be dropped accurately. Others, not prepared to take their chance amongst the heavy concentration of tracer shells, banked their aircraft and flew past without dropping their torpedoes at all, whilst others still simply let theirs go at random in order to lighten their loads and escape more quickly.

Just one ship was hit as the random torpedoes sped haphazardly through the convoy ranks, but that with spectacular and terrifying results. The *Mary Luckenbach* was blown to pieces with the most horrendous of explosions, which seemed to rock the very heavens with echoing sound waves reverberating upwards and outwards. From the bridge of the *Empire Snow*, all that could be seen was a vast column of smoke, flames and water which rose high into the frigid air, carrying an enemy aircraft along with it which simply disintegrated in the fierce heat of the gargantuan blast. The ship, so my father told me, simply vanished into thin air as though she had never existed. She had been the last survivor of the ill-fated ninth and tenth columns.

In the subdued silence and inertia that followed, time seemed to have stood still, as the men aboard the other ships that were close enough to be able to see, watched an enormous column of smoke billow upwards, slow, thick and black, interlaced with long tongues of crimson flames. Gradually, from the overhanging top of the pyre, there drifted down a thick veil of dust, just like a shower of volcanic rain after an eruption, amongst some larger pieces of debris. Two gunners who had been badly wounded by flying debris aboard the *Nathaniel Greene* were taken off by HMS *Onslaught*.

Lieutenant Billings of the *Nathaniel Greene* recalled:

> All the cargo boxes on deck were smashed by the concussion. Some ten doors and bulkheads were blown in and smashed. The insides of many cabins were a shambles. Cast iron ventilators had buckled into the most grotesque shapes. Shrapnel and scraps covered the decks. A piece of angle-iron penetrated the starboard four-inch ready-box and went through a shell, missing the primer by less than an eighth of an inch. Glass ports were smashed, the hospital aft was practically demolished. All compasses had been put out of adjustment. The pointer's platform on the 4-inch gun had completely disappeared and the pointer's sight almost ruined. A side plate about two feet square was found on deck. Bullets were being picked up all over the decks. There was tank ammunition everywhere. How everyone topside wasn't killed or seriously injured was a minor miracle.

When the convoy was off Hope Island, reports were received that the German battleship *Tirpitz* was missing from her anchorage in Altenfjord. Twenty-three Hampden torpedo-bombers were consequently scrambled at 05.00 hours and flew in reconnaissance with the intention of intercepting and attacking the German ship if she was at sea. They found nothing, however, and returned to Vaenga at 15.00 hours. The *Tirpitz* was not at sea at all, but in an adjacent fjord on a training operation.

At 08.00 hours on the 15th, another attack by German torpedo-bombers developed, but Sea Hurricanes were immediately scrambled and, combined with a devastating rate of fire from the anti-aircraft guns of the convoy, rendered the three-hour attack erratic and fruitless.

The day was quiet and calm with a monochrome, leaden grey sea under a lowering curtain of dark cloud. Sea-smoke rose in wraithlike tendrils as U-boat alarms went on throughout the day. By 16.00 hours, the weather began to worsen and, as the wind speed steadily increased, the lumbering merchantmen began rolling and pitching into the rising sea. The smaller escort vessels suffered even more. The massive seas went inboard flooding mess rooms and accommodation, and the crews were always soaking wet, intensely cold and always hungry, having to exist on corned-beef and hardtack because the seas extinguished the galley fires.

At 03.30 hours on the 16th, *Korvettenkapitän* Brandenburg in U-457 was depth-charged and sunk by Lieutenant-Commander Roper in the destroyer *Impulsive*. At 09.00 hours, under an escort of Russian-based RAF Catalinas, the convoy altered course to the south and ran into a light but very cold mist which had blown up on the rising wind. The ships ploughed steadily south into the teeth of a south-easterly gale of force 8 accompanied by freezing rain and mist. The penetrating cold, exacerbated by the severe wind-chill and exceedingly cold rain and mist made life a misery for the unfortunate seamen of both services, especially on the open bridges of the warships.

During the eight to twelve watch on the 17th, the Russian destroyers *Gremyashchi* and *Sokrushitelni* joined the convoy, and twenty-four hours later it was further reinforced by the *Kuibyshev* and the *Uritski*. At 06.00 hours on the 18th, lookouts sighted Cape Kanin, and the *Luftwaffe* made a further attack. Twelve He 111s made low-level runs from astern whilst Ju 88s of KG30 joined in. The Heinkels swept in, almost skimming the sea at masthead height, and divided just astern of the convoy before dropping their torpedoes. Just one ship was hit in that attack, the American freighter *Kentucky*, struck on her starboard side just below the bridge. The resulting blast threw tarpaulins and hatch covers off the Number 2 hatch and high into the air, demolishing a part of the port bridge wing as they flew in all directions. Fire then broke out as electrical circuits were wrecked and water poured into the ship in an unstoppable flood. The engines then stopped and the crew abandoned ship. They were all later picked up in small boats from the rescue vessels despite the adverse weather conditions. A salvage party was then arranged and were actually in the process of preparing to pass a tow line to the crippled vessel when a lone Ju 88 dropped two bombs into her. They exploded aft and started further fires, so preventing any attempts at salvage. HMS *Sharpshooter* despatched her with gunfire.

As was usually the case with Allied convoys in those far northern waters, the promised Russian air support did not materialise when it was most needed, and the CAM ship, *Empire Morn*, PQ 18's one remaining air defence, was obliged to launch her Hurricane fighter. Rear-Admiral Burnett in the *Scylla* had joined with QP 14, the returning ships of PQ 17, in order to give them some extra protection from heavy surface units of the German fleet, taking with him all his destroyers, plus *Avenger* and her two hunt class destroyers.

By late morning, the attack had faltered and petered out. The Germans had lost three aircraft with one badly damaged. Overall, the convoy had lost thirteen vitally needed ships and their cargoes against the *Luftwaffe*'s loss of forty-four aircraft, thirty-eight of which were torpedo-bombers.

There were to be just two more torpedo attacks before the German bombers eventually gave up. There is no doubt that the presence of the four Russian destroyers was a significant factor in the defence of the convoy, and the appearance of Petlyakov fighters late on in the day finally convinced the German pilots that further interference was not a good idea. The balance was finally tipped in the convoy's favour by the worsening weather conditions.

By 16.00 hours that afternoon, the ships were fighting their oldest and most deadly enemy of all – the savage, uncompromising environment of the high Arctic seas. Wreathed in a swirling grey mist, the ships battled through high winds and heavy seas as they made their final approach to the Kola Inlet in two columns. At about 16.20 hours local time, they were met by the local escort group, made up of HMS *Salamander*, HMS *Hazard*, HMS *Britomart* and HMS *Halcyon*. As soon as arrangements had been completed to lead the convoy through the shallows and over the Devina Bar, they proceeded cautiously against an ebb tide and the encroaching twilight. The light beacons required for that operation had not been activated, and nowhere near enough pilots were prepared to put out in the face of such severe weather conditions, forcing the ships to come to anchor.

The hours of darkness, although short-lived at that time of year in the high Arctic, became a nightmare of dragging anchors and parting cables as the ships rolled and pitched sickeningly over the incoming seas under a low canopy of dark, rolling storm clouds. Aboard the *Empire Snow*, life had become a misery of cold discomfort, producing a hovering melancholy in the freezing night air. Little chips of ice hit the bridge screens with the force of rifle bullets as rain and spray froze instantly in the frigid air. It was the starkest possible reminder of the ever-changing face of the Arctic.

With the weather becoming colder as the northern winter rapidly approached, the dawn found masts, cross-trees, superstructure, winches and gun barrels gleaming with the malicious brilliance of ice, with rigging, stays, halyards and mast ladders thick and glittering like frozen waterfalls. Patches of distorted foam flew high above the bridge, freezing the moment it touched any solid object.

By the morning of the 20th, no fewer than five ships were aground on the Devina Bar, and throughout the whole of that mind-numbing day, ships and crews could do no more than endure the foul weather and freezing conditions as best they could. Knowing of their plight, the *Luftwaffe* launched another torpedo attack later in the day as the wind and sea finally began to moderate. Twelve Ju 88s put in an unwelcome appearance at about 15.40 hours that afternoon and, through the heavy, scudding clouds, proceeded to deliver a long but fortunately unsuccessful attack. Although none of the ships were actually hit, several near misses shook them up considerably.

Like unearthly spectres in the misty, storm-tossed twilight of early morning on the 21st, those ships which had not run aground on the Devina Bar began getting under way as the harbour pilots ventured out to take the ships upstream to the quays. The *Ulster Queen* and a Russian destroyer stayed near to the bar so as to afford some protection for the ships which were still stranded and, at 15.45 hours, they were once again subjected to a prolonged bombing attack by two Ju 88s. That attack also achieved nothing except to further stretch the already taut nerves of those exhausted crews, and they were eventually floated free by the 27th.

A month later, all the surviving ships had been discharged and, after meagre supplies had been put aboard, they were once again ready to face whatever onslaught the *Kriegsmarine* and *Luftwaffe* might thrown at them. After once more running the gauntlet of German U-boats and torpedo-bombers on the return voyage my father returned home in mid-November, just two weeks after my fifth birthday. He was not so much a broken man as a much older and wiser one. At the young age of just thirty-four, he had become haggard before his time. I did not recognise him when he walked through our front door as a tall, almost shuffling figure. The terrible sights he had witnessed had turned his hair white.

After just one week's leave the Merchant Navy Shipping Officer sent for him to join another ship. The doctors, however, refused to pass him as being fit for sea service until he had fully recovered and consequently, that was the first Christmas that I can remember my father being at home. Eventually, however, with money running dangerously low and no income to speak of, he applied to the Alexandria Steam Towing Company in Swansea, who offered him a position of Chief Mate aboard the Swansea harbour tugs, where he remained until May 1943.

# 8  The Sinking of the *Canadian Star* and the Battle for HX 229

This story is dedicated to the men of both the Royal Navy and the merchant fleet who fought their long, wearisome way across the stormy wastes of the Western Ocean in March 1943, in a convoy which was to be involved in the last successful massed U-boat battle of the Second World War. It is not just about the destruction of a convoy, however; it is about one ship in particular – the Blue Star passenger/cargo combination *Canadian Star*, with my eldest brother on board.

The *Canadian Star* was an 8,000-ton refrigerated passenger/cargo combination vessel, owned by the Union Cold Storage Company and managed by the Blue Star Line which, although owned and registered in the port of London, was a frequent visitor to Swansea.

My brother Jim had signed on as an assistant steward in January 1942, and by August of that year had completed his first voyage to Australia and back. She sailed independently because of her 17-knot (31 kph) speed and, being a large, new ship, was well armed. Running the gauntlet of the U-boat war in the Caribbean and

Gulf of Mexico which was raging during the first half of 1942, the *Canadian Star* returned to Swansea in July of that year and safely discharged her cargo of meat.

On 12 August, she sailed 'light-ship' to Liverpool, where she loaded a cargo of arms and ammunition and a deck cargo of crated fighter aircraft for various ports in New Zealand. From there, she went on to Australia where she became engaged for a few months in the transportation of Australian and New Zealand naval officers across the Indian Ocean to Port Said. Because of her superior speed and armaments, she had never been intended for convoy work at all. She had already been engaged in an artillery duel with a German U-boat off the Azores in 1941, and at the time of her sailing from Liverpool on that last fateful voyage, she still carried the scars of that battle in the form of a patch on her distinctive funnel.

After sailing from Sydney, Australia, a terrible accident with *Canadian Star*'s 4.5-inch stern gun resulted in the deaths of three men and horrific injuries to three others when the breech-block exploded. Being a passenger-carrying vessel, she had a doctor on board and he, together with a colonel in the Indian Army Medical Corps, took care of the injured men until they had reached Panama, where they were put ashore. The American naval workshops in Panama, however, were unable to repair or replace the gun, and because the naval authorities did not wish for such an important ship to be sailing independently in the dangerous waters of the Western Ocean without it, she was ordered to proceed to New York, there to become a part of convoy HX 229, which was scheduled to sail from the Hudson River on 8 March 1943.

On that final voyage from Sydney, she also took on board twenty-seven passengers, most of them service families with young children who had escaped from Singapore the previous year.

All through the long, bitterly cold night of March 7th/8th 1943, the wind blew steadily out of the north-north-west, a strong wind of force 7 which blew a little stronger with every passing hour, full of razor-sharp particles of ice. Full of menace, it stayed on the port beam as the *Canadian Star* pitched and rolled gently, tugging at her anchor-chain as though eager to be free of her tether. The wind, rain, sleet and snow had been with them ever since their arrival in New York two days previously, rising and falling away again as though gathering its immense forces to add to the horror yet to come, and stealthily lifting the swell on the Hudson River and Upper New York Harbour. The watch on deck shivered uncontrollably inside their thick layers of sea-jerseys, balaclavas, duffel-coats and oilskins as they kept anchor-watch, and constantly scanned the black surface of the harbour for U-boat infiltrators.

The mercury crept steadily down the glass as the low-pressure area slowly but surely increased, and the snow drifted lazily before settling in heaps against coamings, bulkheads, winches and masts. Although every ship at anchor in the bay and river was blacked out, the dimmed lights of New York reflected eerily off the snow as it gathered in clumps everywhere it touched. The masts and cross-trees glistened like huge Christmas trees, festooned with snow-coated stays and halyards. It lay upon the deck in a soft carpet of pristine white, deadening the sounds of the heavy footsteps of the watch as they paced the decks. It softened the anchor-chains on the forecastle head into huge, fluffy ridges of cotton-wool and drifted high against the bridge superstructure. It piled against the engineroom coamings and blew in eddies through the skylights, hissing to sibilant extinction as it met the rising heat from below. It swished silently onto the bridge wings. It crept silently along alleyways and drifted soundlessly down the deck vents. It sought out the tiniest gap throughout the length and beam of the big vessel. It slid effortlessly under oilskin coats and up under duffel-coat hoods, causing misery anywhere it touched. It coated portholes and hardened into intricate patterns of ice on the wide bridge screens, glittering and gleaming in beautiful malevolence, its siren beauty hauntingly inviting and deadly. The fast-flowing current of the Hudson River carried with it many icefloes and growlers which grated against the ship's side as they sped past.

During that terrible winter of 1942/3, the temperature had dropped so low that even the mighty Niagara River, with its immense waterfall, had frozen. But in spite of the cold, malicious gleam of ice-hardened snow mere inches from where he stood in the wheelhouse, the Chief Mate was more chilled by his feelings of isolation and apprehension than by the cold which was being reflected from the ice on the screens. Looking silently out onto the hauntingly beautiful scene, he shivered slightly inside his heavy-duty winter wrappings as he wondered just what the future held.

It had been very late on the previous evening when Captain R.D. Miller had returned from a captains' conference, but as soon as he arrived in his cabin suite, he ordered his three bridge officers to a meeting in order to brief them on their convoy location and the position regarding the U-boat war then raging in the Western Ocean.

The situation in the North Atlantic at that time was not, to say the least, encouraging. Convoy SC 118 had been badly mauled the previous month, losing twelve ships. The two convoys which had sailed from New York ahead of HX 229, SC 121 and HX 228, had also taken a bad beating by a heavy concentration of U-boats in the Mid-Atlantic Air Gap, or the 'death hole', as the U-boat crews preferred to call it. Those two convoys had lost a total of seventeen merchantmen and one destroyer between them, all for the loss of just one U-boat.

The escorts provided for HX 229 comprised four corvettes – HMS *Abelia*, HMS *Pennywort*, HMS *Anemone* and HMCS *Sheerbrooke* – and seven destroyers – HMS *Volunteer*, HMS *Beverley*, HMS *Mansfield*, HMS *Witherington*, HMS *Highlander*, HMS *Vinny* and USS *Babbit*. The escort commander was Lieutenant-Commander G.J. Luther, sailing in the *Volunteer*. No support group and no catapult aircraft were available to either HX 229 or SC 122, which had sailed three days before them on the 5th with a total of fifty ageing merchant ships, one rescue vessel and nine escorts. Air cover from North America terminated at a range of 850 miles (1,570 km) which was 800 miles (1,480 km) short of where it would be resumed again from Northern Ireland. Their shortest possible crossing time was estimated at seventeen days, four of which would be spent in the air gap. It was estimate that there were more than forty U-boats out in the deep ocean waiting for them to arrive in the 'death hole'.

The wintry sun was invisible above a low, dark cloud cover as the crews of the ships destined to make up convoy HX 229 turned to on the cold, grey morning of

8 March. The black, oilskin-clad figures of the Chief Mate, the Bosun, two able seamen and two efficient deck-hands (EDHs) stood by on the forecastle head, stamping their feet and flapping their arms about in an effort to keep their blood circulating, waiting for the order from the bridge to heave the hook.

Whisps of black smoke spiralled out of the *Canadian Star*'s funnel and were whipped away by a force 6 wind that lifted the grey, leaden waters of the Hudson River and Upper New York Bay, causing ribbons of dirty white foam to be torn from the whitecaps and tossed high into the polluted, soot-laden air. Towering above them, the Statue of Liberty stood proud and staunch, her crowned head almost hidden in the low rolling clouds and her base lashed by sea and spray.

The ear-splitting drone of the ships' sirens blared out across the bay as the vessels began moving ponderously across the wide sweep of the bay to form up into convoy out in the Long Island Sound. The British destroyer *Volunteer*, a 26-year-old veteran built in 1927, suddenly materialised alongside the *Canadian Star*. As she cruised slowly past, the flashing light of her Aldis lamp told Captain Miller that it was time to leave. The massive bulks of freighters and tankers loomed suddenly out of the densely falling wind-driven snow and disappeared again just as quickly. The black-hulled form of the 7,244-ton *Empire Knight* passed quietly by, quickly followed by the 5,848-ton liberty ship *Mathew Luckenbach*.

The forecastle-head steam winch began rattling and labouring as the latter slid majestically by, the rhythmic 'thump, thump, thump' of her triple-expansion steam engine muffled by wind and sea. Slowly and without fuss or hindrance, the massive hook was heaved up from the sea bed, and at a signal from the mate informing the skipper that the anchor was 'up and down', the engine-room telegraph's strident ringing told the engineers to set their valves for slow ahead. The *Canadian Star* began moving towards the Verrazano Narrows Bridge and Fort Worth beyond.

The stevedores of New York Harbour plus quite a number of early risers from the city had taken the time to gather along the many miles of waterfront, and braving the freezing temperatures of the late winter cold, they solemnly watched as the convoy moved out. When British merchant ships entered or left their home ports, they did so quietly and unobtrusively, without fuss or audience; the people of Britain never noticed their comings and goings. Unlike the Royal Navy, the British Mercantile Marine was the silent service. The American and Australian people, however, did things quite differently. As far as American civilians were concerned, merchant ships were no different from warships. In fact, the merchant seamen of America were considered more heroic than those of their armed services, simply because, like their British counterparts, they took their ships to sea virtually unarmed and unarmoured, their lives more at risk because of the cargoes they carried than were the lives of those on the warships protecting them. And the American people saw to it that they left port with a wave and a cheer, and returned to a rapturous welcome.

Breakfast was still being served in the *Canadian Star*'s spacious and well-appointed saloon to those officers not on duty and to those passengers who wanted it. Most of the ship's complement of ninety people, however, preferred to brave the cold and venture onto the decks to watch as New York and its waving, cheering people slowly disappeared into the snow and murk. She began to roll gently as she nosed her bows into the sound, and rose to the scend of the sea as the heavy North Atlantic swells, carrying with them the last ice-floes of winter, rolled inexorably through the narrow channel.

The British flower class corvettes *Pennywort* and *Anemone*, together with the ex-American four-stack destroyers *Witherington*, *Highlander* and *Vinny* took up their positions on the port flank. The American destroyer *Babbit* lingered to take up her position astern whilst the British destroyer *Volunteer*, with stern down and bows up, breasted the waves and cut through the water like a knife as she sped past the convoy to take up her position ahead.

The first week at sea turned out to be a most uncomfortable but not particularly dangerous experience for the crews and passengers of the convoy. As they cleared New York and turned onto a heading which would take them first north to pass close by Halifax, Nova Scotia before raising St John's, Newfoundland, the wind and sea began to rise ominously, still blowing hard from the north-north-west. Black, rolling storm clouds precipitated furious showers of rain, hail, sleet and snow, whilst at sea level, the waves of the Western Ocean rose ever higher as the wind speed steadily increased.

Aboard the *Canadian Star*, the passengers were becoming more uncomfortable as the wintry days passed. 'Old Hypocrites', the ship's doctor, was being kept busy dispensing various pills and medicines against seasickness, but nothing really worked. As the weather worsened, the ship began rolling and pitching sickeningly, throwing everyone off balance. Some of them slid along the decks causing bruising, cuts and abrasions, all of which the doctor treated as best he could under very trying circumstances. It was the children who fared best amongst all that sickness. Whilst most of the adult passengers were kept constantly on the move between cabins, saloon and heads, the children played and sported with the ever-increasing violent movements of the ship, laughing hysterically as they tried to walk upright along the alleyways, and staggering uncontrollably.

By the late afternoon of the 10th, HX 229 was passing Halifax, 500 miles (920 km) away on its port flank. The wind speed was up to severe gale force 9 with the great ocean rollers reaching heights of 40 feet (12 m), breaking at their crests and swamping the exposed decks of every vessel. The *Canadian Star* was 'taking the green' over her bows so badly that every time she dived into a deep trough her foredeck would disappear below a maelstrom of furious white water which, as she rose to meet the next sea, would explode against her bridge superstructure, sending plumes of water soaring high above her wheelhouse. At the greatly reduced speed of 9 knots (17 kph) she was struggling, making heavy weather of every sea that crashed over her bows.

On the afternoon of the 14th, the convoy had passed Cape Race on a heading of 028 degrees. The wind speed had increased to severe storm 11, making life even more uncomfortable for passengers and crew alike. So bad was the storm that by the morning of the 15th, the ships had become scattered over many miles of seething ocean, some of them suffering various degrees of damage in the process. The brand new Canadian-built British minesweeping trawler HMS *Campobello*, which was escorting convoy SC 122 which had sailed from New York three days ahead of

HX 229, was so badly damaged that she had to be abandoned. Somehow the crew of the Belgian *Godetia* managed to take off her crew in the horrendous weather conditions, even as the *Campobello* was sinking under them.

On the evening of the 15th, the storm reached its peak. Shortly after midnight, the 7,000-ton refrigerated ship SS *Coracero*, carrying a full cargo of meat from Argentina, shipped a mountainous sea which swept down her starboard side like a massive river after a flash flood, and broke amidships. The Number 3 lifeboat was smashed to pieces and was reduced to matchwood even before the sea had passed. The following sea quickly removed the wreckage, leaving nothing to show that a boat had ever existed there. At that time all lifeboats were swung outboard, lashed to their davits and ready for instant use in the event of a sudden attack. On a vessel such as the *Coracero* they would have hung some 45 feet (14 m) above the sea, which gives some idea of the height of the seas that terrible night. The storm force winds and corresponding seas were directly astern of the convoy at that point, causing many unpleasant experiences when those seas pooped (went inboard over the stern). A lifeboat aboard the *Walter Q. Gresham* was swept away by a massive sea, tearing out her davits in the process and leaving two gaping holes in her 1-inch (2.5 cm) deck plating.

SC 122 had passed right through the *Raubgraf* group of U-boats unnoticed, whilst HX 229 had simply overtaken them, again passing through their ranks unnoticed. This, however, had left both convoys confined between the jaws of a three-way trap. In the early morning of 16 March, as the worst of the storm was passing, U-653, a North Atlantic veteran commanded by *Kapitän-Leutnant* Gerhard Feiler, was returning to base from its sixth patrol and travelling on the surface, 800 miles (1,500 km) east of Newfoundland. Sometime between 03.00 and 04.00 hours *Obersteuermann* Heinz Theen, a quartermaster on lookout duty in the conning tower, saw a light directly ahead. It was a tiny light, as though some thoughtless seaman had lit a cigarette. He reported what he had seen, and a message was immediately flashed to U-boat Headquarters in Paris.

The message consisted only of three letters, but it was sufficient to place the light precisely in grid fourteen of square BC on the U-boat Headquarters map of the Western Ocean. By conflation of intelligence, German observation service believed it had found the SC 122, but that convoy was in fact about 150 miles (275 km) away to the east, and moving on a slightly more northerly course. The effect of that confusion was relatively unimportant, however, as Doenitz at once issued orders for the fourteen boats of the *Raubgraf* group through which both convoys had already passed to turn east and motor at top speed on the surface to intercept, while the eleven boats of the *Dränger* line and the nineteen boats of the *Stürmer* line, then 400 miles (740 km) away in mid-Atlantic in a north-east and south-east patrol line, turned west to join them. It was a total of forty-four U-boats in all. Although Doenitz thought he had only SC 122 in the trap, both convoys were destined to be caught within the next forty-eight hours.

By dusk on the evening of the 16th the stragglers from HX 229 had closed up once more, and the convoy proceeded on a course of 028 degrees. The storm of the previous two days had blown itself out, leaving almost calm conditions in its wake. It was almost as though even the elements were co-operating with the German

U-boat packs as a hunter's moon peeped intermittently from behind the rolling clouds and cast it eerie light upon the face of the deep.

At 19.25 hours the commodore, Commodore M.J.D. Mayall, RNR, sailing aboard the *Abraham Lincoln* in position 61 in the middle of the convoy, ordered a change of course to 053 degrees, a direct course for the UK. At that point, U-603, one of the *Raubgraf* boats under the command of *Kapitän-Leutnant* Hans-Joachim Bertelsmann, was preparing to surface on the starboard flank to make a surface night attack. Owing to the convoy's unexpected turn, it found itself in the forward position it had intended sooner than anticipated. There were already seven other U-boats in contact, clinging to the convoy at the limit of their visibility, and many more motoring at high speed to intercept.

My brother and several more off-duty men of the catering staff, with a sprinkling of deck hands and firemen, were sitting together on the aft boat deck of the *Canadian Star* having a quiet chat in the lee of the aft superstructure. The news of submarines in the area had already been relayed to the merchant crews, setting already frayed nerves on edge. Then a destroyer passed through the convoy ranks at high speed flying a two-pennant signal, T over S. Bitter experience had told them all just what that signal meant: 'Enemy submarines in vicinty'.

Jim recalled:

> Immediately, we had the most terrible feeling of apprehension and foreboding. A nervous tension had gripped us all, as though some powerful hands were clutching at our throats to prevent us from speaking in anything but quiet monosyllables, a tension which increased with every passing moment as the darkness became more complete. I remember asking myself at the time, 'How many ships will still be afloat in the morning?' It was a fear like no other I have ever experienced before or since. And if that's what it's like to be a hero, then I don't recommend it to anyone.

In the event, HX 229 and SC 122 were to be twelve ships fewer by the next dawn; but the brunt of the disaster was felt by HX 229, whose ordeal began shortly before midnight on the 16th.

The weather by that time had moderated quite considerably and was very favourable for a submarine attack. There was a full moon with a cloud density of 9–10, which meant that the scene was only intermittently illuminated and generally twilight conditions prevailed – ideal conditions for the U-boats, whose low profile made them almost invisible to the searching lookouts, whilst the merchantmen could clearly be seen, silhouetted as they were against the skyline. Visibility was excellent and the ships were very sharply defined at a distance of almost 10,000 yards (9,000 m). The wind had moderated to force 2 northerly at that time, with a comparatively calm sea and a slight south-west swell of sea-state 1–2.

At 22.00 hours precisely, U-603 fired off a salvo of three FAT (shallow-searching) torpedoes, a pattern-running type with a pre-set steering. A U-boat could fire these torpedoes at any angle up to 90 degrees. They would then run a course, fixed by distance to the convoy, at a speed of 30 knots (56 kph). When they reached the end of their pre-set run, they would turn back on their course, and in this way, they could make several fast passes through the columns of the convoy's ranks. After that first salvo, U-603 then fired a single G7e torpedo (mark G, 7 metres long, electrically driven with no bubble track), at the 6,000-ton *Elin K*, a Norwegian vessel carrying wheat and manganese. Five minutes later, an ear-splitting detonation was heard and immediately, HMS *Beverley* and HMS *Pennywort* turned to search.

The *Elin K* had been hit in the Number 4 hold and, losing way immediately, she began settling at the stern as her crew made a mad scramble for the boats and life-rafts. The watch officer on the bridge at the time was First Mate Berge, who immediately sounded four blasts on the steam whistle and ordered that the red mast-head light be lit and two distress rockets fired. By the time her skipper, Captain Robert Johannesen, had reached bridge the *Elin K* was sinking fast and he gave the order to abandon ship. The end came very quickly, and was curiously unspectac-ular. Broken-backed, she simply collapsed in on her stricken midsection, lay wearily over onto her side, and within four minutes, she had disappeared beneath the waves. It was fortunate, however, that she carried an experienced and disci-plined crew, who launched their boats quickly and without panic. This enabled all of them to get away clear from the sinking ship in a calm sea. Almost immediately, they were picked up by HMS *Pennywort*.

Contrary to the usual practice after a U-boat attack, Commodore Mayall did not order an emergency turn away from the direction from which the attack had occurred but instead maintained his original course. Consequently, the other U-boats which were shadowing the convoy were able to continue their intended operations without any difficulty.

Shortly after 23.00 hours, U-758, under the command of *Kapitän-Leutnant* Manseck, reached a position out on the starboard bow of the convoy and turned to launch his own attack. HMS *Beverley*, in the meantime, had resumed her position on the starboard bow ahead of the convoy. HMS *Pennywort*, closing in from astern after picking up survivors, was still 11,000 yards (10,000 m) away. That meant that the starboard flank of the convoy had been left virtually unguarded, and in the good visibility U-758 was able to pick out its targets at leisure.

Meanwhile, the wind had turned north to east and had freshened to force 3, raising the swell along with it to sea-state 3. At 23.25 hours, *Kapitän-Leutnant* Manseck fired off a FAT torpedo at the 6,000-ton Dutch freighter *Zaanland*. In quick succes-sion, he then fired a G7e torpedo at the 7,000-ton American liberty ship *James Oglethorpe*, followed by another FAT torpedo and another G7e. Both were hit. Thirteen out of fifty men from the *James Oglethorpe* were killed when a lifeboat capsized, trapping them inside.

At 00.22 hours, U-435, under the command of *Kapitän-Leutnant* Strelow, surfaced astern of HMS *Volunteer* and fired off a salvo of two FAT torpedoes at a tanker at long range. At 00.30 hours, both torpedoes, having missed the tanker, hit the American liberty ship *William Eustis*, which was in position 22 on the port flank. In that position, she was stationed just 500 yards (450 m) off the *Canadian Star*'s port bow. The men on the boat deck rushed to the forward rail to see what had happened. In the darkness, however, there was nothing visible except the dying flash of the explosion. So fast and furious had the attack been that the *William Eustis* had had no chance of sending up distress rockets and no opportunity of getting off a distress signal before heaving over almost onto her beam ends. With such a heavy list to port, she began to settle quickly at the stern and immediately dropped astern of the convoy.

It has been suggested that the *William Eustis* might have been salvaged and that her American crew had abandoned her too soon. In fact, so quickly had her crew left the ship that her skipper admitted to Lieutenant-Commander Luther that he had left his code books and other confidential papers on board. Luther could not leave the ship afloat with such sensitive material on board and, turning back to where the ship was lying, *Volunteer* fired a pattern of four depth-charges as she passed, lifting the vessel several feet out of the water before she finally sank.

At 02.30 hours, two U-boats surfaced on either side of the convoy and made their attacks from port and starboard. The first, U-435 fired a salvo of two FAT torpedoes and two G7es from the port bow of the convoy. At that point, U-91 under the command of *Kapitän-Leutnant* Walkerling, found itself in a firing position some 1,800 yards (1,650 m) from the starboard bow and fired off two salvos of two G7es and heard, after a period of two minutes, two muffled explosions. At 02.41 hours it fired another salvo at a large freighter of 10,000 tons and, after just eighty-three seconds, two massive detonations were heard.

The vessel was the American liberty ship *Harry Luckenbach*, and two immense columns of smoke and blood-red flames could clearly be seen as she went down in under three minutes. Three lifeboats full of survivors managed to get clear away but because the ship was astern of the main body, they were very quickly left far astern. No less than four of the convoy escorts subsequently sighted them, but for some reason none stopped to pick them up. The survivors drifted away into the night and were never seen again. Fifty-four American merchant seamen and twenty-six American naval personnel lost their lives. Incidents like this only served to widen the already wide gulf between the Mercantile Marine and the Royal Navy.

At 04.50 hours, just as HMS *Volunteer* reassumed her position astern of the convoy, U-600, under the command of *Kapitän-Leutnant* Zurmühlen, fired a salvo of four FATs from the starboard bow of the convoy. Quickly turning away, it fired a stern torpedo. The *Nariva*, in position 91 was hit, then in quick succession the *Irene du Pont* in position 81 was hit by two torpedoes and, in position 72 and just four ships away from the *Canadian Star*, the tanker *Southern Princess* by one.

The *Irene du Pont* started to go down at once, and twelve of her crew died close to the lifeboats which had been cast off too soon so that they floated away. The *Nariva* floated for a little longer with a massive rent in her side. One of the laden rafts floated into the hole on a wave as the ship rolled sluggishly in the low swells. The screams of those men as they were trapped inside the hull must have been terrible to hear. Then, as though by divine intervention, they floated out again with the next roll of the dying ship and were pulled clear by the lifeboats. One cannot even imagine the nightmares which those men must subsequently have suffered.

U-600's torpedo hit the *Southern Princess* amidships, square on her port beam. She was laden to her marks with 10,000 tons of high-octane fuel from the Texas oil refineries, and a massive orange and red flash, followed almost immediately by a tremendous explosion, lit up the surrounding darkness as she began to disintegrate before the horrified eyes of the men on watch aboard the *Canadian Star*. Mere milliseconds after the initial explosion, the night was further illuminated by a vast inferno of yellow and blood-red flames, intermingled with clouds of rolling black smoke erupting from the stricken tanker. With a cataract of burning fuel spewing from the huge gash in her side and plumes of thick, black, oily smoke curling and rolling hundreds of feet into the air, the *Southern Princess* had become a raging inferno from stem to stern within seconds of being hit.

Witnesses recall bloodcurdling scenes and sounds as burning men hurled themselves to certain death in a sea of fire that enveloped the bloated, oil-covered corpses in a writhing cocoon of white-hot flames which were being fanned into a roaring conflagration by a stiff westerly breeze. Decks, bulkheads and companion ladders became twisted and buckled into grotesquely strange shapes by the intense heat. On the main deck, the silhouettes of men could be seen running in all directions and throwing themselves heedlessly overboard whilst the gasoline-fed flames were incinerating the 1-inch (2.5 cm) thick deck plates and collapsing the midships superstructure as the heat-softened steel began buckling under its own weight. Dancing like puppets to the strings of their master, the burning men tried vainly to escape as the steel decks began to glow evilly in a dull red, hissing and spitting like pistol shots as the sea spray boiled away into scalding steam the moment it touched the fiercely burning ship.

In fact, although she was burning fiercely along her whole length, of the hundred men aboard her, twenty-nine of whom were passengers returning home after previous sinkings, only four lost their lives, two of the passengers and two boys of sixteen and eighteen. How fearsome is man's imagination in such circumstances.

With the exception of the greasers and engineers on watch below decks, everyone aboard the *Canadian Star* hurried onto the open decks when the exploding *Southern Princess* jolted them out of sleep. Lining the starboard rails, they watched, helpless, as the horrendous scene unfolded before their eyes.

The convoy moved on, leaving the *Southern Princess* burning like a monstrous beacon in the night as she was left far astern. Then suddenly, she capsized and, still burning fiercely, she sank a little later, leaving behind her a sea of fiercely burning fuel as her only grave marker.

As the grey sky began to lighten on the morning of the 17th, Commodore Mayall and Lieutenant-Commander Luther began to reorganise the convoy, which had been considerably dislocated by the heavy losses throughout that long night and the evasive action taken during the last attack. There were still twenty-eight merchantmen in sight, and as the losses had been largely on the starboard flank and had created considerable gaps there, Commodore Mayall decided to reduce the number of columns to nine and to reorganise the ships on the starboard flank. The captain of the British ship *Nebraska* proceeding in position forty-one was appointed Vice-Commodore in place of the captain of the sunken *Nariva*, and took up his position accordingly in the centre of the convoy.

As the dawn gave way to the monochrome drabness of full daylight, the U-boats melted away to the limits of their visibility and brought the men of the convoy and its escorts some little relief from their attackers. Air cover from Northern Ireland was still twenty-four hours away but the escorts, towards which five ships were even then steaming at top speed as reinforcements, would not have to deal with close-range surface attacks during the hours of daylight, and submerged

U-boats, unless already positioned ahead of the convoy's track, lacked the speed to intercept it.

The massed packs, however, had already inflicted harrowing losses on HX 229 in the form of eight ships sunk in addition to four in SC 122, amounting to a total tonnage of 77,500 tons, with the loss of 143 merchant seamen. Not one U-boat had been seriously damaged, and only twenty-eight torpedoes had been expended. Since it was torpedo stocks rather than fuel which determined a wolf pack's endurance, the night's operation had left the *Raubgraf*, *Dränger* and *Stürmer* groups well placed to resume their offensive when darkness once again engulfed them.

Even the hoped-for respite, however, did not last long. Even though the weather had remained moderate, with a force 5 wind and sea-state 4, more troubles were on the way. The prospects were not good. Even then, black, ominous cumulonimbus storm clouds were slowly building up on the horizon to the north-west and small whitecaps were forming on the crests of the rippling waves. Even the most committed atheist prayed fervently for the storm to break quickly.

By midday on the 17th, HX 229 had adopted its new route formation of nine columns. The port flank was screened by HMS *Volunteer* and the starboard flank by HMS *Beverley*. The weather was cloudy but clear, with visibility up to 8 miles (14 km). The wind had freshened up to force 6 with a sea-state of 5–6. The convoy had maintained its course of 053 degrees since the previous night.

The two escorts were obliged to remain near to the convoy and could make no more sorties to drive off U-boats which had remained in the area. In addition, the use of the *Volunteer*'s Huff-Duff was restricted because the destroyer had to provide bearings for the expected aircraft and also to try and pick up their signals in order to give the first plane the correct approach course.

As the passengers and crew of the *Canadian Star* were settling down to lunch, U-384, under the command of *Oberleutnant* von Rosenberg-Gruszinski, and U-631 commanded by *Oberleutnant* Kruger, were positioning themselves. Having spent the entire morning travelling at high speed on the surface, overtaking the convoy in a great arc at the limit of their visibility, they were now favourably placed for a daytime attack ahead and to starboard. They submerged to await the convoy's approach. At 13.00 hours, they discharged their torpedo salvos.

The Dutch vessel *Terkoelei* and the British ship *Coracero* were both hit on their starboard sides. The *Terkoelei* was totally ripped apart by several torpedoes and sank very fast, taking most of her Asian crew down with her. Although they were in two lifeboats alongside the rapidly sinking vessel, they were so shocked that they refused to row away from the stricken ship, and were carried down with her when she capsized on top of them. The *Coracero* settled very fast by the stern but remained afloat long enough for most of her crew to launch her boats and escape. Five men who were in the engine-room when she was hit, however, died instantly when the torpedo exploded in their midst. The other torpedoes, which had been aimed at a tanker, missed her and every other ship in the convoy, eventually sinking when they reached the end of their runs.

In the saloon aboard the *Canadian Star*, the detonations were so far away that they were barely audible through the steel bulkheads. Nevertheless one of the passengers, a Mrs Atkins, jerked upright. There was fright and uncertainty in her huge brown eyes, and she said in a tight, scared voice which my brother overheard, 'Oh God! Not again! Please, no more. I just cannot stand any more.'

'Don't worry, Mrs Atkins, it's probably just one of the escorts dropping some depth-charges to chase away any diehard U-boat skippers.' The lie, however, registered plainly in Captain Miller's eyes as he rose from the table, just as the mate's tinny, discordant voice echoed through the tannoy speakers: 'Captain Miller to the bridge please. Captain Miller to the bridge.'

At 13.12 hours, the convoy commodore ordered an emergency turn to port in two 45-degree turns, and the convoy veered away from the suspected area of the U-boats' attack.

When the torpedoes detonated, Lieutenant-Commander Luther decided that the time had come to ask for help. With attacks occurring by day and by night, and with the escorts having the dual role of screening the convoy and recovering survivors, there seemed to be little hope of saving any more than a fraction of the convoy. In addition, in the prevailing weather conditions and constant attacks, it had become impossible for the escorts to refuel. The destroyer *Mansfield*'s reserves were already dangerously low and consequently *Volunteer* sent out the following message: 'HX 229 attacked again today at 13.10 hours, two ships torpedoed and sunk. Request early reinforcements for convoy, 51 degrees 45 minutes north, 32 degrees 26 minutes west.' At 14.40 hours, he sent out a second message to the Commander-in-Chief, Western Approaches, and to the leader, *Highlander*, which was then coming up from astern of the convoy: 'Have *Beverley* and *Mansfield* in company. *Pennywort* and *Anemone* coming up astern. Constant attacks will not allow refuelling, and situation is becoming critical. D/F sightings indicate many U-boats in contact.' The convoy then resumed its general course.

The situation would most certainly have become critical during the hours of darkness if the *Volunteer*'s Huff Duff had continued to send out the original bearings. Because the personnel were unfamiliar with the equipment, they were 180 degrees out. However, they were corrected, and at 16.30 hours the Liberator J/120 found them. Between 19.10 and 19.56 hours, it located and attacked no less than six U-boats before having to fly back to its base at 20.45 hours, having remained in the air for a total of eighteen hours, two longer than was normally possible. Although none of the U-boats were reported as having been sunk or even damaged, the air attack, together with the subsequent depth-charging by the escort, did have a demoralising effect on the skippers, who wasted little time in clearing the general area. HX 229 therefore enjoyed a quiet, almost peaceful night.

By morning the wind had freshened to almost 40 knots (74 kph), creating a fresh gale of force 8. With their crest edges beginning to break up into spindrift and foam being whipped away in well marked streaks, the high, breaking waves were causing the ships to roll and pitch uncomfortably. Nobody minded, however, hoping against hope that the weather would deteriorate even further and so keep the U-boats at bay until they reached full air cover.

The morning passed quietly and there were still no further attacks, mainly because the U-boats had temporarily lost them. Shortly after daybreak, however, U-60, commanded by *Kapitän-Leutnant* Freyberg, had once again established contact and had sent off a signal to that effect at 08.00 hours. The destroyer

*Volunteer* had been unable to intercept that signal because her Huff-Duff operators were once again busy receiving bearings from the approaching Liberators, L/120 and N/120, and transmitting Direction Finding (DF) beams to the aircraft.

At 12.00 hours on that stormy, snow-laden day, the change of watch took place aboard the *Canadian Star*. The Third Mate, R.H. Keyworth, was officer of the watch on the bridge, a rather crowded bridge just then because the Chief and Second Mates were also there, together with two lookouts, one on each bridge wing, two gunners manning each of the heavy-calibre Oerlikon machine-guns perched on the bridge wings, and the deck stand-by in one corner of the wheelhouse. Captain Miller joined them there an hour later after snatching a quick lunch. They had all been on the bridge without respite for the past seventy-two hours, and the harshness of their self-imposed duties showed clearly in pinched, haggard faces, red-rimmed eyes and puffed lips.

The First and Second Mates were officially on watch below and, when the skipper arrived on the bridge, were sent down to the saloon. Their instructions were to stay there for a few hours talking to and giving what crumbs of comfort they could to the still-apprehensive passengers.

Chief Engineer Buckwell had gone on watch in the engineroom together with the donkeymen, T. Christie and E. Edwards, the Second Fridge Engineer, C. Marsh, the Chief Fridge Engineer, the Fourth Engineer and the 'Black gang' (firemen and greasers). Most of the catering staff had retired to their respective cabins for their two-hour afternoon break.

Standing on the boat deck for several minutes before going to his cabin, my brother Jim stood at the rail looking out over the heaving sea. Somewhere out there in that wild waste of boiling ocean, a deadly presence lurked, unseen and unheard, waiting to pounce. As he stood there, even the water seemed to be dead, old and evil and infinitely horrible. It was a place of harshness, power and incredible cruelty, beneath which lurked an enemy intent on their destruction. He was over-come with a fear he had never known before, a fear which, even to this day, has left an indelible scar. Thick flakes of snow and little chips of frozen hail being driven before the wind stung his face, and the intense cold cut through the thin garments he wore that day beneath his Mae West. Then at last he moved away with bowed head and leaden feet. This was how he described his feelings at that moment to me.

In the meantime, U-221, under the command of *Oberleutnant* Trojer, had estab-lished contact around midday in a north-west wind of force 8 and a correspondingly heavy north-westerly swell. At 15.00 hours, U-221 had found itself ahead of the convoy on the port flank and had then submerged in readiness for an underwater attack. Propeller noises from the approaching ships could be heard through the submarine's hydrophones, then suddenly, from the south-west, the pitching and rolling steamers came into periscope sight. They were heading directly towards U-221.

At approximately 15.45 hours, *Oberleutnant* Trojer fired one of his stern torpe-does at one of the freighters, then turned to make a bow firing on the *Clan MacDougal*, a 6,000-ton vessel in the next column, but missed. At 15.50 hours he fired off a salvo of four torpedoes – a FAT, then two G7es, then another FAT. After thirty and thirty-two seconds respectively, there were two loud explosions followed by sinking noises, at first subdued then very loud, as though boilers were exploding and being sent crashing through collapsing bulkheads, scything down everything in their path. After a further twelve minutes, another two detonations were heard, so close together that they seemed almost to be one.

The first sign that anyone in the convoy had of the renewed attacks was the torpedoes which detonated at 15.50 hours, ripping the guts out of the brand new American liberty freighter *Walter Q. Gresham*, a vessel of 7,190 tons in position 21. The torpedoes hit on the port side in numbers 4 and 5 holds, tearing a hole in her side 40 feet (12 m) in diameter and ripping open 20 feet (6 m) of her decking. Her captain immediately gave orders to abandon ship and, in accordance with instructions, had secret material thrown overboard. Two of the lifeboats capsized when they were lowered into the rough sea, causing the loss of twenty-seven of her crew of sixty-nine.

The *Walter Q. Gresham* had been loaded with powdered milk, a staple of British children's wartime rations which the rising sea immediately stirred into a thick, creamy froth. The ship settled lower in the water and disappeared beneath the waves a few minutes later. The other ship to be hit by that salvo was the *Canadian Star*. Her luck had finally run out.

Third Mate Keyworth later made the following statement:

> I was watching a liberty ship at the head of the next column to port when it appeared to be struck by a heavy sea throwing spray over the entire ship as high as the funnel but, when it lost way, I realised that it had been torpedoed. I rang the alarm bells and the men came running up to action stations. The gunner on the port wing of the bridge was already tearing off the covers of the Oerlikon gun when I suddenly spotted, coming up between our ship and the next column to port, a periscope about a yard clear of the water; the surface of the sea was a little calmer in the lee of the *Canadian Star*. The captain and I called out at the same time and the gunner started to swing his Oerlikon onto it but, almost at once, we were hit. It felt as though the whole ship had blown up under me. There was a tremendous amount of cordite, I can still almost taste it. The captain ordered 'Abandon ship'. I dashed into the chart room to get my little getaway bag with my sextant and some of my navigation books. I had ideas of a long voyage in an open boat.

The ship was hit first in the engineroom, where the engineers, firemen and donkeymen then on watch were killed almost instantaneously, either by the tremendous blast of the exploding torpedo, the devastating effects of the thousands of tons of freezing sea water which poured in through the 30-foot (9 m) gash in her side, main engines and auxiliary machinery being torn from beds and mountings and being thrown about or from the effects of superheated, high-pressure steam from ruptured 8-inch (20 cm) pipes. Then, just a few seconds later, the second torpedo exploded in her Number 5 hold, ripping a further 40-foot (12 m) gash in the sinking ship's side, which tore her main deck open like a key opening a sardine can.

That double explosion at first produced a stunned silence throughout the vessel as passengers and crew alike stopped dead in their tracks, looking at each other wildly as though for some sort of comfort, or reassurance that they had not been hit at all. Then the alarm bells started ringing. The simple act of living had suddenly turned into a desperate fight for survival.

Since the ship was ferrying service personnel rather than civilians, and had an experienced, well-drilled crew, there was no panic, just an orderly rush towards the open decks where lifeboat crews already were assembling. Even as people were being unceremoniously bundled into their allotted boats the ship started settling fast by the stern. With her engine-room and Number 5 hold flooding fast, it took only minutes for the pressure of sea water to collapse both bulkheads of the Number 4 hold and the bows started to rise as her stern sank lower into the cold embrace of the sea.

Even as the two ships were sinking, HMS *Volunteer*, HMS *Anemone* and HMS *Pennywort* steamed past them to perform an 'artichoke' the usual move by escorts following a daytime attack, in which they search for the submarine astern of the convoy. As they passed by the men in the water, the skipper of *Volunteer* shouted from the bridge, 'We'll be back.' Whether or not anyone heard him is not known, but even as they were going down, the guns on both ships were still firing in the direction in which the submarine had been spotted. In the event, the 'artichoke' sweep produced nothing but an uncertain contact, onto which six depth-charges were dropped and, after half an hour had passed, Lieutenant-Commander Luther detailed the *Pennywort* and the *Anemone* to rescue survivors.

At the scene of the torpedoing that half-hour had proved to be a desperate time for the men, women and children struggling in the lifeboats, on rafts and in the freezing water itself. Rescued seamen from other ships who were already on board the warships were more than a little angry when those naval vessels steamed past the two crippled ships, and made their feelings known in no uncertain terms.

The *Canadian Star* was the last ship in that convoy to be sunk during that terrible voyage, and this is the story of her sinking as described to me by my brother Jim, then just seventeen years of age.

> I shall never forget that day as long as I live. It was fifty-eight years ago that she went down, but for me she goes down almost every night of the week of every month of every year. The awful explosions of those torpedoes, the ear-slitting din of exploding boilers and collapsing bulkheads, the noise of the steam and smoke being forced up through the funnel and skylights, the steam whistle blowing off, the screams of women and children falling out of capsized lifeboats and struggling to keep afloat in freezing water with up to 30 foot [9 m] seas running before a force 8 gale. Guns firing. People trying to climb up the scrambling nets of the *Anemone* and falling under her keel as she rolled on top of them.
>
> I just get so carried away whenever I think about it. Do you know that even after all these years I still have nightmares. I can still see that ship going down and the people struggling in the water. There was one young couple with an 18-month-old baby. The father was trying to keep the baby's head above the sea, but I could see that he knew that he never had a chance. He knew that he was going down, and his wife and kiddie with him. [That young family proved to be Colonel and Mrs J.H. Ord and their two year old son.] I'd seen quite a lot of violent death as a youngster, what with the three nights' blitz on Swansea and sinking ships, but never anything like

that. The *Canadian Star* was *my* ship, and to see her go like that, it was just pure bloody murder.

We hadn't had any attacks since the previous day, not even through the night, so naturally enough, especially after that Liberator attack on the U-boat packs, we thought they'd all been beaten off. We'd even heard that some of them had been sunk. None of them had been sunk of course, but you know what scuttlebutt is like aboard a ship. Anyway, with more Liberators flying around we thought it was all over. I remember turning to at three o'clock, and everything was quiet and normal – except for the gale of course.

At about half past three, the steward sent me down to the lazarette for some milk and bully beef, and I was actually inside the lazarette when I heard the alarm bells going off, so I just dropped everything and ran like hell for the open deck. I was just passing by the galley when I heard this bloody great explosion. I thought it was a plane or warship dropping depth-charges, but then I saw that a ship had been hit. The *Walter Q. Gresham* it was, just off our port bow and perhaps about a mile away from us. Well, I thought no more about it at the time because our own alarm bells were ringing and I had to get to my boat station. But as I got to the top of the companion ladder on the boat deck, I just happened to look up towards the port bridge wing and saw the skipper there waving his arms about and shouting something that I couldn't hear because of the wind and sea and the guns firing, so I decided to go up to the bridge and see what he wanted.

I got as far as the number two boat and that was it. There was this almighty explosion right under my feet. The deck literally lifted up under me and a column of water shot into the air as high as the monkey-island. As that happened, the boat that I was right against just disintegrated. It just blew apart as though it were made of cardboard. Something hit me in my left thigh [a large wooden splinter] and I flew across the deck half on my side like a rag doll. I was a bit stunned and it took me a few seconds before I realised what had happened. The ship rolled heavily to starboard and I thought I was going straight over the side. Then, just a few seconds later, there was another almighty explosion, and the hatch cover on the Number 5 hold just rose into the air as though it had been carefully lifted off the hatch and thrown overboard. The deck itself just opened up on the port side and carcasses of frozen meat came flying out into the air through the blown hatch cover and a 20 foot [6 m] rip in the deck.

When I was able to get up, I went to the side of the ship where the Number 2 boat had been, because that was my boat station. I didn't know where else to go because I was still a bit dazed. She was rolling pretty bad by then, and as I looked out at the sea, I could see all these sheep carcasses floating and bouncing about on the waves. Of course, the ship was settling pretty fast by then, and she was starting to go down at the stern, and I could hear these screeching noises coming from somewhere below decks – the bulkheads and boilers going. But all I could think about just then was the blokes down in the stoke-hole and engineroom. That torpedo exploding in there must have blown them all to pieces. Funnily enough, though, one bloke did escape from down below. A fireman he was. He must have been well away from the blast at the time, but the water was pouring in so fast that he couldn't get to the companion ladders, so he just trod water as the engineroom flooded and floated out through the skylight. In fact, it was me and my mate, Billy Bevan, who pulled him out and onto the raft.

But before that, everyone had come running out onto the decks as soon as they heard the alarm bells ringing then, straight after that, the exploding torpedo. The women and children were crying and screaming, and the men trying to calm them down as best they could, but none of them were seamen so they was all pretty scared. But the big thing was that, being army and air force officers, they was all trained for emergencies, so that helped a lot and no one actually panicked. Anyway, I asked the chief steward what boat I should go in, because mine had gone, and he sent me over to the Number 3 boat, starboard.

When I got there, there were the ABs, Joey Johnson, Andy Cole, Joe Bradshaw and my mate, Assistant Steward Billy Bevan, all trying to lower this bloody boat, but she wouldn't go. It had gone down so far, but then the stern fall had jammed. There must have been about fifteen passengers in it I suppose, but I never recognised everyone, I was too busy trying to get the boat lowered. I would have been in it myself if I hadn't been helping the ABs to get away. Anyway, it was going down bows first, because the stern fall had taken charge and the damn thing was almost upended. Everyone was clinging on for dear life and the women and children crying and sobbing, it was pitiful to hear them. Billy Bevan just sort of stood there with this bloody great knife in his hand trying to cut the stern fall, but he just couldn't move. It was as though he was just rooted to the spot. Fright and shock I suppose, although I had never known Billy to be frightened of anything or anyone. He was a big lump of a lad and as strong as an ox, but that ship going down had put the fear of God into him. Anyway, I was yelling at him to cut the rope but he still didn't move, so in the end I had to smack him one and take the knife off him. I gave it to Joey and he cut the rope, but by that time it was too late. The bows had gone down too far, but Joey couldn't see this, so what happened after that wasn't really his fault. By the time he had cut through the rope, the boat just tipped and dumped everyone into the sea, and when the rope did part, the boat just upended and came down on top of them all so those who hadn't been killed when the boat hit them was trapped under it. I don't know what happened to most of them, but I shouldn't think that many of them would have survived, if any at all. [A Royal Artillery colonel watched as that boat fell into the sea. His wife and young son were both killed as the boat fell on top of them.]

So there we were, the four of us with no boat to get into and the ship going down by the stern like she couldn't wait to get to the bottom. All the others had gone and left us. Now we knew that there were some rafts left down on the aft well-deck after the explosion, so me, Joey, Joe and Billy all ran down there to try and get one of those rafts afloat. By then, she was well down and the water was almost level with the well-deck, the bows were rising into the air and all four of us had to hold on with one hand while trying to cut away this raft with the other. Anyway, we finally managed to get the raft cut free. Now that only took us a few seconds, but in that time, all we had to do was to step over the side and into the sea. She was that low in the water by then. But no sooner did we get the raft over the side than all these blokes came from nowhere and scrambled aboard, so me, Joey, Joe and Billy lost out again. It was we who had cut the raft free and got it over the side, but it was we who had to hang onto the lanyards around the side. The raft was full, see, and we couldn't get aboard. And

Christ! Was that water cold? I still shiver even now whenever I think about it.

We got away from the side of the ship all right, and only just in time, too, because when we thought we was far enough away and looked back, the stern was almost completely under the water, and the bows were rising so fast it was just incredible. We saw the chippy on the poop deck where huge waves were breaking over the deck and him. He was saying something to one of the bridge officers, then we just saw him walk straight into the sea. It was just as though he'd had enough and wanted it all over and done with. The bows then just rose straight up into the air, and down she went like a bloody stone. We saw the skipper go down with her. I heard later that he had stayed aboard to make sure that everyone had got off all right and missed the boats. He was hanging onto the after rail of the boat deck as she went down. He never stood a chance. Good bloke, too, that skipper was. [The young captain had married shortly before the *Canadian Star* sailed from Swansea and had everything to live for. His only concern was for his passengers and crew. It was the ultimate devotion to duty for which he paid the ultimate price. He was posthumously awarded the Lloyd's War Medal. Chief Officer Hunt and Third Officer Keyworth were both awarded the MBE for their fine work in launching and handling the lifeboats.]

We were in the water for a long time. About an hour I should think. It might have been less, but all I remember is that it was so freezing cold. I saw a destroyer and two corvettes steaming past us. We thought they were coming to pick us up, but they just steamed on past us. An officer was shouting something from the bridge of the destroyer, but we couldn't hear what it was. A couple of the lads had died on the raft and in the water through the intense cold and shock, and they wanted me to get aboard, but I wouldn't go. There was a hell of a wind blowing, and with a wind as cold and strong as that after getting out of such a cold sea, I knew I wouldn't have lasted ten minutes, so I just stayed where I was and kept my arms and legs moving to keep the circulation going. Joey and Andy got in though. Joey survived, but only just, but Andy died on the raft as the *Anemone* came abeam of us. I could see the ship coming, and Billy Bevan was alongside me, hanging on the lanyard but not moving, so I kept saying to him, 'Come on, Billy, keep moving, mate. There's a ship coming to pick us up, so just keep moving your arms and legs.' Billy didn't move, though, and as I tried to shake him to bring him round, he just floated away, dead. He was only nineteen too. Then there was my other mate, Elwyn; he died on the raft, too, poor bugger. Same age as me he was, seventeen and a half.

Anyway, as the *Anemone* approached and slowed down, I saw one boat go alongside. The ship couldn't stop, you see, because there were U-boats about, and they never bothered about rescue ships picking people out of the sea. If a ship had stopped they just put a torpedo into it no matter what was happening. But she did slow down so that we could jump from the boats and rafts and grab hold of the scrambling nets which had been slung over the side. I remember seeing Dr Atkins and his wife and two children in that boat, and the rest were made up of crew members. As the lifeboat got alongside and everyone was standing up waiting to jump onto the net, I saw the doctor jump first. He grabbed the net all right, and then turned back, holding his hand out ready to help his wife and children. Just as he did, a bloody great wave swept in from nowhere and smashed them into the side of the ship. The boat just seemed to take off. Almost lifted itself clear out of the water and capsized. There was just nothing that anyone could do. The doctor just had to look on as his whole family were swept away under this bloody lifeboat. The corvette was rolling something cruel in that sea, of course, because those corvettes were built to the same design as the deep-sea whale-catchers, and every time she rolled to starboard, the breaking waves were going straight over the doctor, who was still hanging onto the net. Shocked the hell out of him seeing his whole family going like that. Then another huge wave came as the ship rolled, and when she came up again, he was hanging upside down with one of his feet caught in the net. That must have been the most horrible thing I have ever had to witness as, every time that ship rolled, he was being crushed under her keel.

[The man was, in fact, Colonel A.C. Craighead and not Dr Atkins, who survived. There is no official record that I have seen of two other young children being killed under a capsized lifeboat, but bearing in mind the anomalies which very often occur in historical records, it could well have been that the colonel's wife and son died under the lifeboat that my brother saw capsize alongside the *Anemone* and not in the lifeboat which capsized as it was being launched.]

After that, another boat went alongside with Wing-Commander Wrigley and his family aboard. Colonel Crouch was there and Mr and Mrs Dobree. They were a civilian couple going home to the UK. The colonel went first because he was a big, strong bloke, and he held onto the net with one hand while he helped the women and children to get on. The Dobrees went first, and they got to the deck with the help of the corvette's crew, then Wing-Commander Wrigley's little girl, Maureen, and she got to the deck by one of the ship's stokers who leaned right over the side and grabbed her by her hair and just yanked her aboard like she was a little rag doll. Then Mrs Wrigley jumped, but she slipped and was crushed between the lifeboat and the ship's side. Broke her back she did and died on the deck a few minutes later. [When the colonel was hauled unceremoniously aboard, he stood up and announced to all and sundry in words loud enough for everyone to hear who and what he was. A Geordie seaman standing nearby said, 'What the f—— do you expect me to do about it? Get forward!' The crew referred to him thereafter as Colonel Blimp.]

All the rest of them got picked up and the boat was left to drift away. Then it was our turn, but we were right up near the bows, and just there there was a thick lanyard slung from the bows and another from the stern to hold the net in place. As we floated alongside, all the lads on the raft were singing, 'She's a Lassie From Lancashire'. I thought they had all gone bloody mad, but there you are. People say and do the strangest things in situations like that. [Second Officer G.D. Williams from the *Nariva* heard the singing and said later, 'We didn't know whether to laugh or cry'.]

Stan Williams jumped first, he was another steward, but he jumped just as the corvette's bows were rising on a wave, and he missed the rope and fell under the bows as the *Anemone* breasted the wave, and as she came down again going into the trough, she just slammed down on top of Stan. He didn't stand a cat in hell's chance. So then I thought – and don't ask me how I was thinking straight at that time after being in the water and frozen stiff – I had to get onto that lanyard and work my way across to that net. I knew, you see, that if I waited for the ship to pass, I might not be able to jump in time with all those other blokes on the raft waiting to jump at the same time, and if I missed on the first go, I wouldn't get a second chance. I was still in the water at that time, but as the ship's bow came abeam of us, I got into the raft and stood on one of the thwarts. I waited until a wave raised the raft and the corvette was on a starboard roll, then I jumped.

How the hell I was able to hold onto that lanyard I'll never know, but I did, and began working my way towards the waist of the ship. Well, I managed to get there, but by the time I did I was all in. I just looked up at the men lining the rails and I knew that I couldn't have climbed that net, not if hell had me, and I was just hanging there, trying not to fall back into the sea. The next thing I knew was that someone had grabbed me by the hair and was yanking me aboard. It might have been the same sailor who rescued that little girl in the same way, I just do not know. Next thing, I was lying on the deck and saw a shadow bend over me; because that was all I could see by then, just shadows, and I heard someone say, 'I don't know about this one, sir, he seems to be in a pretty bad way. I think he may have some oil inside him.' And of course I was in a bad way, and I did have oil inside me. I'd been in the water for a long time and my legs were so cold they had just seized up. But anyway, I'm still here and that was it.

When I did come to, I found myself in someone's bunk, freezing cold and shivering like a bloody jelly. I was there for three days before I had the strength to get up and go out on deck. The weather had moderated by then. The sun was shining over a calm sea with warships all around and planes circling overhead, and that's the way it stayed until we docked a few days later.

*Oberleutnant* Trojer was later informed by wireless that he had been awarded the Knight's Cross for his successes against HX 229. However, he did not live long enough to boast about it. He and all his crew were lost in the Bay of Biscay later that year after a successful attack by a Coastal Command Halifax bomber.

The survivors aboard the *Anemone* huddled miserably in alleyways, under the lee of superstructures or engine-room bulkheads, or under gun mountings. Others who were not so fortunate merely stood about the open decks, their shoulders hunched and hands thrust deeply into greatcoat or trouser pockets in a vain effort to glean whatever warmth they could. Clothes which had been provided for them by the *Anemone*'s crew, although as welcome as they were generously given, were totally inadequate; there were so many survivors needing warm, dry clothing after their own had been soaked in oil and sea water. Prey to wind, rain and sea, those men simply stood around the crowded decks, cold and miserable, kept going only by the thought that soon their ordeal would be over and they would be going home.

Women and children were given priority where accommodation was concerned, and officers' cabins were made available whenever possible. Aboard the tiny corvettes, however, accommodation, as well as being at a premium, was very basic to say the least. Food was also basic, and never enough to feed all those hungry mouths. But the simple acts of kindness and understanding from the crews speak volumes for the integrity of the men who served aboard those little ships; they were prepared to forgo even the simplest of necessities in order to offer little acts of self-less compassion to those in need.

At 19.30 hours on 18 March, HMS *Anemone* and her sister ship, *Pennywort*, turned away from the wreckage of the *Canadian Star* to rejoin the convoy. The majority of the survivors had been taken aboard the *Anemone*, and at that point, like the *Pennywort*, she was so overcrowded with survivors – about 240 altogether – that she could take no part in hunting the U-boat which had sunk the *Canadian Star* and the *Walter Q. Gresham*. Out of the ninety people who had been aboard the *Canadian Star*, twenty-three crew members and seven passengers, including four children, perished that day in the North Atlantic. Some of them simply drowned, others died of exposure or crush injuries from lifeboats and the keel of *Anemone*, whilst others still simply disappeared into the wild Atlantic wastes. Those who were in the engine-room when the torpedoes struck were perhaps the most fortunate, in that they died almost instantly in the sudden frigid darkness of inrushing sea, their remains still inside the rotting hull of the ship in which they had served.

No more ships were sunk during the night of 18/19 March and no further attacks on HX 229 took place. Moreover, to the relief of Commander Luther, the protection of HX 229 was no longer left exclusively to the escort vessels. The convoy was far enough advanced to be within easier range of the Liberators operating out of Aldergrove and Iceland, and very close to the operating range of Flying Fortresses from the Hebrides and Sunderland flying-boats from County Londonderry. Doenitz's U-boats, however, had not quite finished with HX 229.

In the evening of 18 March the 8,848-ton *Mathew Luckenbach* disobeyed strict orders for all ships to remain on station and, using her 15-knot (27.75 kph) speed, she forged ahead of the convoy in an effort to reach safety as quickly as possible. On the morning of the 19th, *Kapitän-Leutnant* Uhlig, commanding U-527, took a report from his listening room of the noise of ship's screws. Through his periscope, Uhlig saw the two masts of a merchant ship which, having left HX 229 far astern, was then overhauling SC 122. He closed up under water to get into a firing position on what he thought must have been a transport vessel or, because of her armament, an auxiliary cruiser. It was in fact, the *Mathew Luckenbach*.

At 09.47 hours, *Kapitän-Leutnant* Uhlig fired off a salvo of three torpedoes at extreme range of 4,000 yards (3,650 m). After four minutes, the listening crew of U-527 heard one of the torpedoes explode near the area of the ship's aftermast. A huge geyser of white water shot skywards as the *Mathew Luckenbach* seemed to rise half out of the water as though she were arching her back from a mortal wound. The sound of her threshing screw stopped at once, and through his periscope Uhlig could see vast plumes of black smoke emanating from the stricken steamer as she settled fast by the stern.

At the precise moment that the *Mathew Luckenbach* was hit, the watch officer on board the destroyer USS *Ingham* was scanning the sea through his binoculars prior to making a zigzag turn and happened to see, on the horizon, the huge column of water which had risen high into the air after the strike. With no aircraft visible in the sky, he concluded that it could not have been a bomb, and at that point he saw a white distress rocket. He immediately ordered a turn in that direction and, proceeding at high speed, he soon came across the *Mathew Luckenbach*. There were three boats and two rafts in the water with swimmers all around, but no attempt was being made by either boats or rafts to pick them up. With a U-boat in the vicinity, Captain A. Martinson of USS *Ingham* could not stop and was obliged to wait until HMS *Upshur* arrived on the scene.

Having observed the destroyer approaching, U-527 had prudently submerged.

The *Upshur* circled the wreck and lifeboats so that the *Ingham* could take the survivors on board. Within the space of thirty minutes, all sixty-seven survivors had been rescued, but the *Ingham* had been obliged to manoeuvre up to each boat and raft in turn because the American seamen did nothing to help themselves. The *Mathew Luckenbach* looked as though she might have been salvaged, but her crew steadfastly refused to reboard her. Captain Martinson then called for a deep-sea tug and proceeded, with the *Upshur*, back to the convoy.

The tug, however, failed to find the *Mathew Luckenbach*, and she was left to the tender mercies of *Kapitän-Leutnant* Pietzsch in U-523 and *Kapitän-Leutnant* Uhlig in U-527, both of whom began their attack runs simultaneously without knowing of each other's presence. U-523's torpedo hit the wreck mere moments before U-527's at 19.08 hours. The freighter sank some seven minutes later.

Convoy HX 299 had thirteen ships fewer than four days previously, while SC 122 had lost eight. Three hundred and seventy-two merchant seamen and passengers had lost their lives. One hundred and forty-six thousand tons of shipping, and 161,000 tons of vitally needed cargo went to the bottom of the Atlantic with the torpedoed ships and the men trapped inside them – all in just four days.

By the evening of 19 March, the surviving ships of HX 229 and SC 122 were sailing in close company as one vast convoy. After four terrible days of running wild in the 'death hole', round-the-clock air cover finally drove the attackers away.

The relaxation of the tension that came with the sudden departure of danger quickly translated itself into a kind of euphoria aboard the surviving merchant ships. Mess-mates gave each other haircuts in readiness for their home-coming, whilst others were singing, skylarking and ragging each other and looking to the day when they would be reunited with friends and families. Men who just hours before had been fighting for their very lives, no longer gave a thought to the terrible dangers they had fought and lived through, even though the rescue ships were crowded with 1,100 survivors from the many torpedoed ships. The vast majority of the men who had survived torpedoes, exploding ships and the unbelievable terror of the U-boats, lived to sail again, and many of them were outward bound again within the month.

Constant delays due to adverse weather conditions and U-boat engagements meant that both convoys were at sea for a further seven days. The storms had melted away, however, and for the remainder of the voyage, calm seas, cloudless skies and warm sunshine prevailed. Day and night, Allied aircraft circled overhead, driving away any last-ditch, die-hard U-boat commanders who were still dogging the convoy in search of easy kills. The surviving ships finally reached their destination on 25 March.

A number of the vessels which had made up convoys SC 122 and HX 229 had already departed for the Icelandic anchorage of Hvalfjordur. There they were to become a part of another convoy, JW 58, bound for the Russian port of Murmansk, deep inside the Kola Inlet. Other ships which had survived the murderous attacks left the convoy at various points as they approached the coast to sail alone or in much smaller groups to their various ports of discharge.

On their approach to Greenock, the battered warships and war-weary crews were greeted by vast flocks of seabirds, wheeling and diving and crying out raucously in the late March sunshine as they fought each other for whatever scraps of food were available. The surface of the grey, murky water of the anchorage was dotted with the curious faces of grey seals as they surfaced for air, gazing around them in innocent curiosity. It was an idyllic scene of peace and tranquillity which greeted the survivors that day, but the terrors they had endured they could never forget.

HMS *Anemone* and HMS *Pennywort*, overloaded with survivors, finally came to rest in Greenock Bay seven days after the sinking of the *Canadian Star* and almost immediately arrangements were made for the survivors to be sent home. My brother Jim, quiet, depressed, no longer the happy-go-lucky young 17-year-old who had set sail aboard the *Canadian Star* seven months earlier and not as sure of himself as he had once been, boarded a whaler along with other surviving members of the crew, and were rowed out to where three paddle-steamers rode at anchor in the centre of Greenock Bay.

Boarding one of the vessels, each man was provided with either new or second-hand clothes which, even though they were not quite the height of fashion or a perfect fit, were at least clean, warm and dry. After kitting out, they were directed to a table in another part of the ship where they were issued with travel warrants and some money for their train journeys. Within twenty-four hours of coming to anchor, Jim, together with quite a few other Swansea and West Walean men who had survived the sinking, were on their way home. In gratitude to the crew of the *Anemone*, survivors of the *Canadian Star* presented every man with a suitably inscribed silver ashtray.

Even though it was a civilian service and a reserved occupation, the merchant navy was not subject to the regulations which existed for other reserved occupations such as miners, dockworkers, farmers and factory workers. Having come under the authority of the Ministry of War Transport in 1939, they were under the command of the Admiralty and were therefore subject to the rules and regulations of that body. There was a blanket shutdown on information about the movements of all merchant ships. Being a skipper on the Swansea Harbour tugs at that particular time, however, my father was in a position to learn a few details about specific ships entering or leaving Swansea docks, as such information was vital to his work.

Sometime between 19 and 25 March, word had filtered through from the Admiralty to the Swansea Port Authority that the *Canadian Star* had been sunk. However, the report had said that she had gone down with all hands.

My father was a deep sea sailor who had taken up a temporary post with the tugs in order to be as close as possible to his young family at a time of extreme danger. He therefore knew the confusion which can occur with coded signals. He also knew that the probability of sixty-three crewmen and twenty-seven passengers going down with a torpedoed ship was, to say the least, remote. He therefore kept the news of the *Canadian Star* from us all for several days.

However, when it became known that she was overdue, people began asking questions and news began filtering through that she had been torpedoed and sunk with all hands. No longer able to withhold the truth from her, my father told my mother all he knew. Mother, of course, was distraught, almost inconsolable in fact. I, childish and perhaps not quite understanding the gravity of the situation, felt virtually nothing except perhaps for a certain sense of loss. As a young child throughout the war years, death and destruction were normal, everyday events to me. I had known no other way of life. Swansea had ceased to exist as a town and as far as I was concerned, that was how it was supposed to look. In fact, I had witnessed the corpses of several people who had been blasted apart by a German bomb during the heaviest of the three nights' blitz on Swansea between 1940 and 1943, so death was no stranger to me and never meant very much to me. Therefore, the apparent death of a dearly loved brother was a normal, everyday event.

By 25 March, the sinking of the *Canadian Star* had become the talk of the town. A number of men from Swansea and outlying districts had sailed aboard her, and what with the number of people who had been killed in the air raid of the previous month Swansea, as well as having ceased to function as a town, was a town in mourning. Then, on the afternoon of 28 March, the train from Glasgow steamed into High Street Station.

On the platform that day was a woman who had known Jim since birth. Mrs McGrath was there waiting for her son to arrive home on leave and, in common with everyone else in the town, she was aware of the loss of the *Canadian Star*. She suddenly caught sight of Jim and several other men who she knew had served aboard the same ship. That was when the myth of all hands being lost was finally exploded.

It was a cold but bright, sunny day, and my mother, younger brother and sister and I were standing on the doorstep saying goodbye to an aunt who had been visiting us. Suddenly my mother's eyes almost popped out of her head and she threw her arms in the air, shouting and screaming as she ran down the road. Jim was home.

During the following five months, Jim continually failed medicals by naval doctors, who would not pass him fit for sea service because of the mental and emotional traumas he had suffered. Towards the end of August, however, they reluctantly agreed to allow him to sign on a ship called the *Darlington Court*, a troopship bound for the Mediterranean. He had no sooner signed on than a heavy hand fell on his shoulder and a detective asked him, 'Have you just signed on?' Jim said he had.

'Just as well you have, mate, or you would have gone down for six months,' said the detective. That was the official reaction, in spite of the fact that naval doctors would not allow him to go back to sea because of the mental scars he had incurred. He and thousands of others like him had put their lives and sanities at risk in order to keep civilians workers and their families fed and safe, but such was the way that merchant seamen were treated.

## ROLL OF HONOUR

### Passengers and Crew-Members Lost at Sea

Captain R.D. Miller.
*Penybont, Radnorshire.*

W.E. Bevan.
*St Thomas, Swansea.*

Chief Engineer, E.G. Buckwell.
*Crosby, Liverpool.*

Donkeyman, T. Christie.
*Liverpool.*

Cadet, J. Coghlan.
*Liverpool.*

Fireman, D. Connor.
*Liverpool.*

Donkeyman, F. Edwards.

2nd Refrigeration Engineer, J.A. Forbes.
*Bluff, South Island, New Zealand.*

Junior Engineer, J. Gee
*Blaydon-on-Tyne, County Durham.*

Greaser, W. Greaves.
*Rush Green.*

Donkeyman, T. Hughes.
*Treharris, Glamorgan.*

Second Cook, L.F. Humphries.
*Lower Peacedown, St John, Somerset.*

Donkeyman, R.S. Jones
*Caernarvon.*

Chief Cook, H. Mack
*Wallsend-on-Tyne.*

Chief Refrigeration Engineer, C. Marsh.
*Sunderland, County Durham.*

Assistant Cook, J.B. O'Reilly.
*Old Trafford, Manchester.*

Junior Engineer, A.I. Towers.
*Bolton, Lancashire.*

Fourth Mate, V. Trillo
*Wellington, New Zealand*

Electrician, K. St. C. Vincent.
*Leigh-on-Sea, Essex.*

Carpenter, J.G. Watson.
*Whitehills, Banffshire.*

Assistant Steward S. Williams.
*Swansea.*

## RN Gunners

AB E.H. Hayward.
*Andover, Hampshire .*

AB. S. Slater.
*Hyde, Cheshire.*

## Passengers

Colonel A.C. Craighead and Miss A.E. Craighead (12 years old).
*Simla, India and Forfar, Scotland.*

Mr H.T.W. Early.
*Melbourne, Australia.*

Colonel and Mrs J.H. Ord, Master Ord, (2 years old).
*Duntroom Staff College, New South Wales and London.*

Mrs M. Wrigley.
*Newcastle-upon-Tyne.*

The battle for HX 229 and SC 122 was over, but the Battle of the Atlantic was not. Between 3 September 1939 and the end of December 1940, the German *U-boot-waffe* had accounted for some 16.8 million tons of merchant shipping. By March, 1943, nearly another million tons had gone to the bottom. By mid-May of that year, however, the U-boats had enjoyed their last fling.

The final defeat of the U-boat packs came with a small, slow, westbound light-ship convoy, ONS 5, Commodore Rodney Stone commanding in SS *Gharindi*, which left Britain in late April of that year. Three days later, after battling through high winds and heavy seas, they were just to the south of Iceland when the first attacks began. As a result of excellent detection work by the escorts, the attackers were driven off for the loss of one merchant ship. On 3 May, four of the escorts were forced to leave the convoy because they were running short of fuel. On that day, the convoy was again experiencing heavy weather with severe gale-force winds whipping up the seas to heights of over 50 feet (15 m). Ten of the merchant ships became disorganised just as the U-boats were gathering for further attacks. By that time, however, the Canadian Air Force had found them. Spotting the pack on the surface, and despite the foul weather conditions, they managed to sink one U-boat and severely damaged another just south of Greenland.

On the afternoon of Friday, 4 May, the U-boats attacked in earnest. *Kapitän Z. See* Hartwig Looks, commanding U-264, slipped through a gap between the depleted escorts and, with a fan of four torpedoes, sank two ships, one of which was the commodore vessel, *Gharindi*. During the following eight hours, the convoy was to suffer no fewer than twenty-five attacks, during which a further eight ships were sunk. The outlook for that convoy began to look very bleak as more U-boats were ordered in to the attack. Fortunately, however, they were saved further losses when a thick, grey blanket of fog suddenly descended over the ocean. The U-boats had lost them. The escorts, however, had not lost the U-boats.

During the night of 4/5 May Captain Raymond Hart, commanding HMS *Vidette*, received a firm Asdic contact some 800 yards (730 m) away from the nearest ship in the convoy. Without hesitation, he rang down for full revolutions and, roaring through the rough seas, he fired off a salvo of forward-throwing 'hedgehog' bombs, being short of depth-charges. As his vessel passed over the attack site, a vast column of air and sea raised the stern of his vessel into the air as the U-boat broke apart. Throughout the remainder of that night, another six U-boats were destroyed and several more damaged to varying degrees. Demoralised at those severe losses with the odds firmly on their side, the pack withdrew and no more ships were sunk.

On the homeward-bound convoy, the fully laden SC 130 was escorted by the same escort vessels which had escorted ONS 5. Several days out, they were attacked by a large U-boat pack. A furious battle then ensued between U-boats and escort vessels during which no less than twenty U-boats were destroyed with no loss to the convoy. The Battle of the Atlantic, although not quite over, had been won, and never again did Doenitz risk his U-boats in the Western Ocean.

# 9   The Sinking of the
## *Clan MacArthur*

History informs us that the most successful German U-boat ace of the Second World War was *Kapitän-Leutnant* Otto Kretschmer, who sank 250,000 tons of Allied shipping in the first eighteen months of the war. It has been claimed that no other German U-boat commander ever sank such a large number of ships in so short a time. However, he was depth-charged to the surface and taken prisoner just eighteen months into the war. There was another U-boat commander who it is claimed surpassed Kretschmer's record, partly because he survived for longer than Kretschmer, but mainly because he had a tendency to exaggerate the tonnage of the ships he sank.

*Kapitän-Leutnant* Wolfgang Luth, who in spring 1943 was the holder of the Knight's Cross with Oak Leaves and Swords, claimed to have despatched more tonnage than Kretschmer, but after close scrutiny of the ships he claimed to have sunk, his total tonnage for the whole of the war was only in the region of 230,000. He survived the war, only to be shot and killed by one of his own guards after the German surrender.

He was a confirmed Nazi, and the destruction of merchant ships and their crews was to him a crusade for the greater glory of the Third Reich. His first command was in the Iron Cross boat U-9, and his first two kills of the war took place in the North Sea on 16 January 1940 on his first patrol as skipper. The two ships involved were the Swedish coastal freighters *Patria* and *Flandria*, both small ships of around 1,200 tons (which he exaggerated to 4,000 and 8,000 respectively).

There were many other kills after that in U-9, U-138 and U-43, before he took command of the U-cruiser, U-181. Perhaps the most infamous came on an early spring night in the Western Ocean when, in command of U-43 he sank a large, unarmed three-masted schooner. U-43 was at the time four days at sea in a black, empty ocean. It was a freezing, star-studded night with a bright yellow moon reflecting eerily off the Stygian surface of the heaving water. The four lookouts on watch in the conning tower were bored, tired, wet and cold, longing for something to happen to relieve the monotony, when one of them spotted the schooner sailing serenely as a sea-sprite as she heeled over to port under a full spread of canvas.

Luth decided that such a vessel did not merit the expense of a torpedo, but that he was going to sink her anyway. The schooner and her killer were just 300 yards (275 m) apart when U-43, without any warning whatsoever, opened fire with the 105-mm cannon forward of her conning tower, the 20-mm machine-gun on her bridge and a 37-mm gun on her main deck aft.

The schooner's pilot house was hit first, its timbers collapsing in an orange tongue of fire and rolling smoke as the men inside died. Other hits were scored all along the length and beam of the doomed vessel as what was left of her crew poured from her burning interior and began to launch her boats through a hail of heavy-calibre shells and bullets. The schooner's wooden deck, with its pitched oakum seams, was ablaze from stem to stern with angry red flames bursting from her shattered hull and fierce fires licking up the masts into the rigging like St Elmo's fire gone mad. Burning sails and pitch-filled yards fell to the deck, sending the conflagration higher as shell after shell was pumped into her, until the entire ship was a blazing inferno, lighting up the night sky and producing a blood-red reflection on the heaving ocean.

The stench of burnt cordite and burning, pitch-filled timbers hung heavy in the still air whilst the shells and machine-gun bullets reaped a terrible harvest of defenceless men as just two lifeboats managed to get away from the burning hulk. A vast column of smoke and flame and a forest of sparks like gigantic fireflies rose above them as the masts began collapsing and the surviving crew pulled frantically away through the smoke and murk.

At one point, a particularly high sea washed one of the 105-mm gunners overboard from the U-boat and, as he hung there by his safety harness, his shipmates stopped firing to haul him inboard. 'What the hell do you think you're doing?' roared Luth, pointing to the burning ship. 'Keep firing and let that bastard swim.' He thought they were trying to pull a survivor on board. The gun resumed firing with a mixture of HE and incendiary shells for almost an hour. Then, with smoke and flames billowing out from her shattered hull, the schooner rolled tiredly over onto her side and sank.

Luth did nothing for any of the survivors in the frail lifeboats, and they floated away into the night to whatever fate awaited them. Such was his attitude. Codes of behaviour at sea were forgotten.

Luth and his crew undertook the longest ever U-boat cruise, seven months in 1943, patrolling the area around the Cape of Good Hope and into the Indian Ocean as far north as Lourenço Marques (now Maputo), Mozambique and it is there that the tragic story of the sinking of the British passenger/cargo combination *Clan MacArthur* unfolded.

On 11 June 1943 Luth, then commanding the 1,500-ton U-cruiser U-181, left the general area of Lourenço Marques where he had been patrolling for several weeks, in search of easier and quicker kills elsewhere. The vast expanse of the Indian Ocean had become his chosen killing-ground. At that time, he claimed that he had already accounted for 200,000 tons of merchant shipping, and as the Inhaca Light faded rapidly astern, he eagerly looked forward to increasing that tonnage. First however, he needed to replenish his depleted supplies of food, water, fuel and torpedoes.

U-181's replenishment vessel was the *Charlotte Schliemann*, a supply and prison ship for the *Kriegsmarine*'s surface raiders. She was homeward bound from Japan when her skipper received orders to refuel and revictual U-181 in an area of the Indian Ocean that was just a small dot on the chart, a remote point far off the general shipping lanes about 700 miles (1,300 km) south of Mauritius and 1,700 miles (3,150 km) east of Durban.

Her replenishment was completed by 15.00 hours on 26 June and, with full bunkers, fresh food and water and a full stock of torpedoes, Luth headed north towards Mauritius. Arriving off that island's capital, Port Louis, in the early hours of 1 July, he began his lonely patrol. He did not have long to wait. Just a little before midnight on the 2nd, he sank the small British steamer *Hoihow* with two torpedoes, leaving the only four survivors alone without food or water on a fragile raft in the shark-infested sea. On the 6th, a large, unidentified vessel which Luth had been shadowing headed toward Cap Est on the coast of Madagascar. Finally intercepting the vessel, Luth fired a salvo of two torpedoes, but sharp-eyed lookouts saw them in time for avoiding action to be taken. Luth was forced to abandon the chase as the freighter easily outpaced the pursuing U-boat. It was during the unsuccessful pursuit of that vessel that Luth was informed by the BdU that his operational area had been increased yet again to include Madagascar and the Mascarenes and extend north along the East African coast to the borders of Tanganyika. Ranging much further north and west then, lookouts in Luth's U-181 sighted Tromelin on 8 July and Tamatave on the 12th.

In the late evening of the 15th, a lookout in the conning tower of U-181 sighted the British collier *Empire Lake*, and after shadowing her for the remainder of that night in high winds and heavy seas, Luth finally sank her at first light with a salvo of two torpedoes. The only survivors were five men who were left clinging precariously to a piece of wreckage in the high seas 180 miles (330 km) from the nearest land. How those unfortunates survived in those shark-infested waters with no food or water is a mystery, but they did.

At 09.30 hours on the following day, *Kapitän-Leutnant* Luth sank the British steamer *Port Franklin* just 50 miles (90 km) south of where he had sunk the *Empire Lake*, and over the course of the following three days he sank two more British steamers, the *Dalfram* and the *Unvuma*. By that time, however, Port Louis had become aware of Luth's activities, and following an Asdic search by a British destroyer, he decided that he may have been extending his luck too far and left the Mauritius area.

The 10,500-ton passenger/cargo combination *Clan MacArthur* was launched on 15 October 1935 by the Greenock Dockyard Company, and was the first twin-screw vessel built for the Clan Line, and the first to exceed 10,000 tons. Fitted with two triple-expansion Bauer-Wach turbine engines and six oil-fired boilers of 220 psi (15 kg/cm²) each, she had been designed for a speed of 16 knots (30 kph), which also made her the fastest in the fleet. A three-island steamer with well decks fore and aft and an expansive poop deck, her Numbers 2, 3 and 4 holds were refrigerated, whilst her Number 1 hold had been enlarged to cater for such large cargoes as locomotives. Completed on 16 January 1936, at her sea trials she exceeded 17½ knots (32.4 kph). In service, however, that speed was drastically reduced to around 14 knots (26 kph).

After a long and tortuous voyage in convoy from Glasgow, the *Clan MacArthur* finally arrived in Durban on 1 August 1943. Her crew, consisting of 150 hands, had become nervous after rounding the Cape of Good Hope and entering into the Indian Ocean because of rumours that there were U-boats operating in that area. Indeed, they had every reason to be nervous, because quite a lot of ships had been lost between Durban, Mozambique and Mauritius during the first six months of 1943 and, at the time of her sailing from Durban, the situation was worsening. Although there were no U-boat packs involved as there had been in the Western Ocean up until June of that year, there were a number of lone wolves which had been causing havoc amongst the independently sailing ships.

After taking on board water, stores and fuel, the *Clan MacArthur* left Durban on 5 August but, because of a U-boat scare in the area, turned back to spend another night in port. She finally left on the 6th with a cargo of livestock and medical supplies bound for the UK via Mauritius, the Red Sea, the Suez Canal and the Mediterranean. At approximately 11.45 hours on the 11th, she was at 39°30'E and 28°S, on a north-easterly course some 350 miles (650 km) east of Farafangana on the southernmost tip of Madagascar when she was spotted by the eagle-eyed lookouts aboard U-181.

Because of her low profile, U-181 was able to follow the *Clan MacArthur* on the surface without being observed by the British ship and, keeping a safe distance between them, Luth decided to stalk the vessel until the moon had set early the following morning when the sea and sky would be at their darkest. Unlike his Italian counterparts, Luth was too canny a U-boat skipper to take any unnecessary action which might endanger his boat, and would not risk a surface engagement with a heavily armed merchant ship. He could not make an underwater attack at that time because of the vessel's pronounced zigzag, hence his decision to wait until just before dawn. By 01.00 hours, he had correctly calculated the *Clan MacArthur*'s base course and, in an almost leisurely pursuit, gradually passed the big ship in a great arc at the limit of her crew's visibility.

At 03.00 hours on the 12th, U-181 was in position ahead of the *Clan MacArthur*'s starboard side and submerged to periscope depth to await the arrival of its un-suspecting victim. At 03.30 hours, the vessel came into Luth's cross-hairs and, as she did so, he fired a salvo of two torpedoes. The first hit her amidships, and the second struck astern with merciless, indiscriminate swiftness. Crew members on watch below were flung unceremoniously out of their bunks, coming instantly awake, terrified and bewildered, whilst those on watch were thrown about like rag dolls as the torpedoes exploded with a tremendous roar of smoke and flames. The ship was ripped open from midships to stern. The first torpedo had exploded in her Number 4 hold just between her twin funnels, and with both propeller shafts broken by the tremendous blast, she stopped dead in the water, wallowing like a mortally wounded leviathan as the second torpedo slammed into her aft section. A vast cataract of water poured in through her ruptured hull, killing almost instantly the livestock in the aft holds.

With only enough power to start the pumps, the *Clan MacArthur* was going down by the stern as the guns' crews stood by ready for instant action should their killer surface. The canny Luth, however, had no intention of doing so. Knowing full well the danger posed to submarines in a surface battle, he watched from 14 feet (4 m) beneath the surface as the ship's lifeboats were launched. Although she was settling by the stern the *Clan MacArthur* was dying slowly and, detecting a distress call from the ship at 03.50 hours, Luth delivered the *coup de grâce* with a third torpedo which exploded in her Number 1 hold. With thunderous noises she began to slip much more quickly into the lifeless, frigid abyss of the Indian Ocean.

The sinking of a ship in the deep oceans is both unpredictable and highly dangerous, and with urgency lending strength to their aching limbs, her surviving crew pulled hard on their oars to get clear before she finally went down. Just eight minutes after the first explosion, and on an even keel then because of the inrush of water into her fore hold, the *Clan MacArthur* was sinking fast. With a tremendous eruption from deep within her hull, as though a whole consignment of high explo-sives had exploded all at once, her decks finally slipped beneath the waves.

At that time, U-181 was still submerged and lying 1,000 yards (900 m) away from the sinking ship. Nevertheless, she leaped in the water, causing many items to fall from shelves and her crew to stagger uncontrollably as the *Clan MacArthur* was ripped apart by that last blast from deep within her hull. Several of her lifeboats that were already in the water were instantly destroyed by the severity of the explosion and the resulting turbulence of the surrounding sea, killing or maiming most of their occupants. Another lifeboat which was still hanging in its falls and fully laden was blown apart, instantly killing every man aboard. The men in the boats who had been fortunate enough to get well clear before that last violent explosion watched in horrid fascination as she went down on an even keel with a cataract of white and green water pouring over her well deck bulwarks and through her rails.

It was thought for a long time that this explosion had been caused by another torpedo, but in 1984, when U-181's log was made public, it was realised that it must have been caused by another, unidentified cargo besides the livestock and medical supplies which the *Clan MacArthur* had been carrying. It was known to the bridge officers that she had been carrying another consignment which had been classified 'most secret', but its nature was unknown to them. Enquiries by other historians and by myself have gone unanswered, so the mystery remains.

When the *Clan MacArthur* had finally slipped beneath the waves and U-181 was safe from her 4.5-inch naval guns, *Kapitän-Leutnant* Luth brought his boat to the surface. He stood proudly on his bridge as his chief officer, Engel, descended to the weather deck to greet the survivors with, 'Good morning gentlemen. I must apologise for sinking your ship but, unfortunately, it is the fortunes of war.' Then still using the same pleasant tones, he asked a battery of questions. 'What is the name of your ship? Where were you bound? When did you leave England?' and many more. The survivors replied with a load of gibberish mixed with the very best Anglo-Saxon insults possible, but he got nothing from them except for one crew-member who called him a 'cheeky bastard', a term which he readily understood. Unusually for Luth, the wounded were taken aboard U-181 where they were given treatment and some sugar and water before being returned to the boats and an uncertain fate. That was the first time that Luth had ever been known to show any form of compassion to survivors of a ship he had destroyed.

Luth did get the information he was looking for. It is not clear how he was able to convince some of the survivors to tell him what he wanted to know, but he did. Having received that information, and knowing that a distress call had been sent, he decided to leave the area as quickly as possible. Dawn was about to break and at any time British destroyers might appear on the horizon in answer to the call for help. As the lifeboats were being cast off, Engel wished them all good luck, gave them a course to steer for the nearest land and, with a swirl of water from her twin screws, U-181 began to dive.

The remaining lifeboats, surrounded by up to sixty men in the water, many of them suffering from varying degrees of injury, drifted off through gelatinous fuel oil across a speckled sea under a powder-blue sky and a rising sun already hot, despite the early hour. They were at least 300 miles (550 km) from the nearest land and their options were brutally stark. Luth, again unusually for him, had promised to signal Mauritius and inform the authorities there of their plight and, after steaming a safe distance from the scene of carnage, he did just that. The survivors, however, were destined to lose many men over the course of the following three weeks as a result of their injuries, through lack of proper sustenance and medical care, from heat-stroke under the pitiless tropical sun or from the terrible cold of clear nights. Most, however, were lost to that most dreaded of all seamen's nightmares, sharks, before they were finally picked up.

Throughout that first morning, the boats drifted aimlessly over a calm sea. As the sun rose higher into an almost colourless sky, the energy-sapping heat burned cruelly into their aching bodies, many of them only half dressed as they had tumbled, bleary-eyed from warm bunks when the torpedoes struck. They were the men who suffered most as their skins first turned pink, then an angry red. Not knowing when or even if rescue would come, food and water had to be strictly rationed right from the start and if, as turned out to be the case, they were adrift for any length of time, they would have to rely on rainwater and the possibility of catching fish or turtles to supplement their already meagre diet of hardtack biscuits, corned beef and a limited supply of water. It was a grim prospect, made no easier by the fact that they were all too aware that their future hung in a very precarious balance.

As many of the men who were in the water as possible were taken into the boats whilst the remainder hung onto the lanyards around the sides. After three hours, however, the number of men clinging to the lanyards began to dwindle as their strength drained. Exposure, exhaustion and loss of blood from wounds they had received all took their toll as, one by one, they released their fragile hold on life and slipped away.

As the westering sun dipped towards the horizon, its fiery rays reflected off the surface of a calm, oily sea, the first sharks, attracted no doubt by the amount of blood in the water, began to appear. The little red lights attached to lifejackets began to appear in the semi-darkness as men, too exhausted to hold on to the lanyards any longer, floated free in the water, all of them surrounded by the sinister fins of the circling oceanic whitetip sharks which were the first on the scene. These slow-moving but very dangerous creatures have the unnerving habit of persevering fearlessly when investigating potential prey, and will circle distressed humans in the water for very long periods before finally attacking. So it was on the evening of 12 August that the sharks circled, slowly and determinedly, smelling and tasting the blood in the water, and becoming more and more agitated by the minute.

From the lifeboats, those little red dots of light were clearly visible, but as they made towards them in an attempt to pick the men up, the shark attack began. As the first boat closed onto one of the lights, the man gave out a bloodcurdling scream of agony and a great frothing of blood and water swirled around him as the little red light disappeared beneath the surface in an ever-widening circle of crimson. There was another terrible scream and frothing of water, then another as the feeding frenzy began in earnest. Very soon, blue sharks began to appear.

Like the oceanic whitetips, blue sharks are highly dangerous in the deep oceans. Some shark experts would have us believe that blue sharks are not the man-eaters of the deep they have been portrayed to be, but that is not the experience of survivors of the USS *Indianapolis*, the *Clan MacArthur* and the many other vessels which have been sunk in the deep oceans. They are in fact a highly dangerous species which hunt mainly in packs on the surface, and are known to have been the cause of a great number of deaths at sea after a sinking. Reports from survivors of the *Clan MacArthur* tell of lifeboats homing in on red lights, only to find the lights suddenly disappearing beneath the surface as they draw near. In other instances, when a boat arrived at a light and tried to pull its owner inboard, they would find just the top half left.

The dreadful slaughter continued well into the night, until there were no lights left to be seen. The sharks, however, having scented blood, continued to circle the boats, as though aware that more food would shortly be available. They stayed with them throughout the three weeks of their terrible ordeal.

With the setting of the sun on the evening of that first day, the deepening night began to grow cold as the tropical daytime heat gave way to frigid darkness. Scantily clad men shivered uncontrollably under their thin coverings. Covered with a thick, sticky mantle of deadly fuel oil, many of them had suffered horrific injuries in the initial torpedoing and in the intense cold of a tropical night at sea in an open boat, they died very quickly.

With the rising of the sun on the morning of the 13th, the first corpses were found, either sitting bolt upright on the benches around the inside of the boats or lying in whatever positions they had slipped into on the duckboards. Some few words of respect and reverence were spoken over the pathetic bodies before they were tipped unceremoniously into the sea. As each corpse hit the water it was immediately seized upon by the ravening sharks and quickly disposed of. Although it was a hideous sight for those men to have to watch as their shipmates were being devoured, those survivors had no choice. Corpses could not be kept in open boats in tropical seas and needed to be disposed of as quickly as possible. And the sharks continued to circle, their ominous curved fins cutting through the water as they anticipated their next meal.

That first day adrift in the vast, empty wastes of the Indian Ocean became an agony of thirst, hunger and depression. Under the dome of a brassy sky and savage sun they were burned agonisingly. The new dawn revealed a sea alive with the fins of the ever circling sharks, a sight which caused otherwise tough, resilient men to shudder. With no sails to catch any breath of wind which happened along, no navigational instruments to guide them and no charts to give any hint of their position, those men who were fit enough pulled half-heartedly upon their oars in the general direction where they hoped they might find a shore, but after the severe shock of having their ship blown apart from under them, and the subsequent death and mutilation of shipmates and friends, their pathetic efforts were wasted.

Painfully hot days gave way to frosty, star-studded nights with not even the sight of a seabird to break the monotony of sea and sky, just the boats, the dying men and the omnipresent sharks. Sometimes the sea would rise ominously as though to remind them of their precarious predicament, whilst at other times it would be a flat, oily calm with no hint of even a light air and no cloud on the horizon to bring the promise of refreshing, life-giving rain. As the days and nights passed in painful monotony, the meagre supplies with which they had started out began to run short, and they were in desperate need of water. Some of the men made heart-rending attempts to try and catch some fish, but with so many sharks in the water, it was just another wasted effort. Saltwater boils and open, suppurating sores developed in horribly sunburned flesh, and after a few days some of the men began to suffer from dysentery.

Four days after the sinking, the survivors discussed whether or not they should use one of the boats to try and make landfall on either Mauritius or Reunion. Those islands are quite small, however, and they decided that without navigational aids, the chances of missing them were far too great. Instead, they would lash the remaining boats together in a chain before they became too weak through exposure, illness and lack of proper sustenance, so that they could at least all stay together. In the light of subsequent events, it proved to be a fortuitous decision.

By the end of their first week adrift, the South-east Indian Drift Current had them firmly in its grip, pushing them inexorably towards the vast, empty wastes of the central Indian Ocean, then the north-east trade winds began to rise. As the wind grew stronger, so the heaving ocean began to rise and on the morning of the 17th, they were being tossed about in the fierce grip of a severe gale of force 9. Unfortunately, however, as with most gales in tropical waters, there was no rain, and with drinking water at an almost critical level, that could have proved disastrous. However, by cutting their already meagre rations, the majority of the men who were left did manage to survive their savage ordeal. For two long, agonising days they fought to stay afloat amidst the high winds and heavy seas, baling constantly as 40-foot (12 m) seas battered them.

With the passing of the long, hot days and freezing nights they became ever weaker. They saw no birds which they might have had the remote chance of snaring, they caught no fish, mainly because of the ever present sharks, and not even a turtle came close enough to be snatched from the sea. Water and medical attention, however, were their main concerns. With so very little to drink and absolutely no medical aids of any sort, the wounded became more and more restless and weak, and began dying one by one.

At the end of their second agonising week adrift, with their sick and wounded in an appalling state of physical, emotional and mental health, the surviving boats were finally spotted by a patrolling Catalina bomber. It flew low, waggling its wings to let the survivors know that they had been located. It circled for a little while, dropping whatever supplies happened to be on board and, after radioing their position, flew off again, leaving the men with renewed hope of survival.

For a further five days, the Catalina returned each morning, supplying their immediate needs from the air, then, after almost three weeks adrift under the most horrendous circumstances imaginable, the Free French sloop *Savorgnan de Brazza* arrived on the scene and, after taking the survivors on board, landed them at Tamatave, Madagascar. Out of a crew of 150 men, just fifty-two were saved from a slow, agonising death. The *Clan MacArthur* had lost more men to the torpedoes of *Kapitän-Leutnant* Luth than any other merchant ship which he destroyed.

U-181's celebration of the sinking of the *Clan MacArthur* was capped by a signal informing Luth that, owing to the significant blow the sinking of such a valuable ship had caused to the British Mercantile Marine, he had been awarded Diamonds to his Knight's Cross with Oak Leaves and Swords, effective 9 August 1943. It was the highest military award that the Third Reich could bestow. Luth became only the seventh man in the *Wehrmacht*, and the first in the *Kriegsmarine*, to receive it.

# Epilogue

These are just a few of the stories of the merchant navy during the almost six years of the war. There was, of course, far more to the war at sea, but the tales I have chosen to tell indicate the kind of war fought by our 'non-combatant' merchant seamen.

Mankind has always dared to challenge the sea in vessels of all conceivable shapes and sizes. The stormy North Atlantic has been a particularly wretched place for all those who set sail upon its violent wastes in pursuit of a living. It is a cold, inhospitable sea, often plagued by violent storms and massive seas which can reach heights of over 80 feet (25 m) of green water topped with many feet of boiling white foam. Rarely at rest, the Western Ocean has long been the seaman's worst nightmare. In winter, each raging tempest follows so closely on the heels of the last that they merge to give an area of 4 million square miles (10 million sq km) of enraged, leaden grey water, constantly heaving under a dense blanket of dark, menacing storm clouds, unbroken from horizon to horizon. In summer, the storms are muted and spasmodic, but foolish is the sailor who would ignore their warning. And it was upon that watery battlefield that some of the fiercest actions of the war at sea were fought, and eventually, won. 'Battles might be won or lost, enterprises might succeed or miscarry, territories might be gained or quitted, but dominating all our power to carry on the war, or even keep ourselves alive, lay our mastery of the ocean routes and free approach and entry to our ports.' Thus did Winston Churchill describe the issues underlying the Battle of the Atlantic.

The work of the merchant seamen was extremely dangerous, even without the attentions of Germany's U-boats, surface raiders and bombers. It was, however, essential for victory. The Battle of Britain was more immediate and far more dramatic, capturing the imagination of the British people as nothing else had ever done. 'The few', the pitifully young but incredibly courageous men of the RAF in their 'string-bag' planes defeated the overwhelming might of the *Luftwaffe*, a battle which could be seen by ordinary civilians in the skies above London and the southeast coast. And while the battle was raging, the ships of the Royal Navy stood by in readiness to repel Operation Sea Lion, the invasion of Britain by sea. Those warships could also be seen from the southern shores as the people of Britain waited with bated breath for whatever nightmare was to come. But in the euphoria of the success of the battle, nobody ever stopped to consider the men of the silent civilian service who had made it all possible.

The beating heart of any island nation is its merchant navy. Destroy that service, and one destroys the nation. Karl Doenitz was well aware of that and, from the very first day of the war until midway through 1943, his U-boats reaped a terrible harvest of men and ships – and often women and children. Without the Mercantile Marine to bring in the arms and ammunition, the foodstuffs and raw materials which were so vital in keeping Britain alive and free, the RAF would have had no planes to fly, let alone fuel to fly them. The ships of the Royal Navy would have been confined to their home ports, our armies would have been impotent and immobile, and the population of Britain would have been starved into submission within six months. Yet nobody, with the exception of the families of those intrepid men, ever stood and watched as merchant ships put to sea. Nobody was ever there to cheer and welcome them when the re-entered their home ports, often with massive damage from German bombs, mines, shells and torpedoes. Nobody ever saw the sadness in the war-weary faces of their crews as they came ashore, many of them with terrible wounds. What horrendous memories were reflected in those haggard faces, memories of savage, inhuman battles. Those men, who so gallantly faced a fate too terrible to contemplate, wore no uniform, even though they were in the forefront of the war at sea; indeed, they became the subject of ridicule because they were civilians. They are now old men. Yesterday's men. Forgotten men. Men who deserved far better than they received.

Even had the RAF lost the vital Battle of Britain, the success of Operation Sea Lion would not have been assured because of the powerful naval units which had been deployed to counter that proposed invasion, and the shore batteries along the south coast. But far out in the cold, wild wastes of the stormy North Atlantic, week after week, month after month, year after war-weary year, a hideously violent battle was being fought on whose outcome depended the very survival, not just of the British forces, but of the entire population of Britain, and perhaps even the world.

Between September 1939 and the late spring of 1943, the merchant navy suffered harrowing losses which, by the summer of that year, totalled somewhere in the order of almost 19 million tons. The liberty ships provided by America under the lend-lease agreement and such new ships as the British shipyards were able to build barely provided the capacity necessary for the British war effort. Having entered the war in December 1941, the American merchant fleet provided a much-needed boost to Britain's ocean transport, but even after the defeat of the U-boats in April/May 1943, the war at sea continued to the bitter end.

By 21 March 1943, the losses to British shipping were so great that some senior commanders firmly believed that the convoy system had been defeated. There was one man, however, who never even contemplated the idea of defeat. Admiral Sir Max Horton, Commander-in-Chief, Western Approaches, based at Derby House in Liverpool, had every confidence that the successes the U-boats were then enjoying would not continue.

For a little while, changes in the German naval codes had confused British intelligence, which tended to give the pessimism which was being felt in high places more credence. What the commanders were unaware of at that time was that the massacre of convoys HX 229 and SC 122 between 16 and 19 March 1943 was to be the last of the successful massed U-boat battles of the war.

Less than two weeks after those code changes, the new U-boat cipher had been broken. From then on, convoys could be rerouted around known wolf-pack positions. What was more, the output of the American industrial war machine had suddenly, and with dramatic impact, soared to unprecedented levels. The increased air support being provided by the new, very long-range American Liberator bombers which went into service at the end of March finally sealed the Mid-Atlantic air gap. Good intelligence, new and more powerful escorts equipped with the most up-to-date anti-submarine weapons and the closure of the air gap, all combined to make a sudden and decisive impact on the course of the battle.

As we have seen, just a few weeks after the battle for HX 229 and SC 122, a massed pack of U-boats was forced to break off an engagement in which they had lost six boats in an unprecedented counter-attack by units of the Royal Navy. Shortly afterwards Doenitz withdrew his U-boats from the Atlantic, never to return. By stopping the U-boats travelling on the surface where they could use their superior speed to overtake the convoys, the Allied navies finally defeated their menace. During the last week of March, just two more ships were sunk. Suddenly, there was no longer any part of the Western Ocean where the U-boats were safe from escort ships and aircraft.

The Allies then set to work to destroy Doenitz's fleet once and for all. Bombing raids on the U-boat pens were increased, and on one raid on Bremen alone, nine U-boats were destroyed at their moorings. Air patrols became increasingly frequent in the Bay of Biscay and, for the first time in nearly four years, the convoys were used as bait to attract the U-boats, which warships and planes then hunted down and destroyed.

In March 1943, sixteen U-boats were destroyed, and ninety-five merchant ships sunk. The following month, seventeen boats were destroyed, and although in May of that year there were more U-boats roaming the Atlantic sea lanes than ever before, the Allied navies destroyed an incredible forty-seven boats. For the first time in the entire battle, more U-boats had been destroyed than merchant ships sunk.

The destruction of so many vessels in the spring of 1943 had left Doenitz's U-boat arm so badly damaged that, on 24 May, he ordered the withdrawal of his surviving boats from the Atlantic. The *U-bootwaffe* had suffered one of the most dramatic defeats ever. With victory almost within their grasp, more than a thousand of its very best officers and men had been killed in a single month. The Allied closure of the air gap, the brilliant use of intelligence and with the new and deadly sub-killing escorts of frigates had ensured that never again could the U-boats ever hope to win the Battle of the Atlantic.

Nevertheless, Doenitz did not give up. He committed himself to building new, bigger and ever more deadly U-boats, and these were launched and commissioned at a rate of seventeen per month. But every new development was defeated. Victory had been secured by the courage, fortitude and determination of the Allied naval and air forces and by the massive effort and sacrifice of the men of the merchant navies of both Britain and America.

Altogether, Germany produced and commissioned 1,162 U-boats, of which 941 had either been destroyed or captured, one of the latter by an aircraft. As in the First World War, however, the defeat of the U-boats was the nearest-run thing of the entire war. The Germans came closer to victory at sea than anywhere else after 1941. The *U-bootwaffe* eventually lost because every development came just too late. For example, they had a new, long-range torpedo which could be fired outside the scanning range of the victim's detecting apparatus and could therefore strike before being discovered. They were building new, faster U-boats than ever before, all equipped with a revolutionary device called the *Schnorkel* which enabled them to use their superior speed underwater to overtake and outdistance the ships which were previously immune to that tactic. The *Schnorkel* was nothing more sophisticated than a long tube which just broke the surface of the sea, so remaining virtually concealed from sight and radar. However, those innovations had no effect upon the final outcome of the battle because vital breakthroughs in Allied science and technology beat the U-boats back to a position from which there was no recovery.

Theoretically, Doenitz's U-boats had started the war in a winning position simply because they were so difficult to detect and destroy, and Britain simply did not possess adequate naval escort vessels, nor the sophisticated technology to detect them successfully. Sailing faster and deeper than the U-boats of the First World War, the later versions were far sturdier and, unless they suffered a direct hit, they were virtually impervious to depth-charges which had not improved very much over the previous twenty years. Fortunately for Britain, however, the U-boat of the Second World War was still, essentially, what it had been in the First: a submersible surface craft which did not have the capacity to stay permanently beneath the sea. The U-boats' main weakness lay in their inescapable need to surface in order to recharge their batteries and maintain radio contact with their home base, so betraying their position.

Britain's lead in radar technology and information-gathering was central to the success of the war at sea. Whilst radar was used for detecting U-boats on the surface, a variant of radar – Asdic or sonar, as it later became known – probed beneath the waves to find submerged vessels. Massive breakthroughs in intelligence and radar technology robbed the U-boats of their invisibility, and as Coastal Command acquired more and more long-range aircraft, the U-boats could be detected at greater ranges and with greater accuracy. Carrying more lethal weapons than ever before, the U-boats were forced from a position of offence to one of defence from which they could never recover.

In the South Atlantic and Indian Oceans, however, U-cruisers of between 1,500 and 4,000 tons roamed almost at will, even after the Allied victory in the North Atlantic, replenishing their supplies from supply ships. Although the pack tactics used against convoys were no longer appropriate, the deadly U-cruisers operated as lone wolves against independently sailing ships, notably around the east and west coasts of Africa, Madagascar, Mauritius and well out into the Indian Ocean. Independently operating U-boats were also active along the coast of Brazil and all over the South Atlantic. Those boats, most of them large U-cruisers capable of very long cruises, were responsible for many sinkings in the southern hemisphere. With the Western Ocean swarming with Allied naval and air forces, Doenitz concentrated most of his boats south of the Equator. Just a year later, however, the *Luftwaffe* and *Kriegsmarine* surface fleet had been all but annihilated, and the once formidable and seemingly invincible German armies were in full retreat all over Europe.

The eternal sea, once filled with so much blood, so much sorrow, has long since washed away the stench of the riddled corpses, the mangled, burned and bloated bodies of 27,000 German submariners, 30,000 Royal Navy personnel, 56,000 airmen and up to 50,000 British merchant seamen. The raw, untamed ocean has accepted them all into its cold embrace, and the black, abyssal depths have become their winding sheet. The families of those seamen had no clear concept of exactly what had happened to them. Like apparitions from hell, the U-boats came, stalked and destroyed. The men of the Mercantile Marine gave their all, asked for nothing in return, and ended up forgotten. There are no winners in a war. When the bullets begin to fly, there are only victims. Most of what we see we see when we open our eyes, but some things are more elusive, and only to be seen when we open our hearts and minds.

# Index